RICH KIDS

RICH KIDS

by
John Sedgwick

WILLIAM MORROW AND COMPANY, INC.
NEW YORK

Library of Congress Cataloging in Publication Data

Sedgwick, John, 1954-
Rich kids.

1. Adult children—United States—Case studies.
2. Children of the rich—United States—Case studies.
3. Inheritance and succession—United States—Case
studies.   4. Upper classes—United States—Case
studies.   I. Title.
HQ799.97.U5S42 1985   305.2'3   85-3025
ISBN 0-688-05011-5

Printed in the United States of America

First Edition

1 2 3 4 5 6 7 8 9 10

BOOK DESIGN BY JAMES UDELL

For E.L.S., M.M.S., and S.M.S.

ACKNOWLEDGMENTS

No book is ever a solitary effort, and I owe a great deal of thanks to the many people who helped me. First and foremost, I would like to thank the fifty-seven heirs and heiresses who so generously opened up their lives to me. They made this book possible, and I will never forget them. For their hospitality on my travels about the country, I am also deeply grateful to Pepe and Carey Karmel, Rob Sedgwick, Danny and Kathy Davison, Steve Givens, Bill Larkin, Steve Riffkin, Bob and Marilyn Smith, Elva Marshall, and Alessandra Stanley. For their many helpful comments on the manuscript, I am further indebted to Corby Kummer and Pepe Karmel. Matthew Curtis proved an indefatigable researcher. The staff of the Bit Bucket kept my word processor up and running. John Brockman, once again, was a diligent agent. My editor, Pat Golbitz, and her assistant, Jennifer Williams, provided unstinting enthusiasm and support. But as always, the biggest help came from my wife, the writer Megan Marshall, who stood by me, watching over my shoulder to make sure this book came out right.

CONTENTS

Money is a kind of poetry.

—WALLACE STEVENS, *Adagia*

PROLOGUE: A Guide to Life

Among the papers left by my father when he died in 1976, my mother found a document that was a revelation to me. It was titled *A Guide to Life*, and it explained about my inheritance and what my father expected me to do with it. Typed up by his secretary and signed, like a memo, with his initials, the *Guide* was an open letter from my father to his three children, although it didn't address any of us by name. While the copy I eventually received was a carbon on crinkly onionskin paper, it seemed to promise the kind of frank father-to-son talk that, even though it had always made me squirm when I was a kid, I had already come to miss now that he was gone. True to form, the letter charged at the broader questions raised by inheritances in the head-on fashion that was typical of him.

> Fundamentally, I believe there are but two basic goals to life (1) personal happiness and (2) a determination to help make the world a better place to live in. It is my observation that long-term happiness *cannot* be obtained by seeking it directly, but only as a biproduct of success in the second objective. Of course, immediate happiness can be secured and rightly by a good dinner, a good tennis match, an interesting trip, but if one spends one's entire life doing that I suspect, though I never tried it, that no matter what the variety of amusements eventually a life devoted to them would become boring.
>
> The other goal has a thousand different ways of accomplishment. Develop a successful business like Harry's [my entrepreneurial half-brother who had developed a grocery-store

9

price-labelling device called Trig-A-Tape]. . . .
To be a good teacher and educate the minds
and hearts of young people is another road. To
be a useful public servant, a writer, an actor,
or an historian are admirable and satisfying vo-
cations. There are literally hundreds of others.

Then he outlined the financial details of the inheritance
which he termed "no great fortune," explaining that I could
expect $100,000 on turning twenty-one, $20,000 more when
he died (he didn't know that those two events would coincide
in my case), and possibly even more on the death of my mother
"depending on the growth of the economy and the length
of mummy's life." Then he went on:

However, in order to succeed in any role one
must be willing to work long and hard. Of this
you have given fine evidence, it is a quality almost more important than brains. You are ambitious, which is a good thing. Personally I made
a mistake in thinking that ambition, which I
always had, was an ignoble quality. This all stemmed from a line about fame in Milton's "Lyci-
das":

"That last infirmity of noble mind."

I never deluded myself into thinking I had a
noble mind, but I knew I had some ability. I
thought it wrong to be ambitious.
I hope all the foregoing will prove helpful
to you now and in the future. Never forget we
are very proud of you and love you very deeply.

It was a touching letter, and, although I might quibble
with some of his high Victorianism, it addressed some of the
questions naturally raised by an inheritance, things that in
our family we had never discussed before, like the value of
a "good dinner" as against, say, a career in public service.
We had talked about politics, family lore, business, religion,

even sex. But we had never talked about the one thing that bound us all together as tightly as our common heritage: money.

On my father's side, I now know, the money came down from his ancestors, the Minturns, a prosperous shipping family. Among other things, they had acquired the clipper ship, the *Flying Cloud,* said to be the fastest of its day rounding the Horn from New York to San Francisco. There were pictures of the ship all over our house, and we named our tubby Beetle-cat sailboat after her, but it was not until recently that I realized that the *Flying Cloud* had a large financial significance in our family's past. And my mother was descended from the founder of the Ames Tool Company, which flourished in the westward expansion and the gold rush in the nineteenth century, greatly augmenting the family fortune. All of this I have learned only in the last few years; when I was growing up, my parents never quite got around to explaining.

As it happened, many of the assumptions on which my father had written the letter ten years before had failed to pan out by the time he died and I turned twenty-one. The hoped-for $100,000 was reduced to nearly $70,000 by the long stock market slide of the seventies, and the additional $20,000 was absorbed into my mother's holdings for tax reasons. Plus, the money that ultimately did come through had been so watered down by inflation that it hardly bestowed the freedom he had envisioned, by which his children could pick a career without much heed to the financial consequences. All that I got from it was $250 a month to supplement my income as a free-lance writer.

Although my inheritance from my father did not in the end prove very large, nevertheless it had an influence. As Dad had anticipated, the money allowed me some leeway in selecting a profession and probably encouraged me to embark on a writing career whose financial hazards might otherwise have proved too formidable. Because I do have to work to support myself, I do not include myself in the ranks of the rich kids who are the subject of this book. But the money I possess, along with my upbringing, has certainly given me a feeling for the life of freedom and independence that a great sum of inherited wealth can bring. Living on the verge of wealth in this way, I have always been intrigued by the question: what would life be like with a lot of money, a real flood of it, enough so that I didn't have to work? Would it be lovely? Would it be different? Would it be fun? These are the questions that I have set out to answer in this book.

As it was, when I turned twenty-one I received enough money to begin to ponder what I have come to see as a funda-mental rich-kid dilemma: what is the money *for*? Was it really mine, or was it somehow still my parents', or, for that matter, their parents'? Was it really free, a pure windfall, like lottery winnings, or was there a hidden contract by which one some-how had to "earn" it? Did it make me "rich"? In short, what *did* it mean? Such questions may seem like needless self-ab-sorption, and perhaps I should have just relaxed and spent it. But there is something about inherited wealth that seems to require an elaborate philosophy, in the way that certain more complicated games require detailed instructions. Inher-ited wealth inevitably raises vast questions, for money per-vades so much of one's life. In quantity, it establishes one's class, no small thing in American life; it pays for travel, educa-tion, houses, sumptuous dinners; it broadens one's scope, attracts friends, gives power; and it affects career plans, widen-ing the range of possibility even as, perniciously, it slackens ambition. All this my father saw.

I was only sorry that he didn't live to deliver this message in person, for I felt we had a lot to talk about. But that would have been a lot to expect from him, since he was born in 1899 and he was fifty-five when I finally came along. He was a man of the nineteenth century, and in some ways this letter has the clarity, along with the naïveté, of a nineteenth-century view of the world. That's the way he was. In those mysterious ways that parents pass their attitudes on to their children, I am sure I inherited some of his beliefs; and, no less subtly, I expect that some of his ideas have slipped into this book, too. So that readers may more properly be on their guard, let me enlarge a bit on him, and on the way he raised me.

Called by his middle name, Minturn, and nicknamed Duke, my father was a big man, six foot four, and very handsome

and gallant. Besides playing right tackle on Harvard's unde-
feated Rose Bowl team of 1919, he also boxed, which he
termed "the manly art of self-defense," and he was thrilled
to be mistaken once for Jack Dempsey. I remember as a child
walking with my family across Boston Common one evening
when we were accosted by a drunk. Although he was in his
sixties, Dad quickly squared off with his fists up. "I know box-
ing," he declared. The drunk didn't know what to make of
that at all, and staggered off.

So with this letter, it was all unmistakably Dad: no pussy-
footing euphemisms about death ("When I die," I can remember him saying, "I am going to *die*. I am not going to 'pass
away' "); little concern for appearances, which came out here
in the way he has no embarrassment about referring to my
mother as "mummy," lower case and all; and a general impatience with the subtleties of life, so that he could, for example,
reduce the full range of human ambition to "two basic goals"
and then number them "(1)" and "(2)." Reading the letter,
in its inimitable style, heavy on the noblesse oblige (Kipling's
"If" was one of his favorite poems), I felt a little that it might
have been written by George Apley.

If my father sounds solemn in this letter, it's because inheritances to him were no joking matter. In his view, by coming
into money I was assuming a great responsibility. It was part
of growing up. I was joining the aristocracy, with an implicit
code of ethics that was as obvious to him as it was mysterious
to me as a teenager in the late sixties. To be a true aristocrat
was selfless, honorable, lofty, and somehow timeless. To Dad,
a line from Milton could be a personal directive.

As clearly as my father must have understood the duties
and obligations of wealth, he must have been troubled to act
on them. He hints at that in his lines about ambition and
how he felt betrayed by Milton for discouraging it. Although
he would have bridled at the term, he was a rich kid, first
by birth and then by marriage, and like most rich kids he
never did get entirely comfortable with his riches. He was
torn between what he should do and what he wanted to do,
and not until he retired in his sixties did he discover a way
to use the money to bring those two things together.

For nearly forty years he worked as an investment adviser

in a downtown Boston firm, and he hated every day of it. He lived for vacations with his family and for his work after hours for a range of what he fancily termed "eleemosynary" institutions in New England, ranging from the Massachusetts Society for Prevention of Cruelty to Children to the Riggs Foundation, a psychiatric hospital. So devoted was he to Groton School, which he attended and then served as a trustee for nearly half a century, that he treasured his double-breasted blazer emblazoned with the Groton School crest. He wore it so often, in fact, he covered the inside of the breast pocket with leather to keep it from wearing out on the crest's prickly golden threads.

In a moment of great candor, probably in response to my badgering him, he once told me how much money he made. It was $30,000 a year. "Now, don't tell your friends about this," he said in a pleading tone I can still hear. While the implication that this was a vast and intimidating sum was clear enough to me then—I who had only my twenty-five-cents-a-week allowance to compare it to—looking back on it now, I think he may have been distressed that it was so little. I didn't know then that we weren't living on his salary, but on family money.

I was in public school then, which I attended through the third grade in a little white schoolhouse with a steeple across the street from where we lived in the Boston suburb of Dedham. Most of my friends from school lived on the far side of town in small tract houses. When I visited them, their houses always struck me as strangely compressed, the way the kitchens merged with the dining areas which in turn flowed out to the living rooms. Our house was big enough so that everything had its own distinct place—a living room, dining room, playroom, TV room, library, study. And everyone had his or her own place, too. The three kids all had their own bedrooms, and there was still a considerable number of guest rooms, room-sized closets, and undefined areas left over.

At the time, I didn't feel that a bigger-than-average house distinguished our family so much as the great weight of tradition that hung about us. I caught on to that quite early. We journeyed out to Stockbridge, Massachusetts, every fall to visit the family mansion built in 1785 by Judge Theodore Sedgwick, my great-great-great grandfather, the first Speaker of the House of Representatives and founder of the American clan. There, I'd play touch football Kennedy-style in the backyard with all my relatives. Inevitably we'd stroll down the street to take a look at the celebrated family graveyard, which was called The Pie, arranged in concentric circles emanating outward from the Judge. When I was very young, I played hide-and-seek there with my grandmother among the granite stones shaded by high hemlocks. My father is buried there now.

In fourth grade, I went off to a preprep school, Dexter, until I was old enough to follow in the footsteps of my father and brother (and dozens of other Sedgwicks) to Groton and Harvard. I suppose I was subtly being trained in the ways of the aristocracy, but all I felt was an occasional prickle of embarrassment. All the Dexter kids were required to wear maroon caps. That was awkward. Townies used to hang about by the wrought-iron fence that surrounded the school and tease us about our "Dexter beanies." On Fridays at Dexter, all the seventh-graders were bused to dancing school at Miss Souther's in Boston, where we learned to waltz and foxtrot to the old standards as played on the piano by an aging black-haired fellow we called Dracula. That year I was in love with a girl I'd met playing tennis at the country club who was a head taller than I. I used to dread dancing with her, since only by dancing on tippy-toe could I clear her shoulder with my chin.

Going to Groton was strangely like going home—not to one's own home, but to an older, ancestral home that was even more commodious, and even more mine than the Stockbridge house. I didn't fully realize that until I got there and recognized the school buildings from pictures on our dinner plates. And I was now finally able to place the watercolor that had always hung in my room: it was the Groton School chapel. My father had painted it when he was a student. Besides teaching there and serving for so long as a trustee, my father had taken as his first wife the daughter of the school's founder, The Rector as he was so forbiddingly referred to around campus when I was there. (To his grandchildren, including my half-brother and -sisters, he was known as Doodoo.) The woman was my "Aunt" Helen Peabody, whom I never knew.

So Groton was family. Helen's two sisters still lived across from the school. I called them Aunts, too, and they invited me over to breakfast on Sunday mornings occasionally. Actually, the school was an extended family. Sedgwicks had been going off to Groton for so long, their names were everywhere—inscribed in memoriam on the walls of the chapel hallway, on wood plaques recording graduated classes around the study hall in the School House, on lists of football teams in the gym. My father's brother Halla had died there in the school infirmary after catching pneumonia. His name was inscribed on the chapel wall.

In my class, 1972, one of my classmates turned out to be related to me through my father's first wife. But I gradually discovered that I had a kinship with my other classmates, too. They were members of my social class. And they intrigued me, since their styles were so different from my own. One was the son of a Portuguese marquis and playboy who had been killed in a racing-car crash several years before. As editor of the *Third Form Weekly*, the school newspaper, I persuaded him to write a story about it. After describing the accident in oddly thrilling detail, the unsigned account ended, "For the first time, there had been a tragedy in my life." The son later distinguished himself in the eyes of his classmates by leaving school at the end of his junior, or fifth form, year. We were astounded to read the announcement of his marriage in the *New York Times* the following fall. Another classmate's father owned 6,000 acres of prime Connecticut real estate, which the family maintained as a nature preserve. He took me on a pack trip to the Canadian border of Washington State; it was practically the first time I'd left New England. The mother of a third owned the *Atlantic Monthly*, her father having picked it up from none other than my great uncle Ellery Sedgwick, and she held the magazine as a sideline to her real estate and oil and gas interests.

Flush as they were, none of these kids seemed rich, exactly.

Just as none of the rest, even the ones on scholarship from the Lowell projects, seemed poor, although they were. One of the scholarship kids told me later that it wasn't until going to Groton that he'd ever been able to walk around outdoors and feel safe.

This apparently class-free atmosphere was partly Groton's doing. Except for a candy counter that opened up for an hour after lunch, there was nothing to spend money on. And the school enforced an almost military standard of uniformity in which each student worked at identical desks, slept in meager, identically furnished cubicles, and washed out of identical plastic tubs. But the revolutionary times—these were the late sixties and early seventies—also dictated a new sartorial standard. There seemed to be an unspoken competition between the students to see who could obey the school's coats, ties, and no-hair-below-the-collar dress code and look the shabbiest. While I can't claim to have won the competition, with my Afro-like curly hair and thirdhand black overcoat I was certainly a finalist.

After such a sheltered adolescence, Harvard was like high school for me—an introduction to a world that I had never before encountered. Certainly there were groves of privilege in the university, with its private clubs and gangs of preppies, but they didn't dominate and, eager for something new, I steered clear of them. I roomed at Radcliffe because that's where I understood the girls were. I was eager to begin a romantic education long delayed by my years at all-boys' schools. In this, at least, I was successful. But as far as gaining the confidence of the *other* other half, of the kids from average middle-class backgrounds, I'm not sure I fared as well. I once came back to the dorm raving about some nifty leather sneakers I'd just bought, how comfortable and durable they were, when a long-haired dorm mate cut me dead. "We can't all afford leather sneakers, John," he said. I was crushed.

Now that I am a writer, I am sometimes bothered by the thought that I have indeed ended up living the aristocratic life, even if I don't have quite enough cash to pull it off: I am my own boss, and I do what I like. Still, the question lingers: how much of me is my money, and how much of me is me?

I was pondering this question when the oral biography *Edie* by Jean Stein and George Plimpton came out in 1982. Because my uncle Francis, Edie's father, married a fabulously wealthy woman, Alice de Forest, the money on that side of the family put our own to shame. We might have been well-to-do, but they were rich. While we just had a big house in the suburbs, they had a ranch, a vast and beautiful one, in Santa Barbara, California. In reading about Edie, whom I as a small child had met but had no memory of, I couldn't help thinking of her as the rich kid I might have become. Certainly, the money alone did not dictate the course of Edie's spectacular life, the idyllic youth in Santa Barbara, the splashy career as a *Vogue* model and actress for Andy Warhol and his drug-infested Factory. But in it I could certainly detect the glitter, the ethereality, and the enchantment, as well as some of the disaffectedness and ennui, that often come with great wealth.

The question fascinated me: how are the lives of young heirs and heiresses affected by their wealth? Are the rich, as Fitzgerald so famously asserted, different from you and me? My wealthy friends must have thoughts about it just as I did as a rich kid *manqué*. But if so, I hadn't heard them. People don't talk about that sort of thing. But it occurred to me that they might talk to me. After all, I was familiar with the territory of wealth, even if I didn't precisely live there myself. But—more than just fantasizing about what my life would have been like if—I was curious to know about the people who could live their lives on a higher plane. Freed of the constraints that pull everyone else down, could they attain a higher perspective? Did they really know how to live?

I chose to direct my questions at people who were roughly my age, between twenty and forty. I was particularly interested in hearing from my own generation because I felt their answers to my questions would be deeper and more heartfelt than those of the generation before or after. For these people were, like me, still emerging from the shelter of childhood into the open air of adulthood. Having come into it at eighteen or twenty-one, the money was still, as it were, fresh, and fresh in their minds. I wanted to approach them while it was all still new and exciting, and before it had faded into the backgrounds of their life as part of the natural landscape, along with the broad lawn, the English garden, and the towering elms.

Indeed, many of my subjects proved only too eager to discuss the questions I was raising—so eager, in fact, I sometimes had difficulty disentangling myself from them once my questions had run out. Wealth was a whole new world to them, and they were thrilled to find someone with whom they could discuss it. Some of them had as many questions for me as I had for them. But wealth is, still, a sensitive subject, and there were others who were unwilling to broach it with anyone, let alone a stranger writing a book. One young woman burst into tears when I called to ask her if she would agree to an interview. "Now I have to face up to my money?" she exclaimed. "I just can't!" Yet others were snappish, assailing me for my shocking lapse of taste in inquiring into such a private subject. One was indignant that I should have asked her about her wealth so directly. She said that I should have inquired about her status as a member of an "establishment family." Then she would have been glad to tell me whatever I wanted to know.

In the end, I spoke to fifty-seven people in seven cities: Boston, New York, Washington, Dallas, Houston, Los Angeles, and San Francisco. While New York City is undoubtedly the rich-kid capital of the country, beyond it, the list was fairly arbitrary. Wherever money is made it can be made to excess and then passed on in tidy bundles to turn generations of descendants into heirs. They are born in every region of the country; in city, suburb and ex-urb. I went where my leads took me.

Varied as the circumstances and experiences of the rich kids were, they all bore the unmistakable stamp of wealth. One rich kid retired from his job with an investment bank at age thirty to return to his apartment and "think" for six years. Another quit a rock band to develop a blimp. Another has perfected a special deluxe design for an egg-shaped isolation tank. Still another spends most of her time sailing.

In selecting them, my one criterion, aside from age, was

that they be rich enough so that they didn't have to work, although they might well work anyway, and most of them did. This was necessarily subjective, both from my point of view and from theirs, but considerably less subjective than asking them simply if they were "rich." To that question, I quickly discovered, the reply is almost always negative. By asking them about their working life, however, I was able both to get at the essential freedom of their lives and, indirectly, to set a minimum standard of income from their inherited wealth in the vicinity of $20,000 a year, although many of them exceeded that by a great deal.

As far as the sources of the wealth, those varied wildly. Rich kids may have come from old money, some of it practically as old as America itself, or they may have come from money so new they didn't even know it was there until they inherited it. The sources were as diverse as the national economy, ranging from the old standbys of oil, industry, banking, and real estate to the newer marvels of telecommunications and electronics.

Some of the wealth is so well known that it is practically a national treasure, even though the proceeds flow exclusively to the family holders: the Rockefellers and Pratts of Standard Oil; the Mellons of Gulf Oil, manufacturing, and banking; the Pulitzers of the newspaper fortune; the Pillsburys of the flour company (thereby lending the latest generation of male heirs the inevitable title, the Pillsbury Dough Boys); the Meyers and Grahams of the *Washington Post;* the Hunts of Alcoa aluminum.

But it takes a while for wealth to gather fame, and for many their riches are as little known as others' poverty. Andrew Hixon's fortune came from the tiny plastic clip in the back of the telephone that plugs in the power cord. Put out by a company called AMP that Hixon's great-uncle had the wisdom of investing a half million in at the right time, that little clip and related products have driven a few dozen Hixons into the economic stratosphere.

Many of my subjects have, graciously and courageously, allowed me to use their names. Others have insisted on anonymity, and some have asked me to identify them only by the source of their wealth. In the cases where the individuals were cautious, I could certainly respect their concerns. In the course of writing this book, my name got out erroneously as that of a rich kid, and I became the object of a few unwelcome solicitations myself. One fellow wanted me to back a Broadway musical. Yet even where the names and a few identifying details have been changed to protect their privacy, the essential truth of my interview subjects' lives remains.

The lives of the rich kids are funny, charmed, sad, but always extraordinary. This book is their story.

PART I

Rich Kids

1

Crossing the Moat

She looked like Tuesday Weld, a lovely blonde with a slim figure and a perfect nose, and she was really rich. Her name was Anne Dale Owen, Annie to all her friends. She was everything you hope for in a woman of exceptional means—lively, beautiful, and different. Definitely different. In the course of a few hours at her place in Houston late one night, she gave me the whole Annie philosophy: how she had learned a lot about patience and sensitivity from dogs; how, whenever she was feeling down about her life, she went and sat next to some old lady on the bus and found out what it was like to *really* have problems; how she wished she were myopic because it's so sexy-looking; and how she would like to strike the word *should* from the English language.

RICH KIDS

A lot of it went right past me, she talked so fast. But I was still smitten by her. She wore a clinging sweater, a tight pair of Levi's, and some tall, brocaded cowboy boots with high heels. Her eyes sparkled like diamonds. What else? Her skin was smooth and pure. But it wasn't her beauty, exactly, that entranced me. She had a glow. It was like the glow of starlets in forties movies, except that theirs came from back-lighting. Hers came from her money.

Annie's grandfather was Robert Lee Blaffer, the man who struck a world-class oil gusher at Spindletop, Texas, in 1901 and became one of the original partners in Humble Oil, which has since become part of Exxon. Her mother was Jane Blaffer Owen, a patron of the arts known around Houston chiefly for her big hats and her unexpected points of view. In an early example of her independent nature, Jane married Kenneth Dale Owen, a geologist who had gone to Cornell on a track scholarship and who was the great-grandson of the utopian Robert Dale Owen. (Jane's sister, by contrast, married the prince Tassilo von Furstenberg.) Fascinated by the spiritualism of Owen's famous 1824 settlement in New Harmony, Indiana, Jane applied a major portion of her inheritance to rebuilding it. And she bought a place there to live a few months out of the year.

The marriage never clicked, however, and the couple moved apart. Annie didn't see her father much, but spoke of him warmly, calling him Daddy, saying she got her "Welsh eyes" from him. She called Jane Mother. Mother is worth many, many millions. Someday Annie could be worth a fair number of millions herself, depending on what her mother decides to do with them all. But for the time being Annie was scraping by on a tiny portion of her potential inheritance, a mere few hundred thousand dollars that her Blaffer grandmother had passed on in trust a few years back.

I had heard about Annie through a friend of hers I'll call Emily Montgomery, a cultivated young woman I knew from friends in Dallas. Emily is rich herself and was immediately thrilled with the idea of my book when I called. "I love it!" she exclaimed. When I hung up, she hurried to her address book and started selecting the wealthy young friends she would enlist to my cause. On the back of a postcard, she told me to call Annie Owen, and gave the address and phone number.

I wasn't able to reach Annie from Boston, however, before leaving on the Texas segment of my cross-country research. I didn't in fact manage to get hold of her until nearly midnight on my last night in Houston when I was packing to leave for home. I was staying in a Groton friend's place in a singles complex. A real bachelor pad, it had no pots and pans or matching silverware, and the only glasses I could find were beer steins chilling in the freezer. Eager for relief, I decided to try Annie one last time, and she answered, quite brightly considering the hour. She said she was just back from a seminar in Colorado, but was too "wired" from traveling to sleep, so why didn't I just come on over? It turned out that she lived just down the road. She was used to having people drop in at all hours, she said. Sometimes she found them sacked out on the couch in the morning. She gave me elaborate instructions on how to get there: left at a gas station, another left at a green mailbox. She made me repeat them back to her to make sure I'd gotten them straight.

Emily had once described Annie's place as a log cabin, but I figured she was exaggerating. Even if this was Texas, I didn't think log cabins were in fashion. Besides, Annie lived in a prominent residential area not far from what passes for the downtown in no-zoning Houston, and what would a log cabin be doing there?

It was a drizzly night, and the windshield wipers on my rented Chevy weren't handling things too well. But I found the first key turn at the gas station and located the critical mailbox. I took a left and plunged in between some bushes, and suddenly I entered another world. The sounds and bright lights of the city dropped away behind me. Everything was still and dark. With a thump I crossed over a stone bridge spanning a little creek—I learned later the family calls it the Moat. There was no road on the far side, just a floor of matted pine needles. I was driving through a forest. I crept along, my headlights flashing on a few dark houses. And then up ahead I spotted a cabin made of genuine hewn logs, all gnarled and uneven, and caulked with what looked like mud. Lights were on, and there was gentle folk-rock music coming from a stereo inside. I parked and knocked on the door.

Annie answered right away. She was all smiles. "Hi!" she said. "Come on in!"

She led me through a big living room with a large stone fireplace, throw rugs over the floor, and some knockabout furniture. I imagined we were way off in the mountains. The rain pattering gently on the roof sounded like a stream running by. And, except for Bonnie Raitt singing sweetly on the stereo, the cabin was quiet. Annie sat me down on her brass bed with a glass of ginger ale while she went back to work polishing the bedroom floor where a trunk had scratched it and smoking cigarettes. A big TV pointed at me, and there were some dried flowers rising out of a large clay pot to my right, beside a life-sized statue of a dalmation. A couple of real dogs, fluffy little creatures, scampered about, skidding on the stone floor. "That's Thistle," she said, pointing. "She's got terrier, poodle, schnauzer, and a little Lhasa in her. This one here is her daughter Tigerlily. Her father is Frito, up at the main house. He's half Yorkshire and half schipperke." Bloodlines mattered to Annie.

Dominating the room was a big post-office desk off in one corner. It was covered with papers pertaining to her current business, managing her trust fund. For want of anything better to do, Annie had been playing the stock market with her grandmother's money, and, remarkably, she had been winning. Acting on general know-how taken from the business press and some key tips she picked up from oil-company executives she met at parties, Annie said she had upped her money by 36 percent every year for the last six years. She called her stocks her "things." "I feel you can either leave your things in safety-deposit boxes or you can work with them," she said, "and I prefer to work with them. My friends are trying to get me to turn over my things to a professional, but I say, 'No, let me screw up this year and then I'll do it.' But I haven't screwed up yet. Managing my stock portfolio isn't my ambition in life, but right now it's all I do. For me, it's a game, like playing the horse races."

I complimented her on her cabin, but the words didn't

seem to register. It was as if I'd praised her dress, and she'd said, "Oh, this old thing?"

"This cabin was here when my parents bought the property from the Goodriches," she said. "Old man Goodrich used to play poker out here with his buddies. He lived in the main house and kept a bunch of cats in a special cathouse. I guess he was kind of eccentric. His granddaughter used to live just down the street and she'd come over here sometimes, wheeling her baby carriage. She'd say, 'I wish Grandpa had never sold this place.' I'd tell her, 'I know how you feel.' "

Annie was right—she *was* wired. She kept right on working what looked like shoe polish into the floor, and she kept right on talking.

"I didn't move in till fairly recently," she said. "This was the place we used to come to let it all out after football games in high school. Mother didn't care if we all drank or got drunk, just so long as no one drove. People used to pass out on the barbecue pit outside, and it was fine. One time, my friend Gary—who is now dead unfortunately; he used to race cars—he took a Christmas tree in the other room and javelined it into the big fireplace. He picked it up with one hand—he was about six-five, two sixty, and a linebacker—and he just rammed it in.

"This place was never, you know, *decorated*. It just is. That bed you're sitting on just got there somehow. The Martha Mood tapestry over there I rescued from my sister's apartment because the moths were getting it. So I sent it to Washington to have it restored. I love Martha Mood. I have lots of books on her."

"Does this place represent anything to you?" I asked, fumbling for a question to break up her monologue.

Annie looked around at the furnishings and pondered for a moment. "I think it represents what everybody wants," she said.

As a child I once dreamed that I found a long row of silver coins on our lawn. It was as if someone had been carrying a big sack of change, and the sack had ripped open as he walked, and he'd left behind a trail of silver. I was delighted at my discovery. There was no one else around, and I eagerly scooped the coins up in both hands and stuffed them into my pockets as fast as I could. I remember thinking, "Ah! Now I'm set for life!"

I don't think I'm all that unusual. Who doesn't fantasize about a sudden windfall? Lots and lots of money, yours for the taking. Appealing, isn't it? The miners who headed west in the California gold rush knew the feeling, and they knew the anguish of seeing their golden dreams turn to dust. But the idea isn't foreign now. Finding buried treasure, striking a gusher, hitting the jackpot—these are still the images of instant happiness. Think of the patient souls who come out at low tide to comb the beach with their metal detectors, or the oddballs who send those chain letters demanding a dollar (or more) by return mail and threatening you with the most horrifying case of bad luck if you don't come through. Then there are all the gamblers, game-show contestants, and lottery addicts. And those are just the ones working the fringe methods of getting rich quick. Others play the more respectable numbers games we term investments. And finally, of course, there are the slower-acting methods that nearly everybody goes for, namely regular work at a regular job and hoping that someday it will all pay off. But the goal is still the same.

Everybody wants to strike it rich.

Rich kids like Annie, though, are different. They hit it big at birth. They have started out their lives at the apex of the pyramid that everybody else spends a lifetime climbing, pay raise by pay raise. As Marisa Berenson, one of the more famous rich kids, once put it, "I started out at the top and I have been rising ever since." Since the Constitution specifically outlaws the creation of titled nobility (in Article I, Section IX), rich kids are the closest thing America has to royalty. Movie stars may outdo them in glitter, but stars have to work for it. The rich kids' greatest accomplishment has simply been to be born, and the fascination is built in from the start. Like Annie Owen in her log cabin, rich kids live in a fairy-tale world, and they decorate their lives as they please. They will never have to work. If they choose, they could go on an endless vacation, flitting from beach to beach, slope to slope. Their peers strive to create their opportunities; rich kids spend much of their time fending off opportunities from chance acquaintances offering them stakes in oil wells and mineral deposits. Middle-class kids strive to carve out an identity for themselves; rich kids have one ready-made. Many of them bear household names like Rockefeller, Mellon, Pillsbury. The rest are likewise clearly defined: they are rich. They are set for life.

I call them rich kids, but they rarely use the term to describe themselves, since to them it means "spoiled brats"— they might see their peers that way but never themselves. If pressed, though, they will sometimes offer up the terms "lucky-genes kids," or "trust-fund babies." The society newspaper *W* calls them "Proper Young Things," but those are more the new generation, led by *Life* magazine-proclaimed Debutante of the Decade Cornelia Guest, who have taken to the old rituals of coming-out parties and fancy-dress balls with gusto. The twenty-to-forty set—my generation—are still shaped by the antiestablishment sixties and admit to their privilege more shyly. With a shrug, they say they "picked their parents well" or are the beneficiaries of an "accident of birth." Or, as one heiress explained, "My family is just where I got put."

It's hard to tell how many rich kids there are with the half-million-dollar inheritances it takes to generate what I think of as enough money to live on without working. Although the IRS keeps track of large estates, it doesn't know how they are ultimately distributed, and it doesn't particularly care, since the estate pays taxes, not the recipient. The Bureau of the Census inquires only about income, not wealth. But it is still possible to arrive at a ball-park figure. New York City's U.S. Bank and Trust Company, which does take an interest in locating the wealthy as a first step toward enticing them inside its doors, counted up the number of millionaires in the country in 1980 and came up with a grand total of 574,342 (nearly a tenth of whom were conveniently residing in New York State). The company did not distinguish between earned and inherited wealth, nor did it consider the age of the holders. However, with that figure as a benchmark, there could be as many as a few hundred thousand rich kids tucked away around the country. A rough estimate to be sure, but because of the very covertness of wealth in America and of the strange limbo that rich kids exist in, it is the best I, or anyone, can do.

Whatever the actual numbers, the economist Paul Samuelson put it most vividly when he wrote that if an "economic pyramid" were to be built to resemble the Eiffel Tower, nearly everyone in the country would be placed within a yard from the bottom. From this broad base, the tower would, like the stem of a champagne glass, thin out dramatically as it rose, growing sharper and sharper until it reached the lovely shallow bowl balanced on a pinpoint at its tip. Way up there at the top of this socioeconomic tower, drenched in affluence from the dawn of their lives, are the rich kids.

At that height, of course, the whole world is at their feet. For them, the very laws of gravity seem to have been suspended. Some of them catch on to the facts of their rare privilege quite early in their upbringing. For example, at the age of two, Elizabeth Meyer, granddaughter of financier Eugene and niece of *Washington Post* owner Katharine Graham, was found scribbling wastefully on some precious watercolor paper. When she was questioned about it rather sharply by a family friend, she responded gaily, "Oh, it's all right. I have a million dollars."

Quite so. Yet in one of the many mysteries that surround these financial princes and princesses, many of them don't grasp the truth about their lives for quite some time. Remarkably, the money that is everywhere around them—paying for the houses, the maids, the art, the horses, the cars—is to them invisible in their childhoods. It is as if they had been wearing green-tinted glasses. The money just disappeared.

In a common analogy, money was like sex. In polite society one might think about it, wonder about it, perhaps even have it, but one might never talk about it. That was vulgar. Sarah Pillsbury's mother taught her to dodge the persistent questions of her schoolmates about whether she was rich by saying, "Yes, I am rich. I'm rich in happiness." Sarah didn't say how her little friends responded.

So, in the early years at least, these children enjoyed lives that were fabulously rich without fully realizing it—possibly that was the best part. As far as they knew, everyone lived like this. They had nothing to compare their experience *to,* that was the main thing. The rich life was the only one they knew. Off in the gilded ghettos of Westchester County or Beverly Hills, they were surrounded by children fully as rich as they, so they never guessed they were anything more than average.

But they should have guessed again. For them, life did not hold its usual proportions and natural restraints. And all rich kids now look back on their childhoods with amusement that they should have taken so much for granted. Shannon Wynne, a scion of the Texas Wynne family, used to order up his father's Lear jet to take him and his schoolmates to any of the Six Flags amusement parks scattered around the nation (his father owned all of them) at a moment's notice, as if he were merely summoning the governess for a walk in the park. An East Coast industrial heiress recalled that for her birthday when she was seven, her father gave her a mint condition Model T for her and all her friends to ride in— driven by the family chauffeur, of course. And a black million-airess I'll call Shiela Waters not only had her own yacht as a child, but also received private scuba lessons from not one but two instructors at a time. "My father wanted to make *sure* I didn't drown," she explained.

And when it finally dawned on them that their lives were indeed quite special—it was like losing their virginity. Most rich kids can recall exactly when and where it happened.

Generally it came by comparison: they suddenly realized how high they stood by seeing, for the first time, how much lower others do. And that discovery often gave them the dizzying sense of vertigo. Indeed, some have never regained their balance. One young heir I'll call Harold didn't make the discovery until his middle teens when, on vacation from his prep school, he was taking a train to Hobe Sound in Florida, where he was going to spend some time with his grandparents on their yacht. He'd grown up on a gentleman's farm, a place so completely in line with his father's pastoral ideal that it had no motorized machinery: all the work was done by hand or by horse. That in itself was unusual, of course, but Harold never noticed. On the trip to Florida, though, he distinctly remembered looking out the window as the train rattled through South Carolina and being astounded to see all the shacks lining the tracks. "I was sitting in the dining car," he said, "with the white tablecloths and the black waiters, and I said out loud, 'My God! I can't believe that people live in those conditions!' And this black waiter happened to be leaning over the table just then straightening the knives and forks, and he heard me and suddenly tears started to run down his cheeks and splash on the tablecloth. It was his people living down there, I guess. I'll never forget that."

For others, however, the rude awakening comes in college, when for the first time they end up mixing full-time with people from far less affluent backgrounds than their own. Having grown up in New York City, Michael Pratt, of the Standard Oil Pratts, was not exactly sheltered. He knew, for example, that it was somewhat unusual to be able to take his girl friends to French restaurants as a teenager. He attended the selective high school Dalton, but unlike his father, who had been driven by chauffeur to the possibly even more exclusive St. Bernard's (the driver kindly removed his uniform for the trip so as not to embarrass his passenger too much), Michael always took the subway. He thought he knew about the world, but it was not until college that he realized quite how much the world knew about him.

"Although my father had gone to Yale," he said, "it was something of a family tradition to go to Amherst. My father would sing the Amherst song at Christmas, because that was something that his father had done. I still didn't know what, if anything, it all meant, though.

"When my father drove me up to Amherst, I noticed that right in front of me there was a building called Pratt Dormitory, and another one called Pratt Museum. Then there was the Pratt pool, and Pratt something else. And I said to my father, 'What the hell is going on?' And my father said to me—I'm not sure he was being disingenuous—'I don't know; let me check and see if we're related.'

"So he did, and of course we're totally related. My family had donated everything!"

And yet—this was the hard part—the Pratt beneficence did not win Michael too many friends among the undergraduate body. "That was the first place I ever felt any real stigma attached to my name," Michael went on. "The Pratt Dormitory was named after a Pratt who had died as an undergraduate, and my father joked that he had been stoned to death after the students found out he was related to *those* Pratts. But sure enough, after I got my freshman package, the first person to look at my name said, 'Pratt. Hmmm. Are you related to *those* Pratts?' It was like that for four years."

Alice K. R. Tatum didn't entirely realize that her ancestors' King Ranch—with its thirty rooms and million-acre backyard in South Texas—was all that spectacular until she brought a friend down from college. The friend, herself reasonably well off by New England standards, knew Alice was a Kleberg but didn't quite know what that meant until she drove out to the ranch. Because the surrounding land is so flat, the two friends caught their first look at the place from miles away. They could see the high palm trees waving in the wind, and the tower of the Spanish-style house gleaming in the sun, and the Texas Lone Star flag flapping on its mast. Finally they reached the wrought-iron gates where an attendant hands out brochures about the property to tourists and directs them to loop around the house for the full 360, and the friend could hold back no longer. "It's just like Fantasy Island!" she exclaimed. Alice has never been able to see the house the same way again.

Michael Pulitzer, Jr., of the publishing family, grew up in a castle in St. Louis. It was a genuine castle, built of stone in the German manner with cast-iron balconies, marble staircases, and generally immense dimensions, that the Pulitzers had picked up from the Busches of the beer fortune. The driveway ran a full mile, making it quite a field trip to bring in the newspaper—the Pulitzer-owned *Post-Dispatch,* of course—every morning. And the surrounding neighborhood was so plush that Michael's task around the house was to keep the neighbor's polo ponies from digging up the front lawn by peppering them with stones when they drew too close. Still, the castle was just home to him, nothing all that special.

RICH KIDS

Doesn't *everybody* have one? He remembers that he didn't catch on until the plumber who had been summoned to plug a leak in Michael's bathroom expressed astonishment that the bathroom walls were eighteen inches of solid concrete, reinforced with steel girders. And the poor man was even more amazed, when he finally dug down through the floorboards, to find that a drainpipe had rusted out years before and an ocean of water had accumulated underneath, suspended over the downstairs dining room. He had to drain it with a sump pump.

Oblivious as the rich kids may have been to them at the time, such enchanted childhoods leave their mark. Like princes and princesses, all rich kids have a certain air about them. It makes them what they are. They have an allure made up in part by their illustrious background, in part by the breeziness that comes naturally to those who have everything, in part by the range of experience they have picked up in their Lear jets, in part by the shining good looks that is another happy consequence of picking their parents so well, and in part by the tragic attitude they bear for being alone with such blessings.

As I sat with her in her log cabin, I could see all this in Annie Owen. She was like the sun, and people were automatically drawn to her radiance. She picked up one boyfriend that way, after she had charmed his mother at a party. "She said, 'I've got a son I want you to meet,' " Annie related. "And I said, 'Oh, dear God, I've seen 'em all.' But I met him and fell in love with him right away, even though I was leaving the next day for Europe." They pursued the relationship when she returned. The man was a rock musician, as it happened, and Annie spent several months traveling with him and hanging out with such rock stars as Kris Kristofferson, Jackson Browne, and Bob Dylan along the way. Despite their fame, they failed to turn Annie's head. "They lived from one joint to the next, one gig to the next," she said. "And there was so much drugs, and rotten hamburgers and filthy vans, that I was just turned off by the whole thing." She moved on to other pleasures.

36

She often found that people were drawn to her, like moths to a golden flame. While I was visiting, a beautiful girl I'll call Denise came dashing in. She was another of those mysterious visitors who drop in for an hour and end up staying the night, or a month. She'd been going out with Annie's cousin, Annie later explained, but preferred to live with Annie. Now the romance had turned sour, and that left the girl with Annie. Denise charged in complaining that the cousin wouldn't give her back her TV. Annie promised to work it out for her. Reassured, Denise went out to get some cigarettes. She never did come back while I was there.

"She's adorable, so cute," said Annie. "She's been here for about three or four months now. We just kind of adopted her. I don't know how long she'll stay. Isn't she sweet?"

I agreed she was. But it was Annie's magnetism I was beginning to feel. It was a sensation I would have often as I hobnobbed with the rich. They hold the Denises of the world in their power. With Annie, the feeling hit suddenly, unexpectedly, when she turned back to me after Denise left, and I blurted out that I felt that I had joined Annie's farm as one of the prize animals.

"Oh, I collect people," Annie replied. To my startled look, she added, "Well, what else is there? People are the most fascinating things to collect."

Annie grew up in the main house nearby that is now occupied solely by her mother. It was one of the dark shapes I saw on my way in. Since Jane was so absorbed in her various philanthropical and artistic ventures, Annie was raised by a nanny. Hers was a kindly black woman—"Not big and fat like the ones you think of," she said—named Goldie who had, in fact, first come into the family to raise Jane. Goldie would dress Annie and plait her hair in the mornings and, whenever her mother was out of town, whisk her away from the family's Episcopal church to get a feel for real religion at the Baptist. As a child Annie spent most of her free time in the kitchen with Goldie watching the black cook whip up the chicken dumplings and corn bread she still has a taste for. "Goldie was serene, but the cook was really jolly, and they'd sing together and carry on," Annie remembered. "They'd always be joking about the yardman because they thought he was so lazy. That kitchen was always a happy place."

When Annie wasn't palling around with Goldie, she was out in the yard tending her animals. "I had a menagerie of them," she said. "I started off with four little buff bantam chickens that grew to about fifty or sixty before I knew it. I used the washer of the house as a hatchery. After the chicks were born, I'd leave them in there like an incubator in the nursery. I gave all the chickens names and tacked up stockings for them all at Christmas. Every morning I'd get up at six and carry water to them, and let them out of the coop so they could run around. And every night I'd lock them back up again so that the owls and rats wouldn't get them.

"I had nine geese and about twelve guinea fowl, and six tumbling pigeons and two peacocks. And we had dalmatians and German shepherds and poodles. And as they all died off we'd replace them. We had all the animals on this one acre, with the geese on one side and the chickens on the other. And there was a chicken-wire fence all around to keep them all in. The dogs helped me herd everybody up at the end of day. I never had to teach them, they just knew."

Although the life sounded solitary as she described it, Annie was one of three sisters in the Owen family. The oldest, Janie, was stricken with polio as a child and went to live under doctors' care in New York City. And the middle child, Carol, became an alcoholic in her late teens and finally committed suicide in 1979 by jumping off a bridge in New Orleans. "I adored her," Annie told me. "She had piercing green eyes, fabulous blond hair, and tiny bones, like a sparrow's. She was practically an Olympic rider, and she could beat just about any guy I knew in tennis. It's so tragic that some people can't see themselves. It's like they have a block. Her death is one of those things you can never get over, can never justify."

ꞏ Jane Owen had built a memorial chapel to Carol on the property, and she had planted a garden for her next to the house in New Harmony. Annie herself paid tribute to Carol in other ways. The seminar that she had just completed in Colorado was on alcoholism, and it marked Annie's attempt to figure out what had gone wrong. She came back with some high-blown theories about certain people's natural inclination toward alcoholism because of various biological factors. And she spoke of Carol's inordinately low self-esteem, despite her beauty and talent. But beyond that, Annie couldn't really explain it.

The story stayed with me as I traveled the country and heard more of the lives of the rich kids. I began to see that along with the vivid intensity of an Annie came a certain darkness that might never be dispelled, and I couldn't help thinking it wasn't the alcohol that did Carol in so much as the money itself. For all its undeniable glory, the money involves hazards that all rich kids have to face. It is like some magic sword: it gives the holder rare powers, but only the mightiest warriors can keep from being nicked themselves by the blade. In myth, of course, a young knight proves his ability to wield such a blade before it is bestowed. For rich kids, however, their sword is presented to them whether they can handle it or not. And wealth is as potent as any sword. When mastered, it can bring the world to its knees. When it is not, it can bring the owner to his knees.

At the very least, wealth exposes its holders to dangerous temptations like drugs and alcohol. But it also creates the conditions that make such chemically assisted escape so appealing. In this, the very rich peculiarly resemble the very poor. They are isolated from the mainstream, often dependent on the professionals—accountants, trust officers, nannies, psychiatrists—who serve them, and generally hopeless about ever being able to improve their lot. Yet, unlike the poor, no matter how bad the rich kids' problems, no one ever gets much sympathy for being too rich. These are the ingredients of despair.

Annie was managing far better than Carol had, but even she was sensitive to the drawbacks of great wealth. They came out when I asked her about her career plans.

"The way I was raised," Annie told me, in words that would echo through many of my conversations with rich kids, "I wasn't trained for much. I was trained to be attractive, polite and make great party conversation; play the piano, swim, and water-ski. It was still the old school for me. But what are you supposed to do with your life? Sit home and watch TV all day? No. You work! There may be another way of doing it, but I don't know what it is."

But work at what? Annie liked animals so much that she once thought of becoming a veterinarian, but she gave up on the idea at college at Tufts when, after her performance on her premed courses, the vet schools were "not kind" to her. Instead, she has drifted from one thing to another. She has held several jobs but never made any one into an occupation. Most of the jobs just came to her out of the blue, and she couldn't think of any reason *not* to do them. For a time she delivered gourmet lunches to downtown Houston office workers trapped by the one-hour lunch limit in a town where, as she said, "It takes a half-hour just to get anywhere and another half-hour to get back." That scheme came about at a cocktail party in Houston when a woman came up to Annie and said, "Annie, what are you doin'?" Annie said not much, and the woman signed her right up as the vice-president of Peerless Gourmet. (Annie preferred to call it the Cantering Caterer but was overruled.) It helped that she knew many of the building owners socially, but occasional problems still cropped up. Once she heard that a jittery building manager had called an owner to report seeing a "Gypsy" delivering sandwiches in the building. The owner reassured him that it was only Annie. Ultimately, though, Peerless Gourmet encountered too many hassles from competing delicatessen owners jealous of the low overhead involved in their shoestring operation and it closed down.

Then she was a model. "That was no big thing," she said. "Every girl in Houston under a hundred fifty pounds did it. It was just runway stuff." But Annie caught the eye of a designer who wanted her to come to New York to model his clothes exclusively. "He must have thought that I had contacts," she said, "but he didn't know that I would never allow him to use them. That wasn't the deal. The deal was simply that I would wear his clothes to parties and be attractive. I said OK."

But a year after she arrived in New York, the designer

went out of business, and that left Annie holding the bag. "I felt so badly for all his customers who had paid in advance and now weren't going to get their dresses," she said. "So I took one of the seamstresses and opened the shop back up." But then, to Annie's surprise, she started receiving more orders, and before she knew it, she was a dress designer for real. She found the experience frustrating. "I didn't know what I was doing," she said. "I never did. My taste was always much higher than my ability, and I was never happy with what I did. The dresses weren't perfect. Finally, my frustration and my motivation equaled out and I quit.

"That was last year," she went on. "Ever since, I have been looking for the next thing. I never know what it'll be. I've never really sat down and figured out what I really should be; no, not *should*. Should is the worst word. Leave that out of the vocabulary. What I really *want* to do. I don't really feel the need to do anything. I don't have to go out and start an oil company or something, because I have that behind me in my genes."

Like most rich kids, Annie had done a lot of traveling in her youth, and it was as a traveler that she seemed to go through life, passing from one interesting scene to the next, but never finding the right place to settle down. Having never made any lasting commitments, she'd never put down roots. That was probably why she kept coming back here to this log cabin, I figured. It was the only real home she had. Still, the nomad's life had its pleasures.

Annie liked to take her dogs with her wherever she went. In Tigerlily and Thistle's younger days, she'd tuck one in a basket and the other in an old briefcase to sneak them past the stewardesses at the boarding gate, and then let them out to roam when she reached her seat. "They'd wiggle around and amuse themselves," she said, "but they'd never bother anybody." Now, because of tighter regulations, she was forced to store them in cages in the hold. "It's tragic what the airlines make you do," she said.

She spent a year traveling around Europe with Thistle after college, and almost came to regret her choice of companion one night when she was visiting a friend named Oliver, the son of the French ambassador to Denmark, at the embassy in Copenhagen. "They let Thistle onto the embassy grounds with a special passport with her nose printed on it," Annie recalled. "Everything was fine until one night Thistle chewed up the cords to the embassy's sound system. She just went crazy. And the next day they were going to have this big reception! So that night until five A.M. Oliver and I were scrambling around the floor of the embassy testing all the speaker wires trying to find the ones Thistle had chewed and then fixing them. It was wild, but I didn't mind. I don't travel just to see the sights."

It was nearly two, and Annie was finally talked out. "God," she said, "I wish I could think of something just *fascinating* to say. Has any of this been useful?" I reassured her it had all been fascinating. I figured it was time to go.

But before I left, Annie took me outside to see the backyard. A gentle rain was still falling and it made a soft hiss as we walked through the trees. While I had expected a leisurely midnight stroll, Annie strode quickly ahead of me and I had to hurry to keep up. We paused to look in the empty swimming pool. A few inches of rainwater and soggy leaves sloshed about in the deep end; it looked eerie and dismal to me. But not to Annie. She was wondering whether to ring it with Spanish tile or to install a heater to make it usable year round. Undecided, we pushed ahead to the trees beyond, where another problem loomed. A gap had appeared in the wall of trees where some of the pines had died out and allowed the bright city lights to peek through. Annie wanted to shut them out with a stand of sweet gum, magnolias, or possibly some wild Mexican plums. She smoked one last cigarette while she pondered the question. Then the rain came down harder, so we went back inside. I gathered up my things and headed out to my car. Annie said a casual good-bye, as though my leaving were no different from my coming and all motion was, in the end, purely random. She didn't see me to the door. Before driving off I took one last look at the cabin and the grounds where the buff bantam chicks used to roam. Under Annie's influence I had almost been able to see them. Now I was a little surprised that the scene still existed at all. The chicks, the log cabin in downtown Houston, my midnight visit—it all seemed like a dream. And even though the house and grounds looked real enough, the place remained an illusion, a figment of Annie's imagination that I could never share. I had thought there was a clear line where the money ended and the real world took over. But now, as I looked out at the dripping cabin and the drenched trees, I was beginning to see what it is to have money that never ends. It just goes and goes, transforming everything, like a long and heavy rain.

PART II

The Money

2

When It Happened to Me

In the 1950s there was a popular TV show called *The Millionaire*. It involved a billionaire industrialist named John Beresford Tipton who, every week, dispatched his executive secretary Michael Anthony to bestow a cashier's check for a million dollars on some unsuspecting individual. It was a "chess game with human beings," Tipton once explained. The fun was to drop this money on someone out of the blue and then watch to see what happened when a regular person suddenly became a millionaire. The only rule was that the recipient could make no effort to contact Tipton himself. Indeed, Tipton was never even seen by the TV viewers. They only heard his voice. His intermediary Michael Anthony conducted all the business of this "inheritance" for him. To the recipients,

RICH KIDS

Tipton was like a Roman god—an unseen force that ruled their lives completely.

The Millionaire, of course, was fiction, but it captures, inadvertently, the strange, out-of-the-blue quality of the transaction by which rich kids suddenly become so rich. The matter is invariably handled by intermediaries, and, to the sheltered heir, it almost always comes as a big surprise. Even though the donor is most often the heir's own father, the rich kid is not likely to hear about his inheritance in any detail until he legally comes of age on his eighteenth or twenty-first birthday, depending on the state. And he will almost certainly get the news from some professional middleman, such as the family lawyer, trust officer, or accountant, whom the heir has probably never met. So the whole affair retains the mysterious air of a visitation. It's a miracle! And when the rich kids told me about the blessed event years later, they often used the same two words, spoken with gusto, to describe their reaction: *"Hoooooooo-llllll-eeeeee SHIT!"*

Those were the words used by an heir to the Paine Webber fortune whom I'll call Roger Elkin. He is a tall and handsome young man living with his wife and child just outside of New York City. I found him through the Boston-based Haymarket People's Foundation, a leftist philanthropical organization Roger helped found, after his first eye-opening talk with his trust officer, back in the early seventies. Even though he ultimately decided to unload a fair percentage of his inheritance, at the time that he received it he felt only the thrill, amazement, and, yes, utter joy of being filthy rich.

"I had always sensed there was some money in the family when I was growing up," Roger told me, "but I had such a regular child-rearing that I never had any idea how much. I felt I was somewhat different from most people, but not significantly different. I'd flunked out of the University of Denver and was living in a communal house in Cambridge, Massachusetts, when I came into my money officially. I didn't think about it much, except the household kept getting all these solicitations from different activist groups for money and it made me realize—I know this sounds dopey—that I had something that a lot of people want. So I decided to go into the trust officer to find out just how much I had.

"It was classic. The place was this fancy brokerage house in Boston. I got reasonably dressed up for the occasion—put on some good corduroys—and went in there. I remember getting in the elevator and the higher it went, the more spaced out I got. When I got off, it took me a while to get my balance, because I felt so distant from everything. I had never been told about money at all when I was growing up. I think my father felt it wasn't his place to inform me because it wasn't his money. It came from my mother's side of the family. But my mom felt it wasn't her place to tell me because she'd never been told too much about it herself, and she was only a little less ignorant than me.

"The trust officer was your average banker type with glasses, and he handed me this big portfolio. It was mind-boggling. I didn't know what market value meant. I didn't know what book value meant. And there were four or five different trusts altogether. But I was trying to stay cool about the whole thing, and I said to him, 'I see, and now tell me, how much does all this come to?' And he said, 'Over a million dollars.' And I said, 'Oh.'

"But in my own head I was thinking, 'Holy shit! I'm a millionaire! Me!' But I still couldn't really believe it. I thought of a millionaire as having a million dollars, right? And all I had was a hodgepodge of trusts. So I said to the guy, 'Can I see it?' And he said, 'Sure,' and he took me down to the bank vault in the basement. And we went inside and opened up my deposit box. There were all these stock certificates inside—Black and Decker, U.S. Steel, IBM. I reached in and touched them. That definitely made it seem more real, touching the paper. I thought of it as a slice of America. I'm part of what made America great and bad. But it was still weird. I mean, there were all my holdings in one little drawer in this huge vault, like ashes in a mausoleum."

While Roger's experience is unusually dramatic—few rich kids can summon the courage to ask anything at all of their trust officers—it conveys the feeling that most rich kids have that first time. In an instant, their entire lives are transformed. I'm a millionaire! Me! All the evasions of their youth give way at the first glimpse of the bottom line. There are seven digits down there, or eight, or nine. . . .

But, as Roger sensed, the truth of the situation is still hard to grasp, and most rich kids come away from the first encounter with their millionaire status feeling dizzy and out of breath, as if they had a sudden case of altitude sickness. And indeed they do, but a lot of the feeling has to do with the setting itself. In going to see their trust officer, they are setting off into a dazzling, and slightly intimidating, new world of corporate finance. Like an encounter with The Millionaire's very proper executive secretary Michael Anthony, the first meeting involves a clash of consciousnesses. The trust officer is so controlled and the rich kid so befuddled, the two undergo a peculiar role reversal in which the rich kid ends up subservient to his employee. Most millionaires, of course, spend a lifetime growing into the role; rich kids have it thrust upon them.

In hearing about their trusts, all rich kids naturally feel a need to rise to the occasion, to deal with these professionals on their own terms and show that they are indeed worthy of this sudden elevation. But the encounter can be bewildering. The trust officer speaks another language, of market value, book value, and the Standard and Poor index. He is older, usually male, and generally wears, along with a rumpled gray suit, a slightly world-weary expression that may come from dealing with so much money that is not his. Besides being outdone, the rich kid is generally outnumbered, since the trust officer usually escorts the new heir on to meet the rest of the battery of officials that handle any individual account— lawyers, accountants, financial advisers.

To try to cope, the rich kids dress up, mind their manners, and sometimes even ride over there in unaccustomed style. One heiress said that her family rents a limousine—the only time she ever rides in one—for the trip through Manhattan to visit the family trust officer downtown. Some of the more indulgent officials, it is true, occasionally offer to meet on neutral ground. One New York rich kid got the word—"multimillionaire"—over dinner at the Harvard Club.

These officials can't be expected to make house calls, of course, or to unbend completely to put the rich kids at ease, but their professional manner makes the clients feel the money is foreign to them, a possession that is not truly theirs at all. Rather, it somehow remains in the hands of the professionals who administer it. And this is a sensation that many rich kids spend their whole lives trying to shake. As one put it, "It's like it's yours and it's not yours."

Nothing brings this home so much as the last act of these introductory meetings, which is for the trust officer to ask about the will. Not the donor's—the rich kid's. Now that he has inherited all this money, has he made any "provision" for it? The question is accompanied by the usual nervous jokes about how the new heir should drive carefully, etc. But it's a real kicker nonetheless, for it impresses upon the heir the fundamental truth of inherited wealth: that any heir is just a temporary carrier. Individual heirs may come and go, but the money lives on.

Such a realization naturally breeds a degree of detachment, and it comes out in the terms that rich kids use to refer to their money, which rarely suggest much intimacy with it. One calls it "the lump"; others say "my funds," "my resources," "my things," or, more colorfully, "the green." One Mellon descendant I'll call Heather, a tall, round-eyed blonde who still feels considerable ambivalence about her windfall, refers to her coming into her money by saying "when it happened to me"—as if it had been a blow on the head.

Yet, adding to their reserve in discussing their money may be the rich kids' sense of decorum; it's impolite to discuss one's riches too gaily. Even if they do enjoy their good luck, they quickly learn to do it privately. Of all the rich kids I spoke to, only one said that he celebrated on receiving the money. All the others may have confided in a close friend about how the lump had descended, but most carried on as though nothing had happened.

The one exception was Steve Graham, son of *Washington Post* owner Katharine Graham, and even he marked the big event fairly modestly. His older sister Lally Weymouth, the journalist, invited him out to dinner when he was in New York shortly after turning twenty-one. When he arrived at her apartment that afternoon, she took a look at him and said that the first thing he should do was get himself some clothes. And to do that, he should call up Morgan Guaranty and get some money. Steve made the call to his trust officer while Lally stood by. "Hello," said Steve bravely. "Ah, I'd like to take out five hundred dollars." "No!" said Lally in a stage whisper. "Make it a thousand!" "Uh, better make that a thousand," Steve said uncertainly. To his amazement, the officer said, "Fine, just come on down." So Steve went down, picked up the money and bought a supply of shirts, and then capped the night off with a very pleasant dinner with his sister. Still, there was something peculiar about it all. "That day felt very strange," Steve told me.

Yet even if the rich kid's attitude toward his money seems guarded at first, that doesn't mean he doesn't care. In the early stages, at least, the relationship has the quality of an illicit affair—with a married woman, say—which the rich kid imagines would be frowned upon by everyone he knows, but which nevertheless has caught him in its thrall. It's a guilty pleasure, but a pleasure nonetheless. Even if the rich kid expresses a certain reserve in discussing his "funds," his words are belied by a sneaking smile that, in guilty liberal and swaggering conservative alike, almost invariably flashes across his face. The look on this shy suitor says: Yeah, she's really the wrong woman for me, but, you know, I kind of like her.

But this affair has its complications, not the least of which is practical. In gaining the money, these rich kids gained a new and rather cumbersome aspect to their lives—a layer of bureaucracy to ensnarl them till they die. Always before, when these rich kids had needed a little pocket money, they'd go to Dad. Now they go to Morgan Guaranty. The trust fund is the rich-kid equivalent of the welfare office, complete with clerks and officials, and strict terms written by higher powers governing how the money is to be spent. And it can be a nuisance.

Trusts come in all shapes and sizes. There is the accumulating trust, which is generally established during the heir's childhood, with dividends reinvested (hence the term accumulating) until the heir turns eighteen or twenty-one. Then it becomes all his to save or spend. Another popular variety is the generation-skipping trust, which a grandfather might set up. It allows his children to take the trust's income during their lifetimes, but upon their death the principal passes to their children. The advantage here is to save inheritance taxes for the intermediary generation; since they didn't control the principal, they cannot be taxed on it. And there is the sprinkling trust, which is arranged to "sprinkle" money to those within a family with a demonstrable need for it.

Yet the most common variety is probably the personal trust, which is handed down directly from one generation to the next, with as many or as few strings attached as the parents wish to devise. Some heirs have such complete access to their trust that it is essentially a glorified bank account, allowing them to make withdrawals at will, without ever having to make a deposit. On the other extreme, some trusts are written so that the beneficiary may not touch the principal of the account—may not, as the elders would say, "invade capital"—but only spend the interest, and in exceptionally restricted cases he may only get at that for certain approved purposes, such as to further his education or salvage his health.

Trusts go back to twelfth-century England and started for much the same reason that they continue, namely to save taxes. In those days, land was the chief possession being passed along. Since there were inheritance taxes to pay if the landowner waited until his death to transfer his property, some property-holders started shifting the legal title to trustworthy intermediaries during their own lifetime. The intermediaries then passed it along to the heirs at a safe interval after the donors' demise. Because the "trustees," as they came to be called, didn't receive any income from the land, they weren't considered responsible for paying any taxes, and the ultimate beneficiaries got off tax-free since they didn't receive title upon the original owner's death. Although this certainly looks like fraud, the dodge was firmly incorporated in English law, after a series of skirmishes with three centuries' worth of English kings, in 1535.

The tax angle is a significant one in the minds of today's generation of wealthy parents and their accountants. Chiefly the attraction is that, because of the progressive income tax, individuals can cut their total tax burden by shifting some of their estate to trusts for their children. While the trust's income is taxed, it is taxed at a much lower rate than it would have been if it had remained part of the huge earnings of the parents' estate.

But another advantage lies in the nature of the trust itself, which allows the donor to maintain control of his money long after he has ostensibly given it away—indeed, long after he has been lowered into his grave. By setting down his wishes in the terms of the trust, the all-important fine print of this legal instrument, he can make sure that his preferences are regarded for three generations and twenty-one years. And in creating the trust, he also empowers a small army of professionals to enforce its terms.

Just as in twelfth-century England, the modern trust has to pass through to the beneficiary only via intermediaries. And all of them, from the appointment secretaries to the trust-company presidents, treat the trust like a business—their business. Ironically, just as the trust is considered its own legal entity, with its own IRS number, and therefore responsible to pay its own taxes, so the trust itself pays for the services of the trust company that can be so off-putting. Hence the lament heard from all of the heirs—whose money is this anyway?

The majordomo of the trust is the trust officer, that rumpled fellow the rich kids first meet to find out how rich they are. In legal terms, the trust officer is the account's custodian, a title that conjures up an image of an otherwise unemployable fellow with buckets of ammonia and a dust mop. After they get used to him, most rich kids come around to this view themselves.

Rich kids may deride their trust officers, but in truth much of the abuse is undeserved. At New York City's U.S. Trust Company, which maintains a well-appointed brownstone designed by McKim, Mead and White at midtown so that clients will feel right at home as they do their banking, the trust officers are reputed to have walked the dogs of their clients. For their younger charges, they have sent allowances and even typed up term papers. According to an article in *Town and Country*, one trust officer has gone even further beyond the call of duty for a rich-kid client who was vacationing with her mother on Nantucket when the old lady died unexpectedly. The woman's husband had passed away some time before, and the couple had always wished to be buried in identical coffins. When the client couldn't find a matching coffin on Nantucket, she let her fingers do the walking and dialed her trust officer. Would he mind looking around for one? He bent to the task without complaint and located a duplicate. Then he drove to a suburban airport where he chartered a private plane and slid his unusual luggage into the hold. Unfortunately, it didn't fit. So the man then hired a cargo plane and pluckily hopped into the unpressurized cabin to ride with the coffin to its destination. He presented it to his client in person. And not a penny extra was charged for his time, just his usual percentage of the account.

Like a psychiatrist, the trust officer gets a rare, insider's view of rich kids. As one officer pointed out, "When you talk about money, you talk about everything." Officers know about the new house, the new car, the new yacht, the new wife, the new hobby, the new job and how much, if anything, the kid is paid to perform it. Having examined the prenuptial agreement, he knows about the uncertainty a young groom may be feeling about his intended, and, processing the alimony payments later, he can see how much that uncertainty was warranted. Since many trust companies place great store in the personal touch, trust officers have been known to travel widely to visit their far-flung charges, in some cases venturing to remote corners of the globe like latter-day Stanleys in search of some trust-fund Livingstons. "We have to understand their needs firsthand," one explained.

Sometimes, because of the unusual knowledge they have of the heir's fortune, the trust officers become the recipient of even greater confidences than they expected. One officer said that one of his file folders was thick with rambling confessional letters. But this intimacy can pose unexpected dangers as well. One trust-fund baby, fresh from a movie about a horseback rider, strode in for a visit to his trust officer wearing jodhpurs and a riding helmet, although the officer knew the kid owned no horse. He was also carrying a riding crop, with which he started to beat the trust officer about the shoulders.

RICH KIDS

The poor officer managed to hold him off and then use his position as the rich kid's personal comptroller to take his revenge. "We kept a tight rein on him after that," he said, without humor.

But despite the best efforts of many trust officers to stay on close terms with their charges, there are inevitable lapses, and they stem from the basic scheme of having such a fellow in charge of the heirs' personal finances. Women feel this more acutely, since they have often been more sheltered than their brothers from the world of high finance. One automobile-supply heiress I'll call Marie didn't realize the most elementary facts about her trust, or her trust officer, until she was well into her twenties. "I didn't know that you could just call somebody up and get money," she says. "I only figured it out when one of my brothers told me. He'd just gotten a big check out of his trust and I was amazed. I said, 'How'd you get that?' and he told me all I had to do was to call up the trust officer. So I did, and sure enough, I got some money, too."

Unfortunately, Marie had trouble keeping it. Not long after she made the first exhilarating discovery of what her trust officer could do for her, she decided that she could do even better for herself by putting it in the hands of an investment adviser she met one day at a spiritual bookstore. His results, however, were hardly divine, as he proceeded to lose all her money, first in an anxiety-provoking gradual slide, then in a final heart-stopping rush. "I find this topic sort of icky," Marie says, finishing our interview. She is now studying to be a lay preacher in a Catholic seminary.

Many families still expect women to stay in the dark. In the Pulitzer family, the trusts were set up around the turn of the century by old Joseph Pulitzer so that women weren't allowed to come into any money at all, nor even were their male children allowed to receive any of the Pulitzer fortune through them. The idea here was twofold—not to overload the Pulitzer women if they were just going to go find rich husbands anyway, and to discourage bounty hunters. But the result was to leave them totally baffled about money matters.

The trust officer is only the front man, the one who handles the day-to-day business of the trust in as cheerful and accommodating a manner as possible. He's the good cop. Behind him, however, stands a more dreaded figure in the pantheon of trust officials—the trustee. He's the bad cop.

Generally the individual is a close family friend, or a relative or a banker with ties to the family holdings, or, possibly, some combination of these. One might thereby expect that the trustee would be someone close to the heart of the beneficiary, but in truth this is rarely the case. Legally, his responsibility lies with the trust, not the recipient. And this has set off not a few epic battles between trustee and beneficiary. A famous one involves Brooks McCormick, Jr., an heir to the International Harvester fortune, who in 1980 sued his trustees, one of whom was his father Brooks McCormick, Sr., after they paid off a $1.9 million bill for a house Brooks Jr. was building for himself in Warrenville, Illinois, with money from his trust. He claimed that the builders overcharged him, and that the trustees should have paid no more than the supposedly agreed-upon price of $400,000. Brooks Jr. wanted the trustees to make up the difference. He also sought a full accounting of the trustees' actions since 1964 to find out if any other assets had been, to use Brooks Jr.'s word, "squandered," without his knowledge. Thrown out once in a lower court, only to be reinstated by an appellate court, the suit was still pending in early 1985 and will probably not be resolved until 1986.

An heiress I interviewed made the same mistake when she assumed that money she had inherited through her mother was safe in the hands of her father as trustee. But her parents had divorced when she was in her teens, and when she looked into her finances on turning twenty-one she discovered that her father had invested her trust exclusively in a poorly performing mutual fund of which he himself happened to be a major partner. Fortunately, the terms of the trust allowed her to take full control on her majority. "I yanked my dad out of there as soon as I could," she reported. "Now I take care of all of that stuff myself."

Even when the trustee is acting properly, a certain degree of distance is bound to creep into the relationship. Since he is there to enforce the terms of the trust, he sometimes acts like the loan officer at a bank that is less concerned with satisfying its customers than with maintaining its assets. *Washington Post* heiress Elizabeth Meyer, for example, may have wasted that expensive watercolor paper at age two, but since turning twenty-one, she has had to be more respectful of her larger holdings. She said that she has to write up a lengthy proposal whenever she wishes to dip into the capital of her trust, explaining precisely what the money is needed for. If it is for a business venture, she has to spell out the exact nature of the business, its prospects and risks. And sometimes she is turned down. Yet she professed not to mind. If it were any other way, she reasoned, her siblings would have the same leeway, and she fears that one of them might blow it, leaving Elizabeth to repair the financial damage.

If it seems the trustees are acting *in loco parentis,* it's because they often are. While an inheritance may seem to be one of life's few unalloyed pleasures, the cruel truth is that you sometimes have to lose a parent to gain it. It's true that parents usually set up a trust for their children to inherit as adults, but the bulk of the money doesn't usually come down until they die. Consequently, many kids are rich at a young age only because their parents have themselves died young, and that often means that they were carried off unexpectedly or even violently—the victims of cancer, or of a car or plane crash, or by some freak accident. One young heir, Winston Goodfellow, came into his money after his father had choked to death on a piece of meat before Winston was even born. Obviously, this dampened Winston's enthusiasm about his good fortune. Not long ago, he told me, when his girl friend was razzing him about how lucky he was to be so rich, Winston cut her off. "You want to be lucky like me?" he asked her. "Why don't you go bump off your old man?"

To a certain way of thinking, in fact, the whole matter is totally perverse. Since the inheritance swells the fewer relatives remain to share in it, the richest rich kid is the one who in all other respects is worst off, the orphan with no brothers or sisters.

When these children lose their parents at a young age, however, they still don't come into their inheritances until adulthood. At that point they aren't likely to make the association between their inheritance and their parents' death too powerfully. One viewed it positively. She was thrilled to discover how successful her father had been. But for the rich kids whose parents die when they are themselves fully grown, it sometimes seems as though the parents have vanished like some characters in a fairy tale and left behind a pile of money for the heir to remember them by. Particularly when that money is then watched over by some strange and possibly tyrannical bureaucrat in a downtown office, that can leave the heir feeling a little peculiar about his supposed good fortune.

That's how the woman I'll call Amanda Holladay felt, anyway, when it happened to her.

"I would rather Father had lived a hundred years and spent all of his fortune himself," she told me. "He could have run through every penny and I would be perfectly happy. I really loved Father. I'd do anything for him to be alive." And she meant it.

A fashionable young woman with good bone structure and a profusion of red hair that ran halfway down her back, Amanda was, at thirty-two, studying to be a stage actress. She admitted to a strong fantasy life—indeed, she appeared before me for lunch at a chichi San Francisco restaurant in the pantaloons and polka-dotted blouse of Pierre le Fou—that seemed to well up from the deepest part of herself. "I love costumes," she said. When I observed that I could see her as Alice in Wonderland, she applauded my insight. "Of course!" she exclaimed with a gleeful clap. "She wore her hair just like mine"—she ran a jeweled hand through her long red locks—"and she wore lots of light cotton Victorian things with sashes. Alice wore pinafores. Little flaps. I used to dress like that constantly in school and college. I always felt perfectly at home." When her father was still alive, her life was a wonderland. She grew up in a Hillsborough, California, castle, complete with turrets and elaborate gardens that were the wonder of the house-and-garden tour. When she traveled with her family to the best hotels of Europe, which she did frequently, she learned as early as age eight to take full advantage of room service. "That was my favorite thing," she said. "I'm just like Eloise, you know, taking room service at the Plaza." That year she went off to a boarding school in the Arizona desert where she learned how to ride and shoot a bow and arrow. On her birthday, she recalled, her parents gave her an ivory fan, a Madame Alexander doll, and a .22 short-barreled Winchester.

As at eight, so at eighteen and all the other years, Father took care of all the financial arrangements and delighted in surprises. Amanda didn't even know where the money came from. She sensed that it might have been "back there" in the family, but she also thought that Father had made a lot of it himself. "The wealth was just a given," she said. "I don't know the sources. It was just there." As for the critical matter of how much of it would someday be hers, she felt that it would have been "tactless" to inquire. "He always told me that I would 'never have to worry,'" she said. "I knew I would always be provided for." The matter became more pressing in the last years of her father's life, when he grew sick with cancer and she had to start planning for the future. But she couldn't bring herself to ask the big question because, as she said, "I didn't want him to think I was curious about his demise."

Amanda was in her early twenties when her father died, and suddenly her wonderland turned ugly. The first thing that happened was that the bloodsuckers came out. "We started getting bills from everybody in the vicinity of the hospital who had ever looked in on Father," she said. Compared to what followed, that was just a minor irritant.

Amanda found out quite quickly that there was no substitute for Father. "Father may have been capricious," she said, "but he was very warm and generous. It was suddenly very awkward for me to go to these strange men at the trust company to get money. The trust never gave me money while he was alive, because Father ran it. He distributed the money at his pleasure. That worked out fine. It meant I had to ask Father when I wanted something. But now I have to ask the executor when I want something, so it's very much different. The executor was one of Father's business associates, but he is not at all like Father. He's very conservative, comes from an entirely different sort of background than we do. He's not poor, but he works for every cent he has. He's very good about it, I suppose. Very professional. But it's still having to deal with a male figure, the older figure, who is paternal. And I find that annoying. When it was Father, it was different. It was his money. It's not this guy's money. I'm still grateful, of course. I mean, Father could have left all his money to an animal cemetery."

While this executor, who had many of the functions of a trustee, seemed willing to dole out money when Amanda wanted it, he was far less inclined to hand out any information about just what she possessed. Eventually this began to nag at her. "I mean, it was my money, right?" she said. To compound her urgency, no one in the rest of the family was making much of an effort to take charge. Amanda's mother was still too consumed with grief, and her brother was lost in fantasies of his own, having embarked on writing a multivolume history of cosmic consciousness.

"Even after the inheritance officially went into effect," she said, "neither the executor nor the accountant ever got it together to explain things to us. I didn't get on them right away because it was a hard thing for me to deal with. Nobody wanted to tell me anything. They expected me to be totally passive like the rest of my family. Gradually I became quite alarmed. I asked my mother if she knew what was going on, if she had any idea what she owned, and she said, 'Well, I trust the executives handling it completely. . . .' She just let it go."

That didn't sit well with Amanda.

"First I tried to get the executor on the phone, and then I tried in person. He just said, 'Wait and see, wait and see.' Now, four and a half years later, I'm still waiting. He continues to try to brush me off. Friends who are lawyers have told me I have the right to demand full disclosure, but I didn't want to push it. At least not right away. I felt guilty. I didn't want to look like I was sweeping down like a vulture. Besides, I didn't have any reason to think that the executor was doing anything inappropriate. After a while, though, I began to suspect he resented us because we'd just inherited all this money, and he'd had to earn his. Gradually, I began to push a little harder.

"So he gave me the runaround. Finally he told me to call the attorneys. I met with one of them and it blew my mind. The guy wasn't sure he should even show me my federal tax return. I found that *very* alarming. I mean, my God! It's my tax return, my money, right? I'd never met him, so I thought maybe he wasn't sure I was the person I was claiming to be. I said, 'If you want to see some ID I can show you. If after seeing some ID you don't wish to show it to me, I suggest you consult your attorney, because this is a *very* bizarre attitude!'

"He turned beet red and started to shake. At that point, I thought, my God, what is going on? All I want is information. This is crazy! Finally he pulled a document out of his files and showed it to me, but I couldn't follow it. And he wouldn't explain it to me.

"Well, it took a long time, but finally I hired some lawyers of my own to lean on these other lawyers who were supposedly working for me, and those lawyers gave the word to the accountant to give me the information I wanted. It took a year for him to prepare a statement of all my holdings. I don't know why it took so long, because these were documents they were supposed to have ready to show the government for tax purposes.

"When the statement finally did come, there were pages and pages. I felt like Sisyphus as I went through them all. When I finally figured out the statement, it made me feel really sad. It made me miss my father. The money represented what he had chosen to give us. It was a great deal of numbers, but it was actually less than I thought. I'd forgotten how much Father had spent. That's how we lived the way we did.

"I don't know why it took so long, whether it's because I'm a woman or just a kid, or what. Supposedly nobody has anything to hide, so I don't know. I finally ended up taking the trust people to court because the figures turned out to be so much lower than we expected. That's where the whole mess is now—in probate."

* * *

Although the money hardly passed smoothly into Amanda's control, it still managed to infuse her with its mysterious power in just a few years. Back when she was still living on handouts from her father—lavish as they might have been—she would never have expected that she would ever be able to stand up to any of her father's associates, let alone hire a lawyer to haul them into court. The money can accelerate their growing up this way. Like a booster rocket, the money can fire these kids into a hyperspace of previously unimaginable possibilities if they can just get a grip on the throttle. Shortly after becoming a millionaire, that is to say, a rich kid often starts to act like one.

A multimillionaire for six years now, twenty-four-year-old "Sonia Belahovski" still can't get over the change.

When she sat by her accountant's desk at his office near the Plaza in New York a few weeks after her eighteenth birthday to hear him explain about her holdings and present her with her extensive portfolio, her head was swimming. She had tried to obtain some financial information before from the family brokerage firm, but never gotten anywhere. "Every time I called over there," she said, "the guy I wanted to speak to was either dying, or dead, or just retired. It was like something out of Dickens." So at eighteen, in her ignorance all she could think of as the accountant rattled on about her vast fortune were the houses, hotels, property cards, and multicolored cash of the game Monopoly. "That was the only way I could make sense of all the money," she said. "And I was extremely concerned with understanding it. I kept telling him, 'I'm sorry I'm so dense, but could you go through that one more time?' "

Six years later, Sonia had an uncanny ease, self-assurance, and sophistication that belied her age. In her bathroom, I found a button that said, "You're a Big Girl Now." But she didn't force it, instead just let her confidence flow in the natural and unassuming manner, I imagine, of royalty. It was no small accomplishment.

Sonia was slim and attractive with a deep Lauren Bacall voice, luscious Mick Jagger lips, and a thick swath of hair that is as black as the carbon black her fortune is based on. On her mother's side, her great grandfather was Godfrey Lowell Cabot, who devised a technique to burn off the cheap surplus gas from various American fields to produce the carbon black—he always just called it "soot"—which was first used to blacken such things as ink and stove polish, and later, far more lucratively, to reinforce the rubber in automobile tires. Godfrey Lowell Cabot added many millions to the Cabot family shipping fortune before he died at the age of 101. Some of those millions are now Sonia's, having been transferred to her in what she called "the easiest possible way," as a portfolio to be registered in her name when she came of age.

She sat smoking herbal cigarettes (to break her addiction to Camels) at a heavy monk's refectory table that she inherited along with her money in the dining area of a small duplex cooperative a few blocks from Central Park. She was wearing a puffy blouse that was gathered at the shoulders and no jewelry except some "Indian things"—a few jade rings on her fingers. To disguise her true identity, she had decided to call herself Sonia Belahovski for this book and wrote it for me on the blackboard she used for messages. Her parents almost named her Sonia, she explained, and Belahovski was the original name of her father's family back in Eastern Europe. Her actual name, however, was comparatively prosaic, and I couldn't help thinking that it suited this down-to-earth young woman far better.

Actually, she enjoyed the anonymity her real last name brought her, particularly the freedom to list herself in the phone book without worry. Yet at the same time she admitted that occasionally she had felt a twinge of regret that more people didn't recognize that she was a Cabot, or if they did know, that they didn't fully appreciate all that it meant. It reminded her of the way that she had been ignored or patronized as a child. Riding in elevators with her elders, she used to feel an urge to stick her bubble gum in the ladies' fur coats in retaliation for the way they accidentally squashed her against the wall. "I wanted to tell them," she recalled, " 'I'm a Cabot! You can't do this to me!' " Now, although she had been given no middle name, she occasionally found herself sticking Cabot in, as a subtle memento of her privileged status. "Usually, I leave it as a C.," she said.

THE MONEY

Like most rich kids, Sonia had had little experience with money growing up. She had spent her childhood on a gentleman's farm in Connecticut's Fairfield County that had a Greek revival main house, a large barn, and several outbuildings including a chicken coop that she occupied as a teenager after her mother had renovated it for her. She never received an allowance as a child, and aside from a stint playing guitar in a local coffee shop, she never held a job. She did have a bank account, but the only money she'd scraped up for it was her Chanukah dimes (she's Jewish on her father's side) and a few odd dollars she'd received for the vegetables she grew in her garden.

But there wasn't much that she wanted to buy, either. She was happy riding any of the several horses; playing with the smaller animals, the sheep, and the goats, penned out back; and, when she was younger, finding "little hideaway places" in the barn. A caretaker handled the animals during the week; Sonia and her brothers would muck out the stalls over the weekends when school was out. The children themselves were looked after by a succession of governesses, one of whom led to the first realization that Sonia's life-style might set her apart from the other kids. The woman was Haitian; she had come to America with her husband to take care of the Belahovski children. The other kids in the neighborhood had never seen any blacks, and as soon as they saw this Haitian couple, they started calling Sonia "Niggerlips." The other kids didn't realize how classy it was to have foreign nannies.

In general, the family operated free from the world of cash. Sonia's mother regularly rode into town in a pony cart that was a holdover from the days of gasoline rationing in the Second World War. And the family practically lived off the food they grew in the garden during the summer. If they happened to catch a raccoon or a woodchuck nibbling at the cucumbers or lettuce, they killed it and ate it, too. "We had a reputation," said Sonia. "We once found a huge pregnant turtle wandering down the road with a knife in her back after she had been stabbed by some of the neighborhood kids. We gathered her up, took her home, and ate her. And we made turtle soup out of the eggs."

Despite the presence of the Haitian couple, Sonia might

have thought her childhood was entirely average if it hadn't been for a chance remark by the Belahovskis' "family counselor," a local therapist who provided the children with low-key psychological advice. When Sonia got on the subject of possible careers one day—she was thinking of becoming either a singer, a photographer, or a jockey—the counselor observed that she would never have to work to support herself. But that was all he said, and she often wondered what he could have meant.

An early boyfriend sized up the situation more quickly and took advantage of it one summer when the two of them traveled together from Paris, where Sonia had spent the winter after graduating from high school, to Morocco. "Jim" was a blond Californian with a strong interest in rock music and struck Sonia as a step up from all the "shaggy kids" she had been hanging out with previously. (The shaggy kids—whom Sonia distinguished from the "rich kids" of the town she liked a lot less—used to gather at Sonia's chicken coop, drink mint juleps and drop acid, then sit on the stone wall to watch the sun go down.) Sonia had been to Europe a number of times before—practically every other summer, it seemed—but always in the company of her parents. This time her mother let her go alone, but sent her a steady supply of travelers' checks so she could manage by herself. Sonia wanted to use the checks sparingly, but Jim had different ideas. "He was really interested in the money," said Sonia. "I wanted to go low-budget, but he kept pushing me into first-class every-thing—first-class trains instead of hitchhiking, first-class hotels instead of camping out. I had about five hundred dollars a month, and to me that was a lot. I'd never *seen* so much money before. My father had always said, 'Don't let a man marry you for your money,' but I had never known what he was talking about. I was starting to find out. It was, 'Uh-oh, wait a minute.' "

Sonia gave Jim the word when they got back, but as often happens with the boyfriends of the rich, Jim didn't take no for an answer and continued to call Sonia regularly for some time afterward, often to berate her for not making more of herself. And he would pay her unexpected visits at odd hours.

Not long ago she was spending a night at the farm when Jim appeared suddenly at two in the morning. He claimed he'd left his wallet in the bathroom after coming to swim earlier in the day, which hardly made Sonia feel any better. This time she told him to get out and stay out. "He was a definite moocher," she said.

It was a few months after she got back from Morocco that, Sonia said, "the huge thing happened" and she went in to talk to her accountant. After noting that Sonia had just come into rather a significant sum, he asked her naturally enough what she planned to do with it. And here was where those many hours hunched over the Monopoly board with her brothers (spent in quantity because the children had been allowed to watch only a few approved TV shows) paid off. For she realized that the income shouldn't just pile up; it should be reinvested. Not in houses and hotels, of course, but in stocks. So that was what she told him: reinvest it, please. When the accountant asked how, Sonia was stumped. The accountant then suggested that she might be interested in an investment adviser. Sonia agreed—grateful both for the idea and the term "investment adviser." She would have had no idea what to call such a person.

One of the first big changes occurred right away, for the accountant told Sonia that while he could suggest advisers for her, she was the one who had to do the actual hiring. Fortunately, she got along with the first one she met. In her interview with the man, he asked her how much she needed to live on. Sonia was taken aback by the question; she had no idea. Since she had spent so little money before, she assumed she would spend little money now and, picking a sum practically at random, said $10,000 a year. As if to explain, she announced, "I'd be completely happy living in a log cabin in Vermont." The adviser could only smile and say he doubted she would stick to such austerity for very long. "I expect to see you spending three times that just for a car in a few years," he said.

The words left Sonia's head spinning with a new sense of possibility. It was as if she'd just realized she had hotels on Boardwalk and Park Place. "That was the first time," she said, "that it ever occurred to me that I had enough money to buy any car I wanted."

It had taken a while for her to act on that realization, but she was making considerable progress, the results of which were visible around her co-op apartment. She pointed to the toaster on the counter in the kitchen and said proudly that it had cost her $10 at a rummage sale. But she also owned a $1,300 Elna sewing machine which, she noted just as proudly, was built with parts made by Rolls-Royce.

She attributed her improvement in managing her finances to the advice of a boyfriend she had met at college in Vermont. Unlike the troublesome Jim, "Peter" took an interest in Sonia's money more for her own sake than for his. Sonia said that she had only talked openly about her inheritance with three or four people in her entire life; Peter was the first. "His reaction was basically 'Wow, that's really interesting,'" she said. "He was sweet." He was studying clinical psychology when they met, and he applied some of it to Sonia. "We lived together for four years in college. I attribute a lot of my growth on the financial thing to him. He was a godsend. I'd go into a clothing store and say, 'These pants are a hundred bucks and I'm really worried about it.' He'd say, 'Do you really like them?' I'd say, 'Yeah.' 'Would you really use them more than a couple of times?' he'd ask. I'd say, 'Yeah.' So he'd say, 'Look, buy them.' That may sound simple, but it really helped. That was the beginning. I remember the pants. They were black silk, and I wanted them to wear for my first time into Studio 54. There are certain pieces of clothing that I use to date my growth. That was one of them. Last year, I had to stop myself from buying a twenty-five-hundred-dollar leather coat. I came very close. I made a pact with myself that if I went to the health club for a month I could buy it. So I did, and then I went back and it was gone. But that shows the progression anyway—from a hundred-dollar pair of silk pants to a twenty-five-hundred-dollar leather coat in six years. That's pretty fast for me."

If there had been a turning point in her purchases during that period, it was probably the car that she bought for herself, just as the investment adviser had predicted. It didn't cost

$30,000, but it was still a big step. It was a Rabbit, and Peter totaled it. He had borrowed it to take a ride into town at college with a friend (without Sonia's permission, which made the accident all the more awkward), gotten a little tipsy from a few drinks, and slammed into a tree. Said Sonia: "My first reaction was—my parents! My parents! He's totaled their car! But then I realized that it wasn't their car, it was mine. It was my money. That was a very interesting change."

If Sonia Belahovski and Amanda Holladay have seen their lives speeded up by the acquisition of so much money at an early age, others have seen theirs retarded by an agonizing wait before they will fully come into their gold. They may have gotten some of it at eighteen or twenty-one, but that was just enough to whet their appetite for the double helping that will be placed before them someday later on. Annie Owen fell into this category, and it didn't seem to bother her very much. But others can be transformed by the delay into the equivalent of aging spinsters—waiting and waiting for life to start. This is the alternative, actually, that Amanda Holladay would have faced if her father had held on, and it is not an entirely happy one. Some trusts are arranged so that the child comes into increasing amounts of money, after that first break-through at eighteen or twenty-one, at five-year intervals: twenty-five, thirty, thirty-five. . . . As one heiress noted, "That kinda makes you look forward to birthdays." The arrangement is more drastic—all or nothing—for the heirs to one of the more common varieties of inheritances, the generation-skipping trusts, in which the principal only descends on the death of their parents. It can, obviously, be a ticklish situation for the child to know that he will profit so handsomely from his mother or father's demise. In families that are more thoroughly aristocratic, where, by provident marriages or a profusion of wealthy ancestors, money comes from more than one source, the situation is eased somewhat. Any one of a number of branches on the family tree can wither to let fall a golden apple. But it's still not easy to be the heir apparent for very long, because it is so much more fun to be the king.

And that situation, a common one for rich kids, is the one

that a Rockefeller descendant I'll call Terry finds himself in. He certainly has enough money to get by, but he's playing the waiting game, waiting for It to happen.

You can see it in his apartment, which could really use some of the green. Despite a fashionable Manhattan address and liveried doorman, Terry's apartment itself was furnished in a surprisingly threadbare style when I saw it—mostly with hand-me-downs from the family rec room. He himself was decked out no better in khaki trousers and a flannel shirt. He sat me down on a sagging couch and served some tea out of mismatching cups. It hardly seemed Rockefeller.

At twenty-nine Terry had not exactly been biding his time. He had worked on a road crew in the Adirondacks, joined a communist work camp in the south of France, herded sheep in Australia, grown tobacco in New Zealand, helped found an award-winning newspaper in Vermont, and labored in the environmental office at New York's City Hall.

But of late, interestingly, he had thrown all that over to spend his days managing what he called "the family assets" that he must devoutly hope (he was too discreet to say) will soon be his. They must loom before him the way Everest did in the eyes of Edmund Hillary before he started to climb.

When I asked, he described the fortune to me one evening before he headed off to a Rangers-Islanders game. Despite the lack of time, he went into the subject in a detail that could only be called loving.

"I'm a descendant of William Rockefeller," he began, "and the difference monetarily between the descendants of William and those of his more famous brother, John D., is that for every two shares of Standard Oil that John D. had, William had one. So my branch of the family started out half as rich as John D.'s branch. Plus, our side has procreated faster so that the money has been divided more ways than it has been on John D.'s. For us, the generation-skipping trusts 'sprinkle' to my mother and her family. But because my grandfather's generation has lived on longer, my mother hasn't come into her money yet. She gets no principal, just interest. That is to say she is an income beneficiary, not a principal or residual beneficiary. Of all the family trusts, I'm a residual beneficiary only of some that my grandfather set up, namely the ones that my mother is a beneficiary of. So basically, I won't see any *serious* money for a while. My mother won't see any until either one of her parents dies. That's one of the gruesome things about wealth. I won't see money for twenty years at least. Through gifts, through estates, I have some value, some assets in the bank more than the huge majority of people in the U.S., but nothing like what people expect from a Rockefeller."

Terry discussed this all straightforwardly, as if he had been talking about nothing more urgent than the prognosis on the Rangers' new crop of wingers. But he also admitted to some impatience in bringing the appearances of his life into their ultimate conformity with reality.

"I think it would be just the *worst* to go through life with some expectations and to always have the realization off in the future. That's the worst kind of delayed gratification. Waiting. It's totally passive. There's nothing you can do to speed up the passage of money. Or at least, there's nothing that you can do that they don't put you in jail for."

We both laughed, but that was before the reports came out about how the Manhattan arts patron Frances Bernice Schreuder persuaded her then seventeen-year-old son Marc to knock off her father, multimillionaire Franklin Bradshaw, to get her hands on her inheritance. She now faces a life sentence; Marc got five years. People do strange things for money.

I asked Terry how he visualized his inheritance. "I see it all as trusts gathered above me like storm clouds," he replied after a pause to take in such an odd question. "And I don't know whether they hold promise or danger. I just can't see. All there is is darkness, but there is a potential to be drenched in a wonderful warm rain."

3

Easy Come, Easy Go

For all their millions, rich kids have a hard time securing
that great American badge of financial reliability and clout,
the credit card. MasterCard, Visa, American Express, and the
other credit companies are geared up only to consider salaries
as they determine credit-worthiness; inherited wealth doesn't
compute. Further, the twenty- or even thirty-year-old millionaire isn't likely to have built up a credit rating to assist the
card companies in their deliberations—either because the kid
hasn't had a chance to make a big purchase yet or because
he has made it in cash, instead of on time in the classic American fashion.

Sonia Belahovski spent two years trying to secure a credit
card with, she says, "my accountant badgering them the whole

time." Her troubles were compounded by the fact that not only did she have no credit rating, but her Cabot mother had none either since she had never in her life taken out a loan. But Sonia, like most rich kids, has the plastic now—for her, a gold American Express card. "They really go wild over it in New York," she says.

And Michael Pratt, who had been so impressed by his first trip to Amherst College, had a similar experience. "When I applied for a Bloomingdale's card," he recalls, "I put down my annual income, which is a *huge* amount, and I wrote in beside it on the space for Profession 'Independently Wealthy.' They sent back a rejection." The other companies weren't any more favorably inclined until they received a phone call from Michael's trust officer at the U.S. Trust Company, who laid the situation out to them in blunt terms. Now, he reports, "Bloomingdale's is soliciting *me.*" But, to get his revenge, he hasn't given in yet.

This small item exemplifies the peculiar, albeit comfy, circumstances rich kids find themselves in after that first, most enlightening conversation with their trust officer: they are far richer than the world would guess. And one result is that the business community, from bankers to realtors to retailers, makes no particular provision for them. Salesmen don't know what category to put rich kids in, and there aren't enough rich kids to make a category of their own. So rich kids fall between the cracks. According to all the normal maps of discretionary income, the moneyed crowd is much older, having worked a lifetime to rise to that cushy job as a corporate VP or law-firm partner. The rich kids are a hidden lode in the stratigraphic record of American wealth.

Of course, rich kids aren't the only youths with some spending money. Some of their talented peers in computers or investment banking may land in the privileged income bracket of the mega-dollar heirs. But they're rare, and they can get so hooked on money-making they never get around to spending it. Not so the rich kid, who draws the big salary and never has to bother with the job. His job is just to spend it.

Some rich kids buy by check, some pay cash, some clear-thinking individuals go on the installment plan (in the awareness that, in their bracket, it pays to maintain a healthy margin of debt), but nothing symbolizes the power of their position so much as the ability to walk into any store, restaurant, or hotel and slap down plastic to get what they want. Now, the same might be said of any of the millions of American card-holders, enjoying the freedom of impulse buying when their wallets hold no cash. Yet most people return to earth when the bill comes in some weeks later. For rich kids the bill *never* comes in. Even if it is not slipped off to the trust officer to be "taken care of," it is paid out of funds that are unearned and, seemingly, inexhaustible. So there is never any pain—the ultimate form of payment—associated with the process. For the trust-fund baby, everything is free.

Given the excitement—holy shit!—with which the rich kid greets his inheritance, one might expect that he would then dash out to the nearest department store and start buying with all the zest of one of those crazed shoppers in TV's *Supermarket Sweep*. But, at least at first, a countervailing force obtains. After that first rush, he has a chilling thought: if the money that has materialized in front of him so magically were to disappear, could he ever bring it back? What does he know about making money? So, like the recipient of a precious jewel, the rich kid doesn't dare flaunt his wealth, for fear of losing it.

But then, as the months pass, it slowly dawns on him that such timidity is silly. What's the point of having it if he can't spend it?

This new daring stems partly from an urge to show 'em. Sonia Belahovski, for example, started to air out her wallet when she found herself staring down suspicious salespeople at hoity-toity boutiques on Fifth Avenue. She needed to prove that, despite her student uniform of jeans and a T-shirt, she really had the scratch. And to do that, she had to slap down her plastic and buy—shoes, pants, jewelry. That hastened her journey toward the $2,500 leather coat considerably.

So, gradually, the rich kid develops a taste for some of the finer things—the designer clothes, the Steuben glass, the occasional Matisse, cocaine—and the taste becomes a habit, and before he knows it, he is launched as a big spender for real. One rich kid thought of her spending in terms of a car's speedometer. Like the novice driver, she started out slowly, but gradually the needle started to rise—five thousand a year, then ten, fifteen, thirty, fifty, a hundred. . . . Soon she loved the freeways. Easy come, easy go.

Sometimes it does go.

Chris Pope was on the lower fringes of my sample to begin with, since he started out with only a few hundred thousand dollars. But the way he has managed it, he might soon have to be dropped from the ranks of rich kids altogether. In his case, though, it wasn't caviar and custom-made suits that did him in; it was real estate. He made one serious miscalculation. He thought that just because he had a few hundred thousand dollars, he was *really* rich.

I met him in the Washington, D.C., office of the *Renewable Energy News,* a bimonthly tabloid based in Ottawa that is dedicated to the cause of solar energy, wind power, and other renewable resources. It's one cluttered room with four desks, where Chris serves as the only full-time employee. He used to do the work for free but now insists on a modest salary. He has to; he lives on it.

It was a few days after the Washington Redskins' 1983 Superbowl victory, and Chris was still wearing his Redskins cap in celebration. He was classically handsome, with thick black hair and eyes that drooped sorrowfully, like a Romantic poet's. True to his prep-school origins (at a school in Poughkeepsie called Millbrook that he described as "a place for Saturday afternoon football games, faculty wives, and dogs"), Chris wore heavy work pants, thick-soled shoes, and an open shirt. He spoke softly, as though he didn't quite have the energy, or maybe the conviction, to speak up.

His money, ironically, came from a natural-gas company that his family owned in a small town in Pennsylvania. He himself didn't make the connection between his own advocacy of renewable resources and the family business until he attended a family board meeting a few years back. "I came into the meeting," he told me, "and one of my relatives came up to me to ask me what I was doing with myself these days. He was just making conversation. But a millisecond before I started to answer, it shot through my mind that this was going to be heavy. Here I was, into solar energy when all these other people were into gas."

Just as Chris had blinded himself to the origins of his money, so had he blinded himself to certain realities about the money itself. "Right now, I'd have to consider that I'm living on the edge," he said. He explained with some shame that the phone company had recently shut off his telephone for nonpayment, and that he was behind on other bills as well. He restricted himself to withdrawing only ten dollars at a time to meet his daily expenses, even if he had to go to the bank several times a day. "I don't plan," he said. "I don't have to. I'm so used to it all working. I don't ever really get afraid. There are times, I suppose, when I've run a little scared because I haven't paid a bill, but those are only the ones I don't have much respect for. I make sure that the people I owe money to, get their money. But when it comes to banking and all that, I'm a bit of a scofflaw. I pay my taxes, pretty much. I have a bank that pays them. If it were up to me, I probably wouldn't."

He attributes his current tight finances to some bad advice from an accountant. When he was a senior in college, shortly after he had come into his money, he decided on an impulse to liquidate all his holdings in the stock market. "My broker wasn't paying attention to the things I wanted him to," he explained. "I kept telling him that I wanted to stick to clean companies, but the broker kept trying to put me in places like Rockwell International. You know what that does? It manufactures nuclear components. It's incredibly trying to find clean companies. So I just decided I didn't want to be involved in the stock market at all."

After paying $8,000 in capital-gains taxes and answering some stern questions from his mother about what on earth he was doing, Chris put all the money in a money-market fund. That actually proved to be a prescient move since interest rates were starting to rise and the stock market was moving into the doldrums. But then he had the conversation with the accountant, who advised him to get into real estate. Unfortunately, after he had given some money to charity and put another chunk down in a separate real-estate partnership, the funds he had left were only enough to buy a single small apartment. Worse, because of the high interest rates, after the down payment he couldn't meet the $1,200 a month mortgage. Chris bought the place anyway, but he could not afford to live there himself. He had to rent it out. He now lived in a not-so-good section of town in a tiny one-room apartment that was barely big enough for himself and his bicycle. "So that's what money can do," he concluded dejectedly. "It allows me to own a home I can't live in."

Fortunately, other rich kids have more money, and they have managed their spending a little more carefully. Still, they all share the urge to go for the big-ticket item like a home of their own. It's the American dream, after all. It's just that it's not too common to plunk down cash for it in your twenties.

When I dropped in on Michael Pratt, for example, he had recently moved into a good-sized condominium in New York a short distance from the Hudson River. It's a fabulous place, and it cost a fabulous amount. The place was so big, he hadn't yet accumulated enough furnishings to fill it. And as he sat in his chair in blue jeans and a work shirt—casual attire that seemed to clash with the splendor of the carved mantelpiece he sat beside—he admitted to some uneasiness about getting too much too soon. Michael wondered about how his friends would react, and also how such a magnificent condo would affect his plans for the future. "I worry about that," he said. "I mean, this is my dream house. I own now what most people spend their lives saving for. What is there left for me to want?" But he was pleased with his purchase anyway; he'd figure something out for the future.

As for other major purchases, the railroad cars so favored by the millionaires of the gilded age have given way, in the space age, to some faster, rarer marvels of transportation. Accustomed to the Lear jets of their elders, several rich kids ended up buying small planes when they came of age, particularly in the Southwest, where the distances (and, often, the material resources) are greatest. Richard Potter, an oil-rich Texan, bought two planes: a Piper Aerostar, which he calls "the fastest piston-prop twin engine on the market"; and its successor, the Piper Super Star. "Take out the Aero's two-ninety horsepower engine and replace it with a three-fifty, then add a whole elaborate computer navigation system and color radar, and you've got the Super." Richard uses the plane to oversee his scattered businesses, which range from Kentucky gold to Texas oil and timber, and to commute from his home in Dallas to his "villa" in south Texas.

Another Texas heir I'll call George Blanchard went Richard one better, however, by picking up a Citaborea, a spunky little craft that he uses to do aerobatics—loop-the-loops and barrel rolls and other devil-may-care sky maneuvers that may well land him in the hereafter someday soon. "I like thrills," he says.

That's typical. Rich kids go for action, and they don't like to be weighed down with a lot of expensive possessions. While they buy their share of what economists call tangible goods—be they airplanes or power boats—they use them to obtain an intangible that economists rarely tally, namely experience. Partly they are embarrassed, in this increasingly democratic age, to acquire many monuments to their own affluence. Anything too visibly pricey would at the very least invite some awkward questions like, "Where did you get the money?" and at the most might make them a target for vandalism and theft. But more than that, rich kids are simply keen to acquire something that lasts only in memories, like the thrills and chills of those barrel rolls. As one daredevil heir put it, "I'm a sponge for experience." So the money doesn't go so much for things in and of themselves as for the sensations those possessions can generate. The bills in their wallets are so many tickets, gaining them admission to a mind-blowing good time.

For this reason, the high-flying Texas kids were exceptions, for rich kids don't usually want to own their own planes. All that hassle. Where would they put them? Nor do they go all that consistently for country houses. The upkeep is such a bother. At their young age, they prefer to roam. Indeed, they view the entire globe as their own private preserve, and, to zip about it, they rely on the more convenient public transportation—like jets. Even on international flights, they sometimes don't bother with reservations; they just head off to the airport, slap down their plastic, and catch the next plane as if it were a flying streetcar.

It was the black millionairess I've called Shiela Waters who indulged in this kind of impromptu vacation most often. I gained the introduction to her through, of all people, a Boston gossip columnist who relied on Shiela for tidbits on Washington high society, of which she is very much a part, and we met one morning in a Georgetown coffee shop. A cheery, giggly twenty-four-year-old with short, loosely curly hair, glowing nut-brown skin, and a slightly pudgy body, she wore a Laura Ashley dress, and she had a convulsive laugh that reminded me exactly of some girls I'd known from the fashionable Virginia prep school, Madeira. The laugh, like Daisy Buchanan's, was full of money. Shiela herself had prepped at St. Paul's. At Yale, Shiela wrote her thesis on Jane Austen and maintains a comic sense of high society.

"There's a luxury-loving part of me that is not extensive," she explained. "But it is there. As a rule, I don't decide things on the basis of expense, since I can afford anything. And it has helped me develop a certain sense of adventure. On a few occasions I have just gone to the airport with my boyfriend and said, 'When is your next flight to Europe?' And then we just got on. Once, it turned out that the next one was to London, but there were only first-class seats. It was ridiculously expensive, but we got on anyway. We drank champagne the whole way. I have to admit I was traumatized about how my parents would react. I thought: 'I'm never going to be able to walk back into my parents' house again.' It took until London to calm down and get over the guilt over what I had done. But I loved it. When we got to London, we couldn't find any place to stay, because we had no reservations. So we caught another flight on to Brittany and hung around there for two weeks. It was fantastic.

"Maybe the best trip was the one I took after I finished my thesis in college. I'd just broken up with my fiancé, a man named Rodney, and I decided that we needed a trip for old time's sake. So we went to Scotland on a total whim. It was wonderful! That was the truest sort of luxury. It was a mending time for us, and we could get out of our world and away from all the people we were related to. And we could concentrate on what we loved about each other. We could have a wonderful trip in a really sublime setting. We went up to Orkney and Skye, two islands off Scotland, and then to Edinburgh. It was lambing season, I remember, and there were all these little lambs around, and all with their little black feet. We were driving over a bleak landscape most of the time. I would doze off as we went along, and Rodney would wake me up from time to time to see something truly beautiful as it loomed up. Wealth gives you that possibility of escape. You can get exactly the right landscape at exactly the right moment. You can create your own universe."

Today's crop of heirs have nearly all caught the travel bug and are likely to have graduated, like Sonia Belahovski, from trips to Europe with their parents to extensive ventures on their own. Their penchant for that getaway vacation, in fact, proved one of my biggest obstacles in lining up interviews. One rich kid I was pursuing took off on a five-year around-the-world cruise. And others were always flying off to various parts of the globe. For them, whole continents are as individual states are to the less-well-endowed, only fewer. Many had roamed Asia, generally with a bout with dysentery to show for it. One heiress paid a visit to Mother Teresa as she traveled through India after her prep school graduation. She thoughtfully took off all but one piece of jewelry beforehand, lest the saint get the wrong impression.

In his travels, the rich kid never takes a package tour. He prefers to go off the beaten track where he can make his own discoveries. He craves the exotic: kayaking in Norway, glacier walking in Nepal, bicycling in China. Ross Perot, Jr., son of the Texas electronics billionaire, made headlines and the Guinness Book of World Records for his thirty-day circumnavigation of the globe by helicopter, accompanied by a flying ace from his father's multinational company. Often, because the rich kid has difficulty finding people with as much free time as he has himself, he goes alone. If he travels with a friend, it is not uncommon for him to pay the friend's way. In one case, an heiress determined ahead of time how much a three-week trip to Greece should cost for two, then presented a girl friend with her half of the sum before they started so she wouldn't have to depend on handouts along the way.

If the rich kid travels to any place as common as Europe, it is generally to some little-known, or restrictively pricey, part of it. It's best to stay with family friends—anything to escape the stigma of being a mere tourist—preferably friends who live in a château in the French Alps. That's always nice. Candace Hooper, as I'll call her, did that one summer for a few months. "When you see what money can buy," she told me with a conspiratorial air, "life is *so drastically different!*" She was amusing herself with some French translations at the time, and she would sit with her manuscript in the garden nibbling pastries the family chef had whipped up for her, and when she'd had too much of that, she would take a nap in the library with a mountain breeze blowing in through the French windows.

Candace and I were enjoying sundaes together in the New York ice cream shop, Schrafft's, and, as the vanilla melted on my tongue, I savored the image of her lying there in cool contentment. Detecting my interest in her tales of European abandon, she let drop the fact that she had once spent time on Aristotle Onassis's private island, Skorpios, in the 1970s. Candace said she shouldn't go into it because she didn't want to appear to be putting on airs. "I have noticed on occasion," she explained, "that when I'm talking to people and say that I've spent five days on Skorpios, it tends to stop the conversation. So I try to avoid it. Like just the other day, I was at a dinner party and we were talking about Greece, and I purposely had to go out of my way not to bring it up. I wanted to tell an anecdote about these wonderful fresh pistachios that we had there. I'd never had them fresh before. But I had to be careful not to say what island it was."

As if to confirm all that she was saying, I saw that, as soon as she mentioned the words Aristotle Onassis, all the ladies around us in the shop swiveled their heads to gape at Candace in silence, openmouthed. Everyone was so busy eavesdropping, in fact, there was scarcely another word to be heard in the whole place. Yet Candace went blithely on.

RICH KIDS

She visited Skorpios just after Aristotle's son had been killed in a plane crash in 1973. "They brought his remains home in a box while I was there," she said. "Jackie wasn't around. She was with her children or something. But otherwise it was a family gathering. I was only there because I was friends with one of Aristotle's relatives. Aristotle was very polite, and very charming. And he was a wonderful host, particularly considering the circumstances. He never cried once. But there was an air of melancholy hanging around. We had a very quiet time. We just had lunch down at the beach, and we had dinner up at the house. There were no festivities, obviously. It was a very beautiful place, but it was a very sad time."

And a very memorable time as well—off on this famous private island on such a tragic occasion. Indeed, the experience was so precious, she had to guard her memory of it nearly as closely as the money that made it possible. Although like most rich kids, Candace had eschewed the expected yachts and Lear jets in favor of these trips, her memory of them had itself become a prized possession. An intangible could be tangible. Much as she tried to hide it, her wealth showed, after all.

For rich kids, it's always a thrill to get out into the world, and the rarer the experience the better. They'll pay top dollar for it. But the trips aren't always made in a questing spirit. Sometimes they derive from a special rich-kid mania to get out there and do something. Possibly because they see no need to exhaust themselves in conventional professional pursuits, they often have a lot of energy left over. They want to plunge out into the world just to burn it up. Otherwise, it might drive them stir crazy.

Elizabeth Meyer, a trim and athletic twenty-nine-year-old, says that with her money, she is "a porpoise in the sea." Such energetic nautical metaphors come easily to her, since the passion of her life is a thirty-nine-foot Concordia yacht named *Matinicus* after an island near her family's island estate in Maine where she loved to sail.

My wife knew her from Bennington College, where, by

the luck of the draw, they roomed together freshman year. They were an odd couple: Megan, a scholarship student from Pasadena, and Elizabeth, an heiress from D.C. But they hit it off, and Elizabeth quickly drew Megan into her confidence about her wealth. At that point, the most money that Megan had ever spent was the $100 for the plane trip east, and Elizabeth tried to relate that to her inheritance, which was to be eight million dollars at twenty-one. They determined that even if Megan did nothing but fly back and forth across the country every day for the rest of her life, she would never be able to spend the entire eight million.

I met Elizabeth a few years later, when Megan and I spent a weekend with her on Martha's Vineyard one summer. The first thing we did was go on a picnic, and Elizabeth wanted to buy some champagne for the occasion. The bill came to two hundred dollars, I remember, for three bottles. "Well," said Elizabeth when we approached the cash register, "shall we split it?" I gulped, and she laughed. "No, no, don't worry about it." A porpoise in the sea.

When we met for an interview at a Spanish restaurant in Harvard Square, Elizabeth had hoisted all her sails—she was decked out in billowing designer clothes, topped off with a flowing silk scarf. Her black hair was gathered in a tight bun off to the side in a chic modern way, she had on purple eye shadow to match her outfit, and a good deal of gold dangled from her ears and about her neck and wrists. She let me know that the diamond on her finger, which was only a little smaller than the Ritz, was worth $30,000.

She babbled on about her fortune outrageously, but I enjoyed it. I felt I was being treated to some of the best of a conversational style honed at dinner parties for the Washington elite. It was full of irony and word play and blazing theatricality as she acted out the parts of the lah-di-dah set she knew too well: Beverly Sills, Carly Simon, William Styron, Edward Heath. She loved dropping the names, then making fun of the people. Yet for all the high-priced chic, Elizabeth let me know she was happiest at the helm of *Matinicus* ducking spray in slickers and Topsiders, her sky-blue eyes fixed on the mainsail searching for a telltale luff.

RICH KIDS

That winter, she was hard at work on her latest project, which was to assemble an all-women's crew to race the following summer in Buzzards Bay and Long Island Sound, then from Marblehead to Halifax, and finally in the cruise of the New York Yacht Club, where she is one of the few women members. "We're going to do it and do it and do it," she said delightedly, "all summer long.

"I'm a cruiser," she went on. "I don't know how to race. I've never really done it. And I am learning how by getting together all sorts of people who are better than me to go with me. Even if I know less, somebody has to be the captain, and that obviously has to be me. That's the way I am."

When I asked her why she wanted to do it, she had to think for a moment.

"One thing about racing is that you are pretty likely to win a prize," she said, "since there are so many of them given out for each race. But beyond that, I haven't raced enough to be able to tell you what the point is. But I know why *I'm* doing it. To sail better. You sail the boat about twice as well when you're racing as when you're not. No matter how much of a sailor you are, it's almost impossible to get the incentive just cruising. At least it is for me. But when you're racing you really work the boat, and make it perform."

Elizabeth has no need to work for any more commercial reward, for she is the granddaughter of Eugene Meyer, the financier, cofounder of Allied Chemical, adviser to presidents, and owner of the *Washington Post*, and the man of whom it was said that he lost more money than his contemporary J. P. Morgan made. There was still a lot left, chiefly generated by the *Post*, and a fair portion of it had ended up in Elizabeth's possession. She was quite unabashed about it. Her trust fund, she told me, was now up to eleven million dollars. Because the trust was invested largely in high-growth *Post* stock (thanks to a father who, when advised that he had overinvested in the newspaper, habitually responded by buying all the more), it currently increased at a rate of about a million dollars a year.

On the death of her parents, Elizabeth had received, as had her brother and two sisters, a share in six houses, ranging from that island estate in Maine and a house in Marlboro, Vermont, that her mother had owned to attend the summer music festival there, to a family property on Kalorama Triangle in Washington, D.C., and a winter retreat in Florida's Del Ray. She owned two more herself, one outside of Boston, which she called home, and another that she recently built on Martha's Vineyard. Besides her interest in yachting, Elizabeth collected art, oriental rugs, and jewelry (including $160,000 worth of earrings) intentionally and a few other things unintentionally, such as people who are interested in her for her money and fine wine. (Rummaging around in her cellar for a bottle not long ago, she was disturbed to find eighty cases down there.) She didn't really mind about the hangers-on; she likes a crowd. But her houses had become, as she said, "a pain in the ass," because of the upkeep they required. Still, she felt it would be heartless to unload any of the six she inherited from her parents, and she enjoyed her own two.

This pointed up one of the big problems with money, she said. "If you're rich, you can buy anything. You can buy fame— by giving parties and inviting all these famous partygoers like Halston. Or you can get attention by doing something eccentric like building a skyscraper in the middle of Arizona. The media are all looking for something. So you can attain glamour, even if you're not talented or don't have great looks. But there's no challenge to it, so who wants it?

"A lot of rich people I know don't know what they want. That's the biggest curse of the wealthy. A gauge of how much you want something is how hard you'll strive for it. If you work for your money, then you know how much your money is worth. But for the rich, they don't know how much their money is worth. So, on a whim, they could say I'd *love"*— she landed on the word—"to have a jet, I think. They don't know how much, because they can have it. Nothing stands in their way. The only thing you find out is how much of a bother it is to have all these possessions. I've seen so many people spending all their time and energy dealing with all the crap they've accumulated because they haven't been able to be selective. 'Oh,' they say, 'the latest things are camelback sofas, I'd better get some of *those!'* And they can get them, because there is nothing to stop them.

"Fortunately, I found that out early, back when about all I had was a ten-speed bicycle. The only thing I really liked was to play with my animals up in my room. I had a pretty big collection of frogs and lizards, and they cost nothing. So when I went away to school, I gave away everything. And now I don't have any crap sitting around that I don't use. If something doesn't fit into my house, it's out. Wssht."

Even if Elizabeth developed this philosophy at a young age, she didn't think to implement it until much later when the full implications of her social standing finally dawned on her. Although it was she who had exclaimed to a family friend at age two that she was a millionaire, Elizabeth grew up with little conception of what it meant to have so much money. Possibly this was because her parents were both academics whose minds were on higher things. After turning down the job of publishing the *Post*, passing it on to his brother-in-law Donald Graham, her father Eugene, known as Bill, taught psychiatry at Johns Hopkins, and her mother also worked there as an epidemiologist.

"I wasn't raised like Little Lord Fauntleroy," she said. "I was raised like anybody else. I raked leaves and shoveled snow for money. That was a major source of income, that and the hundred dollars I got from my grandmother for my birthday every year since I was five. But my parents always kept that money for me. I didn't have any unusual toys, except my animal collection. I always longed for a bike, but I didn't get it until I was thirteen. I felt kind of neglected. Our house was bigger, I suppose, but it was seedy inside. At eleven, I remember thinking, 'This place is a slum!' My mother didn't give a damn. There was art on the walls, but I never really noticed it as a kid."

After Bennington, Elizabeth carried on as if she had no money at all and went out and got a job. Hers was at Hood Sailmakers, Inc. where she stitched sails practically by hand. It was back-breaking and low-paying, and Elizabeth hated it. "It was like an angel had descended when I realized that I could quit," she said. But it had been difficult to decide what to take up since. "I feel like I'm standing in a huge, wide-open space and I can walk in any direction," she said. "But there is no clue to tell me which way to go."

She had done a fair amount of exploring, though. For a while she established herself as a contractor on Martha's Vineyard, building houses for the wealthy. Among her more notable clients was Jackie Onassis, who hired her as the contractor to build a fabulous estate, complete with heated towel racks and a guest house in the shape of a silo, by the sea. Despite her success, she had trouble getting other people to take her seriously. She had, it is true, used her money to capitalize the company, but beyond that she had prospered through her own talent. Still, she lamented, "No matter how hard I work, whatever I do is seen as just a pastime for the idle rich." And that difficulty is compounded by the fact that, as well as she did financially, she would have done better with her money if she had left it invested in *Washington Post* stock.

Now she had recognized that she didn't need to work and resigned herself to making the most of it, and so proceeded from project to project. A while ago she put together a small book on Concordia yachts, compiling testimonials from the 103 owners of the rare crafts, and publishing it. When I spoke with her she had just finished furnishing a house she had built for herself in the woods on Martha's Vineyard. It took three days. "I have infinite energy," she explained. "First I drew up a furniture plan, and then I made my buys. I have great taste, and utter confidence in it. I don't get into any wishy-washy dilemmas. I say, 'I know what should go here. I know what should go there.' I've never made a mistake yet."

With her house all set, and plans proceeding for her summer's racing, Elizabeth was looking ahead to the fall. She was thinking of getting together with a writer to put out a send-up of the sailing world, in the manner of the *Not the New York Times*, in a publication to be called *Yaahting*. But that was as far as she had thought. Without a regular job, she went from season to season, like a true sportsman.

And she went alone, as skipper and crew. Like many heiresses, she has had difficulty finding a boyfriend who was neither excessively attracted to nor put off by her wealth. Further, it has been hard for her to find friends to do things with, since they don't have her own go-anytime schedule. She said that one of the things that attracted her to her Concordia was that it was small enough for one woman to sail alone. She was prone, she admitted, to bouts of depression when all she could do was lie in the bathtub with a bottle of beer and read children's books, particularly the *Jungle Books* and *Danby*, which she described as "an incredible political allegory involving life in the animal kingdom, and it's *just warped!*" Other times, she would lie in a hammock, or stretch out on the foredeck of *Matinicus*. "All solitary, cocoon protections," she said.

But such periods of despair were rare. And she spent most of her time hurrying from one thing to the next. Her biggest worry was not that she would lose her money, although that would certainly be a blow, but that she would lose her energy. "If you have money," she said, "you know that money can't cure fundamental human loneliness. If you don't have it, you still have the hope and illusion that it can. People who don't have it can delude themselves. That's why the wealthy have this incredible despair. They have it all, and they know how little it really is. You know what the worst thing in the world is? It's to go to some rags-to-riches movie and, just when they're getting to the riches part, you start to feel all mushy with how wonderful it all is, and then you stop and think, 'Wait a second! That's the life I lead!'

"It's not that I don't feel my money benefits me enormously, it's just that I know what it is. I've got it. I've attained the mountain peak and seen that it's just so much more Great Plains of the Midwest. The answer, at least for me, is go crazy and keep busy. You have to do what you love to do, and if there's money or no money, then at least you won't be clogged up. That's the biggest fear that I have—that I'm going to wake up some morning paralyzed."

And this explained her purchases, or at least most of them. She bought things not to have them but to use them to keep moving, and that way stay fully alive. There was no pleasure in stability, only in rushing ahead, pushing on to the next thing. Only that way could she attain what she so deeply prized—the rush of fresh sensation. Her latest acquisition, typically, was a set of Mylar jibs for *Matinicus*. And this belief in action explained the delight that she felt fishing. Instead of appreciating the sport's quiet repose, she marveled at the finely honed functionality of each piece of equipment, from her hip-hugging waders to her speckled lures. And her philosophy accounted for the special pleasure of her running shoes as well. "I don't like them," she said, "until I tie them on."

Aside from this urge to do it all, instead of just to *have* it all, there is another significant constraint on these young heirs as they browse in the Neiman-Marcus catalog or cruise Fifth Avenue, and that is the thorny matter of ostentation. Rich kids disdain the gaudy gargantuan displays of old—like Diamond Jim Brady's jewel-studded, gold-plated bicycles—for the simple and perhaps surprising reason that they really don't want to call attention to themselves. Conspicuous consumption may be coming back in for the younger generation of Valley Girls, giddy with their shopping sprees, and their equivalents across the nation, but for the veterans of the antiwar era, wealth is still suspect.

And this shows in their clothes. Rich kids don't dress rich. They dress to fit in, rather than to stand out. That means that for men lily-white suits and Panama hats are cut, although I did find an ascot on one of the kids, and for women there are no ermine coats and peacock feathers. A few heiresses were drawn to outlandish color schemes, to be sure, but for reasons that Thorstein Veblen could never have anticipated. Laura Carpenter, daughter of one of Dallas's bigger real-estate magnates, wore her hair in rainbow colors. But that went with the territory of the *avant-garde* art world, which she was trying to break into with her new gallery, Delahunty's.

It was not just because the Rockefeller whom I spoke to had not yet come into his final "expectation" that he dressed in baggy khakis and well-worn Bean's shirt. That image stated a political identification with the common man. The more liberal the individual, the seedier he looked. (Although these generalizations could be skewed by certain fashion trends, like the Preppie craze that, along with primary colors, called for frayed collars and crumpled Weejuns.) But across the political spectrum, all the individuals in my sample felt that what really put a crimp in their style was the presence of the have-nots in their midst. "For me to dress up," said one heiress, "would be like pigging out in front of a diabetic. You just don't do it."

Because of her race, the black millionaire Shiela Waters has often found herself the unwilling recipient of such consideration. At Yale, she happened to be matched with roommates who were extremely well off. One received a check for $14,000 from her trust fund every quarter and spent every cent. On hearing that they were to be joined by a black, the other girls assumed that she must be a scholarship case, and made arrangements to send home all the expensive stereo equipment and oriental rugs that they had brought with them for fear that they would make the poor girl uncomfortable. On registration day, it happened that Shiela had just come from a morning of sailing on the family yacht at Newport, so she had on only her "grubbies," which confirmed the roommates' impression that they had a ghetto youth on their hands. Thinking that they might start out by giving the girl a decent meal, they invited her out to lunch at a fancy restaurant. It was only there, when Shiela happened to let drop a few little nuggets about the private schools she had attended and her father's oil wells, that they caught on. Their first words were: "My God! We have to get all our things back!"

As these young heirs dress down, they move in the direction of their working peers, who set the standard for what is appropriate for them. A lanky Washingtonian I'll call Max Pearlman, who is one of the heirs to a clothing fortune, had on a corduroy leisure suit at the Washington office where he works for a lobbying organization. The suit looked like something that his family's company might have made. And that might have explained everything. But when I asked him about it, he had to check the coat's label to see if it was one of his own company's. It wasn't.

And a young heiress who works in a magazine art department deliberately foregoes the sensational fashions her money could buy—and that she might like—for fear that if her boss were to suspect that she was wealthy, he might doubt her commitment to the job. So she is always the last to jump on the fashion bandwagons that regularly come rattling through the office. When the trend to wear pearls came in a few years ago, Beatrice, as I'll call her, waited a few months for the trend to stabilize before she looped a set around her neck that had been given to her years before by an aunt. Fortunately, no one realized that they were genuine, not cultured. But she doubts that she'll ever have the opportunity to bring out her sable coat. "It's too extreme a display of wealth," she says. She might get fired.

And if they don't work, they sometimes dress as though they do. One man I'll call Edward, who spends his time renovating his house for fun, makes a point of wearing his carpenter's clothes whenever he goes to the lumberyard. It saves him some awkward questions about what he is doing, and it allows him to make his purchases at the wholesale rate. "They always think I'm doing outside jobs," he says. "And that's fine with me."

By the same token, most rich kids (Elizabeth Meyer being a notable exception) were quite reserved in their jewelry as well. Generally, they wore valuable items only if they meant something to them. The very individuality of the piece negated the price. By displaying wealth that carried their own stamp, the kids were taking it over, laying claim to it as truly theirs. Such practices reversed the ebbing away of identity that began when the money first descended on them. This way they proclaimed to the world that they were themselves first, and rich second. One heiress did so quite freely. She had on two diamond rings that were engraved with her first name, and her kerchief was embroidered with her name as well. Others were less specific and bore, as an upper-class equivalent of the chunky high school ring, the family crest inscribed in gold about their fingers. The Wynnes, Shannon and his cousin Jimmy, both wore gold rings in the shape of interlocking snakes that are the special property of the descendants of the man who first made the Wynnes the Wynnes. That was their great-grandfather, William Benjamin "Buck" Wynne, a lawyer and judge from Wills Point, Texas, who started the family fortune in oil and mineral interests—a sum that was to be substantially increased by his son, Toddie Lee Wynne, founder of the American Liberty Oil Company.

The fingers of their fellow Texan, King Rancher Alice Tatum, were likewise weighed down with gold, and the gold rings, in turn, were heavy with personal significance. I could read her life story on her hands. The largest piece was a Biwa pearl set within a gilded cage practically big enough for a parakeet, which was given to her by her mother. "It was a very appropriate gift," said Alice. "She had designed it herself. She calls it a cuckoo's nest. She never felt quite normal as a Kleberg, you see." Beside it was her engagement ring, which Alice herself designed. It was a band with interlocking jeweled triangles. "That's an emerald with diamonds on either side," she said, pointing. "I chose emerald because I think the green is verdant, which I hope my husband and I will be together. And I picked diamonds because I think we're both as hard, stubborn, and brilliant as diamonds. And it's an equilateral triangle, because I want it to be an equal relationship." She also wore another band of diamonds given to her by her husband. His grandmother had received it from her husband on their fiftieth wedding anniversary. The Tatums hoped to do as well. And Alice designed another ring for herself, this one a "friendship ring" consisting of interlocking hands. "I designed it from a medieval pattern, with clasped hands that come apart. Usually, the heart is in the center of the palm, so you don't see it until the hands are opened up. But I prefer to have my love exposed." One more ring bore the von Roeder crest of an ancestor. And a last one was the baby ring of her best friend in high school. "She gave it to me on graduation," said Alice, "and I've kept it ever since."

About one wrist, the Alice-in-Wonderland heiress Amanda Holladay had clasped a serpentine ruby-and-diamond-studded bracelet that her father had given her on her eighteenth birthday. "It was a surprise that he bought it for me," she said, "but I have to admit that I did push him in the direction of my favorite jeweler." On the other wrist she had a $1,700 silver-and-gold Baume and Mercier watch. "That is a cliché of wealth, I suppose," she admitted, "but I saw it on a friend and I thought it was beautiful. Besides, I can read it, it's sporty, I can go in the water with it, and I don't have to worry about bashing it." The two items showed the balance of her feelings about her wealth—half her love for Father, half her pleasure in the things that money could buy. But she hid her best piece of jewelry under the neckline of her dress as if to prove that her deepest feelings of wealth would always remain unknowable. It was a three-and-a-half-carat uncut ruby hanging from a slim gold necklace. She refused to pull it out to show me. "It cost a lot of money," she said, "but nobody knows I have it." When I asked her just how much it cost, she flushed and replied curtly, "I don't want to say. That's vulgar." Then she turned mystical. "In the material world, in the world of illusion, it is something of great value and it cost a lot of money. But nobody knows I have it. My mother doesn't even know. If she did, she'd probably drop dead that I spent so much money on a rock. But I like it right over my heart. It's not romantic; it's strictly spiritual. It's electromagnetic energy, just as we all are. All gems radiate energy. They're condensations of matter, and all matter radiates energy. It feels good next to my skin."

Rich kids don't all think alike, and they did not all share the belief that money should be hidden. The jewels grew larger the further to the southwest I traveled. Also, the "fresher," as it were, the money that paid for them, the more prominently they were likely to be displayed. Summing up the difference between old money and new money, one trust officer told me that the old-money crowd let their silverwear tarnish while the new-money holders polished theirs every day.

There is something sparkling about the possessions of the young heirs to new fortunes. For one thing, everything is new. In their homes, they have none of the China trade heirlooms that lend a touch of history to a Yankee heir's decor. If there are antiques, they blend in perfectly, for they have been chosen, sometimes by a designer, for a particular spot. But beyond this, the new-money crowd seemed to conform to the clichés about the nouveau riche. They spent their riches on showier items that lacked the critical element in old-money tastes—understatement. Instead, these kids' acquisitions were underlined—wristwatches the size of hockey pucks, cars chosen for speed rather than gas mileage, stereo systems openly displayed like electronic sculpture instead of concealed tastefully behind hand-crafted cabinets.

But such classifications cannot be drawn too rigidly, for there is no guarantee that the parental line down which the money flows will be the dominant one in matters of taste. And there are two sides to every family.

The young Houston heiress Emily Montgomery, who was such a help to me in lining up interview subjects, is keenly aware of one such bifurcation. Her mother's fortune had been in the family for ages, while her father's smaller sum was of more recent vintage. The resulting styles clashed, in Emily's view, as badly as some of the color schemes her father favored. Emily sided with Mom. The father's nouveau taste had been held in check during the years of the marriage, but it gushed forth after the divorce in ways that eastern-educated Emily found horrifying.

"My father's house looks like a lopsided Holiday Inn," she told me as we sat together on the white couch in her tastefully decorated condominium. "He has just about paved the whole lawn over to put in nine parking spaces in his backyard. Nine! It's unbelievable! And he has these two rooms that are filled with these various bits of video equipment and a huge TV screen. The whole house is a gold mine of junk. His ranch is the same way. I tell my brother that when we inherit it, we'll have to rent a U-haul and just off-load the garbage. It would take weeks!

"The trouble with new wealth is that those people have no taste. I'm not talking about clothes or art. I mean what's appropriate for children. Like the other day, I heard about a man who rented a Rolls-Royce for his eleven-year-old daughter and her little friends and took them to the best restaurant in town and gave them champagne. Come on! I believe in saving some things for the future.

"But my mother has perfect taste, and her house is really neat. It has a wonderful library, and all the furniture is very purposefully arrayed. We have one big garden room that has an interesting collection of pieces of modern sculpture, and some African things, and a few animal heads. It's unique. It's a very warm house."

Emily's own apartment, which she bought outright because it would have been too much trouble to convince a bank that she was worthy of a mortgage, was a masterpiece of classic understatement. It was spare, but elegant, with white walls and bookcases containing books and a few bits of sculpture, including a collection of ceramic peapods. Among the pictures on the wall, there was an almost scientifically exact line drawing of an armadillo. Few pieces, but all of them choice. And no clutter.

Because of its fuel efficiency and reliability, Emily drove a Honda Accord. Most rich kids added a touch of class into the bargain and settled on a BMW as the "perfect set of wheels," as one heir put it. Even if they weren't BMWs, the preferred cars were, as a rule, European—Saabs, Volvos, Mercedeses, and Audis were also popular. Unless the heir was intentionally slumming it or trying to be funny, he left the American models in the showroom. The only exception to that would be the DeLorean, if that can even be considered an American car since it was manufactured in Ireland. DeLoreans were purchased by two rich kids I talked to, both of them acting well before the auto manufacturer's celebrated troubles over an alleged, but ultimately unproven, attempt to finance his company with a cocaine deal. The kids just liked the stainless-steel exterior and gull-wing doors. One of the two belonged to Jimmy Wynne, whose left arm was bandaged up to his elbow when I spoke to him because of the car. "I slipped getting out of it," he said. "It's real low. My elbow went one way and my wrist the other. But I like the DeLorean. When you're layin' in it, it wraps right around you. It may be low, but it's big, so you can swing your arms freely and never touch the door."

The purchase of a car is a difficult and important decision, and generally the first major such choice the rich kid has to make. As cars do for the general American population, from the teenage speed freak in his souped-up Mustang to the graying financial vice-president in his air-conditioned LTD, the auto defines the heir and declares to the world who he is. Nothing else quite so dramatically shows the style in which rich kids burn up their inheritance as they roar through life.

Sometimes the style is not entirely to their liking. Shiela Waters recalled riding with a girl friend in her father's "unpretentious and lovely" Rolls-Royce one evening to the theater to celebrate the friend's thirteenth birthday, when the car hit a raccoon. They only knew because they saw a bloody carcass spattered on the road behind them and asked the driver about it. When they learned that their Rolls had squashed the animal, both Shiela and her friend burst into tears. Shiela says they didn't cry for the raccoon so much as for themselves. "It was because we were so insulated," she explains. "The suspension system was so good, we'd run over a poor little raccoon and never felt a thing."

Generally, one can trace a rich kid's progress by recalling the cars that he has left behind, like dead skins cast off by a snake. Young Sonia Belahovski started out with a secondhand Rabbit before moving up, after her boyfriend Peter's smashup, to a brand-new Saab. After buying one for herself, she went out and bought another one for her Peter, which eventually proved somewhat awkward, because they broke up two months later and he felt obliged to give the car back. Sonia wouldn't take it.

A confessed speed demon and daredevil, Elizabeth Meyer liked to take her Saab V4 out for a spin—literally—on the black ice of New Hampshire's Lake Winnipesaukee. There she joined with a band of fellow ice-racing enthusiasts who regularly urged their cars out onto the ice to tear madly around a marked course—and into each other. "I'd usually get in a few fender benders," said Elizabeth gaily, "but that's nothing. That's like saying you get dirty racing dirt bikes." She has, however, found dry land nearly as skittery, and wiped out the Saab on a narrow country road one winter in an attempt to dodge a van that loomed up at her unexpectedly. She was unharmed, but the car was totaled. Claiming now to have reduced her racing fever, if not cured it entirely, she has moved on to a classier vehicle, the BMW.

Charlie Chiara, the grandson of financier John Loeb, and an automobile junkie, remembered being mildly irked as a teenager when his parents only allocated him $4,000 for his first car—precisely what his older brother had gotten many years before. So, while the brother had driven away from his eighteenth birthday in a Triumph TR7, Charlie had to make do with a used Datsun 240Z. What was even more galling, he knew other kids his age, whose families lived off the father's salary, who had made off with BMWs. "And their dads were eating the payments, too," he said, "because they couldn't afford to buy the cars outright." That tainted BMWs for him forever as common. "The background wasn't there," he said earnestly. "The culture was gone. These kids had no learning."

Now, at twenty-four, Charlie owned an English Rover with cloth seats. "It's sleek, good-looking, and it goes like hell," he said. "You see, if you're clever, you can be the only kid on the block with something and still not feel that you got *shafted* by a car dealer. There are only six hundred Rovers in the country. So I was up on the times to know they were there when I wanted one. And nobody else knows what they are, so that makes it nicer."

As Elizabeth Meyer has experienced, these fancy cars can lead to some fancy accidents. Fitzgerald wrote, famously, of the vast carelessness of the rich. That certainly seems to be true of their actions behind the wheel. The fellow I've called Edward, the son of a shipping magnate, had picked up his first car at eighteen, because that was when his brothers had gotten theirs. "I didn't even ask for it," he said, "I just put in an order for a Saab through the purchasing department of my father's company." It didn't take long before he had his first mishap. He'd crossed the ocean to pick up the car in Sweden so that he could take it around Europe. After a stop for some skiing in Zermatt, he went on to Greece to work for a while on a charter boat, and then headed back north again with three friends. On one of Germany's famous autobahns, they opened her up and hit trouble.

"I was sitting in the passenger seat," Edward told me one night at the house he was renovating, "and my friend who was driving said he wanted to look at the map, so I took the wheel, and eventually I sort of spaced out and just let go. It's true we had been smoking some hash, but I don't think that had anything to do with it. But the next thing I know we're headed for the guardrail, so I yanked on the wheel and there was a terrible screeching of tires and we pulled a hundred-eighty and ended up in the fast lane headed the wrong way. And the engine had conked out. If anybody came, that would have been it for us. The Saab had all this ridiculous safety stuff requiring you to sit down and buckle in before you could start up, so we were hopping around like crazy trying to get it going. We were *sure* somebody would come whizzing up and plow into us. But we got out of there safely. That was one great scene."

Sonia Belahovski got her first sense of life's hazards, she said, when she was driving the family VW squareback down a hill on the way into town from her place in Fairfield County. She had a baby goat on the front seat next to her. She was reaching over to get a baby bottle for the goat when the goat slipped off the seat and landed on the accelerator pedal. "The pedal flipped back," said Sonia, "so I couldn't control it anymore. And we were going so fast, about fifty, I couldn't get the car into neutral and pull the brake. We went off the road and flipped over. It was very dangerous, to say the least, but both the goat and I came out of it OK. No one came to help, so I had to walk all the way back to the house. I was the one to call the police, and I thought that was ridiculous. That was my first dealing with the lonely reality of the outside world."

Sarah Pillsbury, of the Pillsbury Flour Company, had a similarly enlightening experience on her first crash, which occurred at the age of twelve. She was driving with her father into town from their house in Minneapolis. As a kind of driver's-ed. program, her father sometimes let her steer with him, and she was holding the wheel from underneath when suddenly, as she said, "I panicked and pulled the wheel the wrong way." The car went off the road and Sarah passed out. "I don't know if I hit my head, or whether it was just the shock," she continued, "but when I came to I got really scared because I looked over and saw my father lying there beside me unconscious. His face was covered with blood and he was moaning." An ambulance took them to the hospital, where it took ninety stitches to seal up all her father's cuts. "I don't feel guilty about what happened. My father does, but I don't. I was thinking about this a little while ago, and I thought how outrageous it was that he should let a twelve-year-old steer a car. Basically, I just feel it was a stupid thing."

Despite the hazards, no one believed more deeply in the joys of car ownership than Winston Goodfellow. He was a tall, lanky twenty-four-year-old who looked like he was still trying to get the hang of his oversized body just as he was trying to come to grips with his oversized bank account. He had come into his money before he was born, when his father, a successful San Francisco attorney, choked to death on a piece of meat in a restaurant while celebrating his wedding anniversary with his pregnant wife. Winston had proceeded to lose over half of it in some unfortunate stock-market investments when I spoke to him, but he vowed to make the money back. He still played the market, but that took up only a small portion of his time and even less of his attention.

A resident of Menlo Park, south of San Francisco, Winston had a case of auto-philia that was, to use his word, "awesome" even by Californian standards. For his own driving needs, he currently owned two Italian sportscars—Iso Grifo Targas— and a Datsun 240Z, which he termed his "daily set of wheels," and he had recently flown to Germany to pick up a third Iso Grifo Targa to refurbish and sell. He was working on a book about a small Italian car company, put together by "the world's greatest postwar engineer" Giotto Bizzarrini, which had flourished briefly in the sixties. And he was developing a local TV show on exotic cars.

Winston's office was in the suburban duplex he occupied with his brother. The walls were covered with racing posters, and the closet was full of three-ring binders holding pictures of just about every sportscar made in the fifties and sixties when, as he said, "a racing car still looked like a car." He showed them off to me with all the pride of the kid with the biggest baseball-card collection on the block.

In a way, Winston's absorption with the sportscar seemed

to follow the tradition of the playboy sportsman, whose choices for objects of devotion were limited to fast cars, fly fishing, big-game hunting, and girls. And Winston did share a few of those characteristics. His cars, for example, were never fully equipped unless they had a good-looking young lady in the front seat, and he had spent a considerable amount of time figuring out how to get him, the girl, and the car together on the perfect date. But in another way, Winston's attitude showed that rich kids don't make their purchases for show so much as for use. His vehicles are vehicles for experience. He had built his whole life around them, from his European jaunts to his hoped-for TV show. They *were* his life, and he talked about them in almost sacred terms. He saw an allure deeper than sex in the curves that ran from the front to the cockpit and the cockpit to the back. And he heard the sweetest music in the roar of the engine. "If you listen carefully," he said, "you can hear a symphony. You know how you can pick out the violins and the horns and the winds in an orchestra? On a Ferrari V-12 you can, if you listen real close, hear the chains and the cams and the pistons. I went to a Carlos Montoya concert a while ago—he's the godfather of flamenco guitar—and I was listening to how he built to a crescendo and how fluid it sounded. Then all of a sudden it hit me. I said to myself, 'Son of a bitch, that sounds just like the Ferrari Daytona when you run it flat out.'"

With that introduction, Winston launched into the tale of the one time that he did indeed run his fire-engine red Ferrari Daytona "flat out" and established his personal speed record. There was a slightly wistful quality to the story, since it was also his last ride in the Daytona. He had to sell the car to cover some nasty losses in the stock market. As was his habit, he dramatized the tale with expressive car noises, which he reproduced with studied exactness, like an ornithologist reciting bird songs.

"It was like this," he said. "I had my mechanic check the car over before I took it out. I told him I wanted to pin the speedometer, and I wanted to make sure everything was OK under the hood. He told me everything was fine. So my friend and I got up early one morning and went to a stretch of highway that I know real well, and I know there are no ramps. It's about five lanes wide, and it's straight as an arrow. At that hour, I figured I wouldn't be likely to find a flashing red light in my rearview. If I did, I figured I could outrun 'em, because at the speed I was planning on, no cop car in the world would be able to keep up with me. Course I'd be in trouble if the cop radioed ahead to a buddy, since even the fastest car in the world can't outrun Motorola. I just had to hope.

"So we got out there at five-thirty in the morning. The sun was just coming up. It was light. I pulled over to the side of the road and waited for a few cars to go by, and then there was a gap, so I pulled out and hit it. Vvvvrrrrrpp—vvvvrrrrrpppppp—vvvvvrrrrrrrrrrrrpppp—va *rooom*! And I just kept going. I had that thing floored, and we kept going faster and faster and faster. It never levels off! It was awesome! You can feel the road through the steering wheel, and you feel the push of the engine behind you the way the back of the seat thrusts against your back. We were really moving.

"A Camaro had passed by about twenty seconds before, and we were on him in no time. The Camaro was only going sixty. This is what it was like: First, *bingo*! there's the Camaro up ahead. Then, *bingo*! now he's right at my side. Then, *bingo*! he's in my rearview mirror. Then, *bingo*! he's gone. Quick as that. I shifted into fifth as I passed him going about one forty-five. I looked down over the hood and saw the lines coming up on me—bip-bip-bip-bip—just as fast as you can imagine. I thought to myself—son of a bitch, we're flying!

"But I'd reached the end of the straightaway, so I hit the brakes and slowed down to turn around and come home.

"I'll never forget it. For me, that was one of the ultimate highs. There's nothing like it in the world. Nothing! You're out of this world altogether. It's like meditating. And the end result is the deepest imaginable satisfaction. You feel the suspension under you, the seat pushing into your back, and you're hearing all that wonderful noise. Then when you stop—errrrrp!—your neck snaps forward and you *know* you've really been moving. Bam! It's totally awesome. One of the world's great experiences."

4

Do the Indians Have a Tax Number?

While rich kids may think they have hidden their vast wealth from the world at large, there is one industry (aside from the IRS) whose delicate antennae will not be deceived. This is the nation's charitable organizations, the good people who mail photos of some gaunt Biafran child whose belly *you* can fill with a modest contribution, or a species of penguin that will be wiped out if *you* don't help, or . . . Whatever. There are few causes, it appears, that couldn't use a smidgen of the green. One need not be rich to be targeted by such appeals, of course. One has to be either a cloistered monk or dead to be entirely safe from them. But rich kids get them in such saturation bombings that they themselves might consider filing for charity status to keep their souls intact.

Like heat-seeking missiles, these missives have an uncanny ability to detect the hot bucks. A rich kid might have chosen to live in cockroach-infested squalor sweating his life away in menial labor, his true financial worth known only to his most trusted friends, but along comes the mailman laden with urgent requests from Sally (*All in the Family*) Struthers of the Foster Child program and a dozen others.

Even though these appeals increase exponentially each time anyone pays out for a magazine subscription, political contribution, and charitable donation, owing to the healthy cross-fertilization as these hit lists are swapped, it ordinarily takes a lifetime before an avalanche of bulk-rate mail tumbles through the door slot of the average citizen six days a week.

For rich kids, who hurry through so much else in life, this dubious social distinction comes faster.

Sometimes the process is hastened by an early training in the gift-giving process by their parents. Several rich kids reported that as children they were expected to donate a significant portion of their allowances to charity—and to keep an accounting of it in their tiny ledgers. This may have been as much to prepare them for the realities of the American tax code later on as to instill humanitarian values. Ando Hixon, the heir to the fortune made in the manufacture of tiny electronic connectors, remembers being aware of the all-important criterion set down by his parents in his early forays into philanthropy: the intended recipient had to be accredited by the IRS. So Ando's first question when a friend approached him about the attractive possibility of giving to the Navajo nation: "Do the Indians have a tax number?"

Even when the parents don't require that their children get in the eleemosynary habit, they often transmit the message by their example. Sonia Belahovski, for one, consequently brought a deluge of what she called "money mail" down on herself by her modest imitations of her philanthropist mother.

Mrs. Belahovski, the Cabot in the family, always used to spread out her incoming mail on a kitchen table three times as large as the sizable monk's table now in Sonia's dining room. Since Mrs. Belahovski was usually behind on her correspondence, the letters were often stacked a foot high. And much of it was money mail. Sonia occasionally amused herself by delving into the pile, pulling out some worthy plea, and putting her own checks in the return envelope. All too soon, of course, she was receiving her own solicitations. Thus began Sonia's career as a philanthropist specializing in environmental and antinuclear issues.

Like many rich kids, Sonia has had to develop an increasingly flinty heart in order to cope with the daily influx of requests from the needy. "The letters are really tough," she said. She was not the only one to be affected by them. Her roommate, a musician without Sonia's good fortune, once came upon a letter that Sonia happened to leave out on the kitchen table calling attention in the usual gut-wrenching style to the plight of some dolphins. The roommate felt moved to make a contribution to help the animals out. "Now she's getting inundated, too," said Sonia with a laugh.

While many rich kids saw no alternative except to reach numbly for their checkbooks or their cylindrical files, Sonia had devised a simple method for dealing with the two dozen letters she said she received every week. As they came in, she dropped them unopened into a large shopping bag. Then in December she undertook the onerous and painful task of evaluating them all in time to register her contributions on that year's tax form. She found it easier to make decisions by contrast—comparison giving, as it were. Her mother and grandmother advised her, but Sonia had established her own criteria for determining which of the hundreds of supplicants to support, chiefly durability and effectiveness. "I know the difference between groups like Clamshell and Greenpeace," she said authoritatively. "Clamshell is very emotional and I don't think they're so effective. Greenpeace is older, more factual and more organized."

Other rich kids had gone further in dealing with the daily onslaught of pleas for money. Said a young woman I'll call Roberta Bernstein: "The best investment I ever made was a big wastebasket." She parked it right by the door, and as soon as the fat bulk-rate solicitations came in, they went right out again.

But for Roberta, the heiress to a substantial department-store fortune, such hardened resolution had been a long time coming. She had been prone to heavy feelings of social responsibility since at least age three when she attended kindergarten on a farm and made the compelling discovery that the cows out in the pasture were related to the beef on her dinner plate. She became a vegetarian and had been one ever since. When she was five, she removed all the clothes from her closet to turn it into a private prayer stall which she stocked with a children's prayer book and a Bible. "I didn't know how to pray," she said. "I'd just go in there."

After boarding school and college, Roberta "kicked around a lot," marrying and divorcing a TV interviewer, starting and folding a greeting-card company, then saying hello to Jerry Brown's presidential campaign. Now she said she had found contentment as the wife of a former literary agent and the mother of their infant son. But the spiritual questions she first went into the closet to face had continued to nag at her. Although she felt that a strong component of her quest had been to reach out beyond the reality of the five senses into another more sacred dimension, she also recognized that her affluence might have been a major impetus compelling her in that direction. She used to feel acute pain everytime a needy organization wrote her for money. "I found each one a tremendous burden," she said. "It used to be that whenever a solicitation was dropped down the mail slot, I felt a strong moral obligation to save whoever was in trouble, or to give to whatever was being threatened. I was totally overwhelmed." But she did give.

Like many rich kids, she found comfort in philosophy. While others' took the form of more homespun ideas about how there is "only so much you can do," hers came in part from the writings of Sri Aurobindo Ghose, the Indian mystic philosopher. She cited most approvingly a passage in which Aurobindo declared that wealth or, as he put it, "the money power" is not truly human coin at all and therefore ultimately not human responsibility. "All wealth belongs to the divine," wrote Aurobindo, "and those who hold it are trustees, not possessors."

"I was really struck by the quote," Roberta said. "I wouldn't say I'm handling my money in that spirit yet, but it is something I'd definitely want to keep in mind. For one thing, it makes me feel less guilty about it. It makes me feel that I have a lot of gifts besides my money, like my education, my health, and my energy. Like my other gifts, my money is something for me to use as best I can, to do with as I see fit. I wasn't given the money just so I could spend my life being burdened by guilt." It was around that time that Roberta invested in her wastebasket.

Age three is a little early in the life of a rich kid to start feeling guilty about his or her unique privilege. Rich kids don't usually discover that they're anything special until the moment of reckoning with their trust officer much later. But the sad fact is that the bubble of giddy pleasure at being so rich is bound to burst eventually. Rich kids soon recognize the miserable truth: for them to be so extraordinarily rich, others must be poor. And that gives the kids a different feeling about the rarefied life so high up the socioeconomic Eiffel Tower. Rather than rejoicing in their luck, they start to worry about all those little people so far below.

Early as it came, Roberta's desire to drop down on her knees in her closet is a classic manifestation of the nagging guilt that most rich kids feel at some time in their lives. They use the term "guilt" to describe it, too. Yet it is guilt only in the loosest possible sense. It is quite distinct, for example, from the guilt that a murderer might feel after he has just bumped somebody off. For rich kids are innocent—innocent as only kids can be. They have done nothing wrong. They have done nothing at all, simply been born and then presented with an inheritance that in most cases they are literally unable to refuse. When Abby Rockefeller tried to tell her father, David of Chase Manhattan, that she would just as soon not receive the $25 million he was passing along to her, he looked stunned, apologized, and said there was nothing he could do about it. The money was coming down in trust from his father. The money would be hers whether she liked it or not.

For all rich kids, the act of inheritance is entirely passive. Yet this sometimes makes the guilt more severe, and more permanent. True criminals, at least, have something to confess. They can receive forgiveness; they can reform; they can put their sins behind them. But rich kids start to feel they are the sin themselves, and every crime that was ever committed out of greed now hangs on their heads. They see the inequity that lies about them, or read about it in their money mail, and they think they are responsible for it. Because they are on top, they must be squashing those on the bottom. This is the true embarrassment of riches.

To clear themselves they often feel, like the young Roberta, an unspecified and diffuse need to do penance, to suffer in some way so as to square things with the almighty dollar. And that often means giving a fair portion of their money away. It's their way of paying for their inheritance. They buy fine things and go to fabulous places, but they also make hefty donations. To them, giving is like doing the dishes at a friend's house after he's cooked dinner. It balances the moral equation.

The urge to atone for one's wealth is not confined to rich kids of this generation, of course. There is a strong tradition of the Lord and Lady Bountiful in American history. Many of these philanthropists, indeed, are the illustrious ancestors of these rich kids. In his famous *Gospel of Wealth*, Andrew Carnegie set forth an idea of wealth not so different from Sri Aurobindo's, when he declared that the rich should be "trustees" of their money. Taking to heart his own motto that "the man who dies rich dies disgraced," he gave away $350 million altogether, much of it to endow the nation's libraries. The most shining example comes with the Rockefellers, in the transformation of the man, John D., once the very embodiment of the thieving industrialist, into something closer to a national saint. He set the family on a path, taken further by his son John D., Jr., that led to the creation of national parks for the California redwoods and Jackson Hole; the reconstruction of colonial Williamsburg, Rheims Cathedral, and Versailles; the founding of the University of Chicago; and, of course, the establishment of the Rockefeller Foundation.

Money-makers, however, have a different attitude toward charity than their heirs. Andrew Carnegie and John D. Rockefeller could feel that they were completing a circle as they restored the money they had taken from the public. Rich kids, by contrast, never made the money. They just give it away. And in giving money they have themselves been given, their lives can take on a peculiarly negative quality. They seem to get it backward: rather than place their windfall inheritance on the credit side of the ledger, they put it down as a debit.

If I hadn't known that Daniel Griswold, as I'll call him, was worth a half-million dollars, I would have thought he was a pauper. He lived with his girl friend in a barren apartment in a noisy section of San Francisco. He furnished the living room with a bricks-and-boards bookcase filled with tattered paperbacks, a few rickety chairs, and a tottering sofa that had been abandoned by the previous tenants. His girl friend, Carole, had re-covered it in a garish flower print. An assortment of pale, leggy plants stood by the window, hungry for fertilizer. When he led me into the room, I was about to take a seat on the couch, but he steered me away because of all the cat hairs that had gathered there. Then he sat down on it. "I don't mind," he said. He didn't furnish himself much better—well-worn corduroys, an open shirt with an out-of-fashion oversize collar, and running shoes. Six-foot-five, Daniel didn't seem to know quite where to put all of himself, and his knees poked up awkwardly as he sat on the couch. "I wouldn't mind losing a couple of inches," he told me sheepishly.

Other rich kids may race through their inheritances; Daniel couldn't bring himself to spend his—at least not on himself. He lived on ten thousand a year but gave away that much to various causes, particularly the nuclear freeze campaign, as well. And he donated his time, too, volunteering as a therapist for wife-beaters at a local hospital. He didn't do this out of the usual rich-kid guilt, he felt, so much as a keen sense of the tensions of the world. "I just have this image of the globe tearing itself to pieces," he said.

As a rich kid, however, he must have been particularly conscious of such tensions. He might have picked them up from his father, along with the money. The elder Griswold, now an English professor at a state university, told him that he used to be so embarrassed riding to school through the slums of Chicago during the Depression that he would duck his head out of sight in the backseat of his chauffeur-driven Cadillac. It wasn't so much that he didn't want to see the poverty as that he didn't want to be seen seeing it. He couldn't take the confrontation. It was the same way with Daniel. He couldn't bear being rich knowing others were poor. By depriving himself so utterly, he was fighting back, returning the hostility that he imagined others must feel toward him for being so rich. Other rich kids spend to improve their circumstances; he gave money away to lower his. He confided that he used to dream of becoming a Buddhist monk and impressing people with his austere asceticism. "I felt I had the power to shame people with my pure conscience," he said. "Now that seems ridiculous to me. But then I thought I could shame people by talking about my plans to become a monk. I felt purer than everybody. I'd talk about it all the time." Now he may not be a monk, but he lives like one, and that is just as good. "It's my purpose in life to tread lightly," he said. Indeed, he was hardly there at all.

Robert Coles once characterized the children of the wealthy by their sense of "entitlement," their belief that the world owed them something. But in many cases, like Daniel Griswold's, the opposite is just as true. There is a feeling of obligation; they owe the world. Only during their spending sprees do rich kids exhibit much insouciance. The rest of the time they feel vulnerable. With the money comes a special sensitivity to the pain they see around them. The average Joe, struggling to make it from one paycheck to the next, can always tell himself that there is nothing he can do. He's strapped. But for these heirs, they know too well that there is practically no limit to what they can do. That's why the daily dose of guilt-inducing solicitations so often succeed. They hit right in their wallets where the kids are so tender, reminding them of the fundamental discomfort of their existence. As many of them expressed it, they have in abundance what most people so desperately lack.

But the letters were not the only things to prick their consciences. The movie *Gandhi* sent a wave of anxiety through many of the heirs, leading several to vow to abandon their wanton materialism (a pledge they forgot about as soon as the lights came up). One wealthy young Bostonian remembers being crushed every Christmas by the newspaper's annual *Globe* Santa campaign which daily highlights the miserable conditions of the city's poor in a campaign to buy the children Christmas presents. "When I read that, I go, 'Oh *God!*,'" he exclaims, covering his face with his hands.

Another young woman who grew up on Long Island always hated to come into New York City because of all the beggars she saw there. "I couldn't bear it," she said. "New York is an open mouth." Now a documentary filmmaker, the woman I'll call Helen Strauss has moved into the city for her work and always tries to accommodate the bums. She ended up befriending one, a man named Frank on 57th Street, who had been blinded when shot in the face with a shotgun. Because of her own shyness, Helen didn't find this out herself; she was walking along the street with a more aggressive friend who made the inquiries. But Helen was immediately touched, because she had spent the first years of her life on a cypress plantation similar to the one where Frank said his accident had occurred, and Helen knew that her own family used to go shooting in the winter. When she heard his story, she went to the South Poverty Law Center to try to press his case but found that the statute of limitations had expired. She'll never know who did it, and she'll never be entirely free of the worry that her own family was responsible.

In general, the attacks on the rich kids' consciences are so various and widespread that many have had to formulate firm policies for themselves to determine how much of their money they should give away and how much they could keep. While some ventured as high as half their income, most settled out at about 10 percent. Roberta Bernstein did so deliberately, observing the biblical idea of the tithe. Usually, somewhere early on in their deliberations, rich kids grabbed for the permanent solution, namely, to give it *all* away. Wouldn't that solve all their problems? Wouldn't they then be free? But, appealing as it seemed, they were all deterred by some sobering thoughts. One was, as Sonia Belahovski put it, "Who would I give it *to*?" Another, favored by the more political individuals, was that since such an act would cost them all further influence, it was even more irresponsible to give the money away than to hold on to it. But most hung on to the money, or at least the bulk of it, for the simple reason that, however much trouble it sometimes caused them, they rather liked having it around.

It is always difficult to compare generations, but from what these rich kids have told me, I can't help thinking that the sixties were a particularly awkward time to come into money. All that railing against the establishment; the squabbling about how university endowments were invested; the automatic lumping together of capitalism, imperialism, racism, and war. Class differences were shameful, and the only acceptable way to discuss them was in the Marxist terms of a ruling class and a working class. In those years it was clear to the rich kids which of the two classes was more honorable—and it wasn't theirs. So the rich kids looked at their passports—their money—to the highest reaches of society with increasing disaffection.

While some of the fortunes were ill-gotten, that was not universally the case. Yet many of the rich kids felt their wealth was tainted anyway. Often this derived from exaggeration, misconception, or outright ignorance. Daniel Griswold's money came from the manufacture of particularly sturdy fan belts for steam engines. Harmless as that may seem, to him that raised images of merciless ravaging of the earth by the steam engines those belts went into. "I picture my wealth as having come from extraction from the earth, and I guess exploitation of other people's work," he said. "But it's a confused thing in my mind." To those who came of age in the sixties and early seventies, the guilt was built in.

And this era, this philosophy, had a profound effect on these heirs. It drove one of them to turn down her inheritance, difficult though it was. And the difficulty was not of the legal sort that blocked Abby Rockefeller. It was of a personal sort, for in choosing to go with the sixties flow, this child had to cut herself off from the family's past. In the sixties spirit she made herself new by freeing herself from the oppressive cash. In her case, she gave it away even before she got it.

Margaret was a tail-ender of the sixties, actually, one of the younger siblings who grabbed on the era even more tightly than her older brothers and sisters. When I met her in the winter of 1983, she had moved on to a new movement, from the looks of her punk haircut and off-the-shoulder T-shirt, but her sixties political views have stayed with her, buried deep inside. They've shaped her life. If it weren't for them, she'd be rich.

In what turned out to be the last summer of her wealthy grandmother's life, Margaret was asked by the aged matriarch to join her on a trip to England. The girl was flattered by the invitation, and a little surprised. The two were not exactly the best of friends. Although she'd grown up in splendor in rural Pennsylvania, with horses and the biggest swimming pool in town, Margaret had always been a rebel. She'd indulged freely in leftist politics—she'd gone to New Hampshire for Gene McCarthy—and made a proud display of leading her boyfriends up the stairs of her parents' house to bed. Her parents didn't dare object. In contrast, Grandmother—everyone in the family always called her that; nicknames weren't appropriate—carried on like the last of the Victorians, insisting on every sort of propriety, no matter how outmoded, during her visits, which grew mysteriously briefer and less frequent as the years passed.

On a lark, Margaret accepted the invitation, and the two flew together to London and spent a month traveling around the British Isles. Her grandmother was particularly interested in taking Margaret to the family's ancestral home outside of London, which Margaret had never seen before. It was a towering stone castle, with crenellated walls and turrets and a river running by, that was still in the hands of their English cousins. Margaret had to gasp when she saw it; she never imagined she had such a place in her past. But she was even more amazed by her grandmother's reaction. "I was studying her more than anything else," Margaret told me, "just watching how she acted. She just seemed to blend into the place.

When I looked at her, I could get a sense of all this history. She could have been a queen or a duchess there walking those grand stone halls. It was like a fantasy, for her and for me. It was like seeing some illustrated manuscript come alive."

On the long train ride back to London over the green English hills, an inner reserve had broken within the proper old lady. Suddenly she opened up and talked with Margaret in a way they had never talked before, a way nobody in the family had ever talked before. "How often do you ever talk to your grandmother about all the things that are really important?" Margaret said. "I asked her about her parents and what they meant to her and what her childhood was like. And she was gaily recounting what it was like to wear pigtails, and stuff like that. It was like something had shaken loose in her. We were just laughing and talking about all these things I never knew about. And then suddenly for the first time in her life, or in my life with her, she looked at me and said, 'I love you.' "

It was raining, and the water was streaking down the windows making the countryside a blur. Caught up in the moment, Margaret and her grandmother both started to sniffle and then let loose with their tears. The whole earth was awash with their crying. And then Grandmother wiped her eyes with a silk handkerchief and turned to her granddaughter with an even more astounding proclamation than her love. She said that she was planning her will and that she would like to leave Margaret a million dollars.

Margaret's heart started pounding. A million dollars! She had never expected this. But, quickly, the cold realization of what such a gift would mean came over her. She said she was sorry, but her answer was no. She couldn't take the money.

"It was weird," said Margaret. "We had gotten so close, I felt like I was betraying her not to accept it, and I was incredibly torn. But at that point I knew I could get along by myself. I was doing fine. I didn't need the money. Strangely, I felt selfish for *not* taking it, because here was this woman who finally for the first time in her life had said, 'I love you,' to somebody, and here I was saying, 'I love you, too, but shove it.' "

RICH KIDS

Although Margaret was being singled out from her brothers and sisters to receive this gift, she was less conscious of sticking out in the family than of being isolated in the greater family of her countrymen. It wasn't fair for her to get a million and them nothing, particularly if the million had come from shady deals, as Margaret imagined, in industry and real estate.

"I tried to explain why," she said, "and I think she understood in the end that it would just really damage me, and I couldn't condone where the money had come from. People had been hurt and exploited for centuries for this luxury. It was outrageous, and she knew that, but I guess she wanted it accepted in the end by someone she loved, and who loved her. I just couldn't take the money. It seemed like a real compromise of my integrity. Even though I loved her, it was just too much."

Two days after the grandmother returned to the United States, she died. "It was just like that," said Margaret, snapping her fingers. "We'd been walking all over England together and then she comes home and two days later she was dead, from nothing. It was like she made up her mind."

If so, Margaret's reaction to her offer might have assisted her deliberation. The grandmother may have sensed that life was ending for her, and the world she knew and loved, with its castles and grand heritage, was far removed from the one of which her granddaughter dreamed. She must have felt doubly spurned—not only was her money rejected, but her past as well. Before she died, her grandmother made a last revision of her will. Instead of leaving the money to Margaret, she left it in trust to the English cousins for the maintenance of the family's ancestral home.

Patty Hearst was the totemic rich kid of the era. Her switch from perfect little Republican to revolutionary and back again shows the suddenness and power with which the guilt can strike. The question still lingers as to whether she was truly a willing co-conspirator when she emerged with the Symbionese Liberation Army to wave a submachine gun around during the holdup of the Hibernia National Bank, or whether she was brainwashed into submission. But for a rich kid like

Patty, who is so often acted on by forces beyond her control, the issue comes down to the paradox at the center of her life. She was responsible, and she was not responsible. In the larger sense of the question, she was innocent and she was guilty just as all rich kids are.

Her tale was acted out by many rich kids of the era, only more quietly. Many were overpowered by a sudden awareness of poverty and injustice in the world and turned, at least for a time, against their class, against their family, against themselves.

I met several rich kids who had taken journeys similar to Patty's, for similar reasons. Isolated, unsure, bewildered by their good fortune, they heard the radicals' siren song and they couldn't resist the message that they had to pay for their privileges. It seemed only logical.

A New York heiress I'll call Lily was dragooned into spending several years in a San Francisco food co-op called the People's Harvest that had most of the qualities of an oppressive religious cult, including a self-appointed messianic leader who laid down strict rules for his minions.

Black-haired and a little chubby still with baby fat, the twenty-seven-year-old Lily never guessed she was rich until one day in her early teens when she opened a letter a lawyer had mistakenly addressed to her instead of her mother. It had to do with her trust. At that point Lily didn't even know what a trust was, let alone that she had one herself. And she was even more amazed to discover that, as the lawyer's letter made clear, she had about a half-million dollars in it. "I went straight to my mother," she recalled, "and I said, Mom, would you run this one by me?" Her mother had to walk it by, the whole idea was so extraordinary, but it turned out that Lily's father, an electrical engineer who had died when she was twelve, had been far more successful than she had ever dreamed. He had invented a delicate scientific weighing device that proved immensely valuable, and the profits had been put in trust for his children. Far from being hit by a massive wave of guilt, Lily remembered being quite pleased with her discovery. "I thought it was neat," she said. It meant that her father had been a big success. And sugarplum visions started dancing in her head of leisurely and stylish European travels and nights out on the town. Since then, however, she had come to have different views.

When Lily was born, she had a skin disease that made her vulnerable to infection. It took months for her to heal from even the smallest cut. At four, she went deaf in her left ear, so that now she had to wear a hearing aid and, at the women's health clinic where she worked when we met, she used a special amplified telephone. She joked about her ailments. "That phone is crucial," she said with a laugh. "You should try having someone explain a vaginal infection to you and you keep going, 'You have a what? Where?' "

She didn't joke about the money, though. Her health problems were nothing compared to her "wealth problems," as she called them. "The money is the major issue in my life," she said. Although by all appearances an open and easygoing person, she never could bring herself to discuss her feelings about money with her friends. "My money cuts me off," she said. "I can't talk to my best friends about it. I can't tell them how hard it is for me to get my taxes together. I mean, I owed the feds more money for taxes this year than most of my friends make in two years. You don't bring that up."

Attracted to the coffee-shop atmosphere and freethinking politics of San Francisco, she moved out with a boyfriend from New York in the mid-seventies. But the boyfriend soon took up with another woman. That made her more vulnerable to the imprecations of the People's Harvest.

The head Harvester, a bearded figure I'll call Al, knew just what to say to win her over. "He told me that the organization was trying to bring the neighborhood together. That sounded pretty good to me. But he went further. He played up the bit about this other guy in the organization I'd gotten to like. He said if I moved in, I'd get to see a lot more of him. But the big thing was, he worked on my guilt. He said I'd come from privilege, and I owed something to the people. I said OK, OK, where do I sign up?"

The co-op's mission certainly sounded worthwhile. It facilitated the distribution of food to working people around the city, but some unsavory aspects began to appear in Al's high-mindedness. For one thing, he acted considerably more respectful of the poor the organization served than of the middle- and upper-class kids he'd gathered to do the work. He got quite caught up in running his followers' lives. "He'd tell us who we could invite for a visit," said Lily, "or rather who we couldn't. He told us when we could come in and go out. It was worse than high school. It was like junior high."

As time went by, Lily began to feel that, because of her wealth, she was called upon to make a special contribution. Whenever money for the group fell a little short, as it often did, Lily's name was the first one Al called. After a while, he skipped the preliminaries and just told her to get her checkbook. But Lily was already paying a heavy tab. She was living a drone's existence there in their "scuzzy collegiate" quarters. The only attractive thing in it, she said, was the top-of-the-line stereo system that Lily herself had provided. Al, meanwhile, was carrying on like the queen bee. He routinely went out for sumptuous dinners in San Francisco's best restaurants while the drones like Lily were confined to quarters, having to make do with the high-protein gruel that they were dishing out to the city's poor. And when Al returned, sated from his feast, the females were obliged to grant him sexual favors for dessert.

She stayed in the organization for four years and put up with everything—the long hours, the hard work, the abuse from Al—because she felt it was her lot as an heiress. Finally, one day she decided she'd sorted her last crates of produce. It came to her in a jolt. She was weighing raisins, she remembered, sticky, gooey raisins. She'd slap them on the scales in a hunk, then peel off chunks to even out the weights. Inevitably the raisins would get mashed under her fingernails and between her fingers. Her milk-white hands would be stained a horrid shade of purple. "It was just gross," she said. "I just told them, 'Forget this!' And I walked out." She never looked back.

But Lily was not the only one to be affected by the era. "Shaped by the sixties?" said one rich kid in total seriousness. "I *am* the sixties." All rich kids are sensitive to the times.

RICH KIDS

Their parents may be able to pass their declining years mystified by, and safely insulated from, the political movements and social forces that sweep past their heavy, brass-knockered doors. The young haven't yet developed any ways to be set into. While their money may ultimately seal them off from the world, in the early stages it opens them up. At the very least, it buys them a good education. In the late sixties and early seventies, it delivered them to campuses swelling with kids from far more varied backgrounds than the young rich had ever previously encountered, and rife with increasingly radical politics, as the events at Berkeley, Columbia, and Harvard proved.

Impressed with the feelings of togetherness and purpose in these political organizations, many rich kids turned to good works with fervor, and many of them have kept at it long after the rest of the country moved on to other things. Their dedication to altruism when so many others have turned solipsistic is admirable, but there is a willful eccentricity to them, too, like a dancer who keeps on sashaying long after the music has stopped.

I'd heard about George Pillsbury for years around Boston, but I'd never met him. He was one of the very few heirs to go public about his wealth for revolutionary purposes, and I had always been impressed that he had been able to find a way to grab onto the sixties spirit while at the same time admitting he was rich. In the seventies, I thought you could be rich or you could be cool. George managed to be both.

An heir to the Pillsbury Flour Company of Minneapolis, and brother to Charlie Pillsbury, reputedly Garry Trudeau's inspiration for the character of Doonesbury in the famous comic strip, George made a name for himself in the early seventies when he helped establish the Haymarket People's Fund in an appropriately run-down apartment near Harvard Square. Started in 1974, three years after food heir Obie Benz had paved the way with a similar organization called Vanguard in San Francisco, Haymarket was designed to provide a vehicle for wealthy young liberals to unload a portion of their trust funds for causes they believed in, chiefly tenants'-rights groups; antinuclear groups like the Clamshell Alliance; and political films such as *Harlan County U.S.A.*, a documentary about a coal-miner strike. Although the first year's outlays totaled only $40,000, Haymarket's grants had an impact, according to its backers, far beyond their amounts since they often provided seed money for leftist groups few other charitable organizations would touch. Haymarket's annual outlay has since grown to over ten times that but still remains a fraction of the amounts handled by the establishment's foundations. For example, Haymarket awarded $500 to a gay-rights organization in Boston to buy a typewriter so the group could put out a newsletter—a small sum, but one critical to the group's effort. Furthermore, the organization made its selections in a rather unusual way—by screening off the actual donors from the decision-making process and leaving it in the hands of a board made up of nonwealthy community activists. The number of these alternative philanthropical organizations in the Haymarket-Vanguard mold has since grown to fourteen.

Other early proponents of the cause of radical philanthropy have since gone on to other careers (the movie business seems to have won many of them away, including George's sister Sarah, who, following George's example, founded a Los Angeles group called Liberty Hill). But George has stayed with it; when I dropped in to see him in the fall of 1982, he worked for an umbrella organization called the Funding Exchange to coordinate the efforts of the fourteen local groups on a national level.

For all the forcefulness of his radicalism, George himself was a slim, mustachioed thirty-two-year-old with much of the genteel grace acquired in his years at the New Hampshire prep school St. Paul's still intact. If anything, he seemed a bit timid, a trait he said he'd been trying to overcome since his prep-school days when he kept getting clobbered by the townies of otherwise placid Concord, New Hampshire. "I must have been beaten up four or five times," he explained. "It was a situation where there were these four local toughs and I was this clean-cut-looking kid. I was scared, and people must have picked up on it." Those run-ins, plus an assortment of household mishaps from his youth in Minnesota—like the time brother Charlie accidentally bashed him in the face with a golf club—have left their mark, most visibly a scar that curled up from his chin and a false front tooth.

After meeting at Haymarket's new offices in Boston's shopping district, festooned with revolutionary posters and cluttered with piles of position papers, we strolled downtown for lunch at a noisy restaurant. Despite the fall's balmy temperatures, George was well insulated in woolen navy pants, a tweed jacket, plus mittens and a long blue scarf.

His career as a leftist philanthropist all started, he explained, when he went to Yale in 1968. Although that was a year of riots and assassinations, the headlines merely primed him for the real story. That was the appalling poverty of New Haven's inner city, a side of life he had never seen before. He'd grown up outside Minneapolis on the family's private estate on a private peninsula called Bracketts Point that sticks out into Lake Minnetonka, and he'd spent his free time with his well-born friends at the Woodhill Country Club. Then came St. Paul's and a year in Australia to beef himself up a bit before college. "I enjoyed all the privilege," he said.

But that first year in New Haven undid everything, and he has since devoted his life to giving away the fortune and dismantling the system that made such a childhood possible.

"I confronted a lot of anger and resentment that I never dealt with at St. Paul's," he explained. "It was the first time I'd ever lived in the city—a real city with housing projects with poor people. I began to see poverty where I never had before. I spent a lot of time in the community tutoring and doing political fieldwork, and then I got caught up in the antiwar movement. I never liked the SDS, but I went to all the moratoriums and everything else there was. Those events had a big impact on me. I saw the inequities and felt them personally for the first time. I felt a lot of guilt at first, but then it became an emotional and intellectual process toward dedicating myself to positive social change."

Positive social change—probably not the term he used at the time. "Revolution" was more like it. At least that must have been the way his parents saw it. George's father was a Republican state senator, his mother a fund-raiser for the GOP and various exclusive secondary schools. He had been trained in a form of social activism, but now he was taking it a little further than his instructors ever expected him to go. "I realized that the solutions proposed by the Republican party weren't going to do it," he said. "Even the Democrats had their limits in terms of throwing money at problems and never doing the basic redistribution of power and of wealth. Mainstream politics lost its appeal for me then. It seemed so ineffective."

Like so many rich kids, George felt that the solution still could be found in his billfold pocket. Suddenly the social position that had seemed so various—ranging from the quietness of life on the lake to the surprise of seeing your last name on Minneapolis street signs—boiled down to just one thing: money. And George did his bit to start the big redistribution of wealth one day when he walked into the New Haven headquarters of the Black Panthers with a lot of cash and said, "I think you could use a little of this." He ended up plunking down twenty dollars. "That was my first sense of the power of money," he says. "I realized that I could toss in twenty dollars, fifty dollars, one hundred dollars. . . . What the hell? That separated me from my fellow Yale students."

He soon recognized that to put the money to work most effectively, he couldn't go it alone, and out of that perception, Haymarket grew. "The power of money is neat," he said. "The foundation was a way I could enhance the power I felt with my money. I could leverage it and get a lot more people involved. It wasn't just me tossing money at worthwhile organizations. It was a whole foundation."

But it was a foundation that seemed to live by his example. An early strategy for spreading the word about Haymarket called for George to come out about his wealth and his plans for it to a variety of newspapers and magazines, starting with the *Village Voice.* And the media delighted in the story of the Pillsbury Dough Boy. While the publicity doubtless attracted heirs to the cause, it also brought a few crazies eager to hit up George for an investment. One of them telephoned to ask for money for a device he'd invented that would bring eternal life. George tried to tell him gently that he only supported groups interested in social change. But the caller would not be deterred. "What could be more important to social change than preventing death?" he asked. He then flew to Boston to press his case in person. Although refused an appointment, he made his way down to George's office anyway. George only managed to elude him by dashing out the fire escape.

At twenty-one, George came into the first installment of his inheritance, $400,000. That's pretty much gone now. "I put in between fifty-thousand and seventy-thousand dollars a year for the first three years," he said matter-of-factly. "But I'm down to twenty-five-thousand dollars a year now."

Yet the principal on the bulk of his ultimate inheritance remained outside his control under the terms of his trust, so he didn't worry too much about how much money he had run through. "I can't run out," he said, "because I can't spend my principal. In my situation the money just keeps rolling in. There's plenty of money left in the family that just hasn't made it down to me yet. I won't lose. The next generation is going to be the one to lose out. We're beginning to really water down the family fortune. It's not just me—my cousins are spending it, too. I'm giving it away. We're all doing it in one way or another. Practically no one is making any money, just one out of the twenty-four members of my generation. That's not enough to keep the money alive."

And so the money will die. Not a bad fate, necessarily. George insists that the money will be well spent if it attains the kind of change he seeks. But it is quite possible that he is buying something else with that money, namely a return from the realm of the rich kids to the ranks of the average American from which his family sprang three generations back. It's a territory, after all, that his secondhand clothes and his battered car already proclaim him to inhabit. Then appearances would finally square with reality, and he would be just a regular guy at last.

George Pillsbury is an extreme case; few others have the power of their convictions actually to take such dire action. Other heirs, however, are under his influence, and in their minds he stands as a kind of larger version of the dreaded solicitation letter. Many resist. One said that she had once had a conversation with him in which she'd asked him just how much he was worth, anyway. When he gave a figure in the low six figures, she said, "You're guilt-stricken over that! I spend that much every *year!*"

But the Haymarket cause, and that of its sister organizations, has its backers among rich kids. It's one of the last bastions of the sixties spirit. But, curiously, rich kids also rely on it to gain relief from the agony that its very existence provokes. Some use it as a convenient answer to the always sticky question, what do you do? "I work for the Haymarket Foundation," they say, and conceal the fact that their work consists of writing checks. Other rich kids, though, are drawn to it as a kind of club where they can meet people like themselves. The Haymarket-Vanguard organizations offer, along with practical assistance to the young rich such as tax, investment, and accounting advice, a kind of networking service through which groups of heirs can get together to discuss common issues informally.

A group from Vanguard, for example, meets every month in San Francisco to share potluck dinners that, in one member's words, "aren't expensive, just elaborately prepared"; and to share thoughts on such predetermined topics as when to give loans to friends, how to deal with one's family, and, recently, matters of etiquette. The last wasn't a big success. "It was about whether or not to send thank-you notes and things like that," says another. "It wasn't fun."

For most heirs, though, such support groups are necessary for only a brief time. Just as Sonia Belahovski figured out how to handle the money mail (by throwing most of it away), rich kids just move on from a total dedication to philanthropy as they recognize that there are other people they'd like to spend the money on—like themselves and their families.

The Paine Webber heir, Roger Elkin, who was so amazed to discover he was a millionaire, falls into this category. He spent some time in the shade of the Haymarket umbrella, indeed helped found it with George Pillsbury. But by the winter of 1983 he had moved on to two occupations that involved him more deeply, caring for his family and producing feature films. He didn't even worry too much about the films' political content. "I won't get into something exploitative," he said, "but if it's reasonably harmless, and it's fun and I could learn something from it, why not?"

He lived with his wife, a television producer, and infant daughter in a house in a residential area that could be Wealthy-ville, USA, but happened to fall just outside of New York City. When the taxidriver dropped me off, he couldn't get over the place. "Wow," he kept saying, "real streets! Incredible! I know people from downtown who take a ride out here just to see these."

A good-looking, athletic young man with a reddish mustache, Roger was in his jogging suit doing warm-up exercises when I arrived, a little earlier than he expected, and he was disappointed that I was going to interrupt his run. But he took it good-naturedly, and we sat in his downstairs study with a view of the Hudson to talk.

Although the money in his life comes from the Paine Webber stock on his mother's side, it was his father's paper mill that determined where he should grow up—in remote Lunenburg, Massachusetts, on what he calls a "country style" estate with one of the town's finest colonial houses, several acres of field, and a big horse barn. Roger himself left the horses to his two sisters while he stuck to his bicycle.

The Elkins were so well established in the area that the local elementary school was located in a mansion that once belonged to Roger's great-grandmother. Her parlor became the assembly hall, and her barn the gymnasium. "Everybody at school knew," he remembered. "Some of them thought, 'Hey, this is a trip! Imagine living in a house this big!' But others didn't really think about it."

The only other residents of the town who could come very close to the wealth of the Elkins were two of their neighbors. One family owned the other paper mill in town; the other ran one of the largest food-distribution networks in the area. Roger was close friends with a son from each family. He'd go bombing around the countryside with them, first on bicycles, then on motor scooters, playing pranks on the local citizenry. "You name it, we'd throw it at cars or back porches," he said. But as adolescence turned to adulthood, both his friends "went crazy," and gave Roger his first lessons in the strange difficulties of being rich.

"For both of them," he said, "a lot of the problems came from wealth and having so many options, so many places to turn to. They just didn't know what to do. One of them, Dick, just felt that everything he touched fell apart—in business, in love, everything. He ended up killing himself in the family garage in a Mercedes Benz with the radio on. He just turned it on, rolled up the windows, settled back, and went to sleep.

"The other one, Norman, has been in mental hospitals for the last seven years, in isolation in one of them, for manic depression. I think it was because his expectations of himself were so high. He'd been captain of the baseball team, high scorer on the hockey team, all through school. Then he went to a big college and was just a number. For the first time, he had a hard time competing. Then the civil-rights riots of the late sixties started to erupt, and he made some black friends and started drifting around in Watts. Then something in his brain just popped. It was too confusing to deal with. Too much guilt, maybe. Too much input. He was trying really hard to be the best at what he did and he began not to be able to do it, and it started to slip away and he went manic. He said, 'I can do anything, I can be anything.' But he couldn't be, and he knew it. And all the time, his social class was a cross for him to bear, as it is for a lot of people."

Both of these stories are classic cases of a rich-kid disease, of being "soft where we are hard," as F. Scott Fitzgerald put it in his story "The Rich Boy." Where so much is free, rich kids don't know what to value, or how to obtain what can't be bought. Roger himself had spent a long time figuring out what went wrong. Back then, he didn't know how to react, except to worry that he might flip out, too. He took life as casually as he could. He went to college at the Hotel and Restaurant School of the University of Denver until he flunked out. Then he returned to Massachusetts and spent his summers as a general contractor and his winters working for the ski patrol on New Hampshire's Mount Watatic. Eventually, he realized he'd better buckle down if he wanted to make something of his life, so he moved into Cambridge to go to the University of Massachusetts at its Boston campus.

And that's where he had what he called "one of the more politicizing experiences" of his life. He had come into his money by now, discovered he was—"holy shit!"—a millionaire, but still hadn't quite put it together about what it all meant, when he happened to take a course in social theory. "The guy was pretty good," he remembered. "We read Marcuse's *Reason and Revolution.* Some students were aghast at communism; others, like me, were sort of interested. One day the teacher was telling us about how one percent of the population controls eighty percent of the wealth, and five percent of the population controls ninety-five percent of the wealth, or whatever the figures are, and I thought to myself—my God, I was one of the five percent. My classmates sure weren't. They were black, white, Spanish. There were working mothers with five children to support, and eighteen-year-olds who worked in box factories and talked with working-class accents. One of them started to nudge me, 'Hey, Rog, do you really *believe* that? Imagine what it must be like to be one of the five percent! Do you know anybody like that?' I said, 'Well, I have a friend who has a friend who lives like that.' That's as close I could get to it at the time. But it really made me think." (Actually, according to Jonathan H. Turner and Charles E. Staines in a 1976 study of American wealth, *Inequality: Privilege and Poverty in America,* for the period from 1953 to 1969, the top 1 percent possessed between 25 and 30 percent of all privately held wealth, and the top 0.5 percent had 22 percent. Millionaires, of which Roger was one, in 1969 comprised 0.1 percent of the adult population.)

At the time, Roger Elkin was living in a collective house in Cambridge with a self-styled philosopher and two students, and he was getting a large quantity of that familiar stuff, money mail, only it had an antiwar theme, this being the early seventies. As is so often the case, the solicitations brought out the millionaire in Roger. As he said, "I realized that I had a lot of something that a lot of people wanted."

One of the first causes he agreed to help fund was an antidraft newsletter called *Resist,* although he now recognized that the journal was "unbelievably boring." Then he made George Pillsbury's discovery that he could get more leverage with his money if he hooked up with an organization, and he joined with George and others to found Haymarket. He was not deterred when, after their first grant to the Dorchester Food Co-op, the first reaction they received was from someone at the co-op one town over in Jamaica Plain, saying, "Hey! We just heard that the Dorchester . . ." He told the caller: "Don't say another word." He was still soft, but he was getting harder. He didn't send a nickel.

Just about as quickly, his generosity put him up against an even more powerful interest group: his personal trustees. Even though one of them was president of a major philanthropic organization himself, the trustees were not pleased to see Roger dipping into capital for charity, particularly a charity they couldn't find listed in the telephone book. They were not reassured, either, when Roger explained that it was so new that the phones hadn't been installed yet.

"They call it a trust fund," said Roger, "but the fact is they really don't trust you. Basically, my trustees couldn't deal with the idea that I wanted to give my money away. They gave me pious speeches about how the president of the family investment company, who was also a trustee, had worked very hard to build the money up, and I shouldn't just wipe it out. They also felt they had to protect themselves, in case I had a change of heart and sued them later on. At first, I ranted and raved, but then I got wise politically and talked their language. We worked out a deal by which I could give away all the income but had to stay away from the principal, and that's pretty good. Those are pretty liberal reins."

On such liberal reins, Roger soon found himself giving money away at quite a gallop—as much as $40,000 a year. Besides Haymarket, Roger went on to bestow his income on the Funding Exchange, the umbrella organization for the Haymarket-Vanguard network, and its media subsidiaries the TV Fund and the Film Fund; as well as a pair of magazines, *New Dimensions,* which grew to become *Mother Jones,* and *Seven Days,* which was intended to become an alternative to *Time* and *Newsweek* but never took hold.

Ten years later, however, he was shifting his devotions

127

back along traditional lines—toward his family and a money-making career. In retrospect, he was glad that his trustees clamped down on his philanthropy in the way they did. "Long-term changes for social progress are expensive," he said. And for all his money, he wasn't sure he could pay the freight.

He didn't talk about this, but I sensed that he wasn't sure anymore that he even wanted to. He had moved up to a higher, more glittering league of social activists, having recently attended a benefit at Lincoln Center with Meryl Streep, Eli Wallach, and Bella Abzug, and that was fun. It marked a return to the conventional kind of rich-kid philanthropy, in which the kid shelled out a little money, but he got to mix with the stars. That way he could still maintain his own standing even as he helped others out. In the end, Roger cared about his standing. It really was a lot of fun at the top. He wanted to live well, and his living expenses had increased now that he was a family man, and there was the mortgage on that splendid house to pay. . . .

Besides, he had developed a passion for the movies. He didn't think of that as any radical departure. Roger told me he felt there were strong similarities between his former brand of politics and the making of a film: both build something out of nothing. "The political is creative," he said. With these rich kids up so high, it takes an act of the imagination for them to grasp the plight of those so far below. But then, maybe the real dream lies in thinking rich kids can help by redirecting their inheritances to the disinherited—the poor, the sick, the hungry. That's the vision haunting the minds of Roger's fellow rich kids, their consciences stirred daily by pleas for equality and justice that arrive at their feet in a flutter of fourth-class envelopes.

PART III

People

5

A Little More Than Kin...

The money stuffing rich kids' Gucci billfolds is different
from the regular kind lining the skinny wallets of the average
citizen. The bills of the rich kids are not adorned with the
usual engravings of Washington, Jackson, and Grant. No, their
cash has Daddy's picture on it, or their great-uncle's, or their
great-great-grandfather's—whoever it was back there who
made the money and then passed it down.

In rich kids' lives, the founder of the family fortune looms
as a far greater figure than any mere president. Large as such
billionaires as J. P. Morgan, John D. Rockefeller, Joseph Pulitzer, and Eugene Meyer stand in history, they bestride these
little rich kids like so many colossuses. Even though the family
founder may be long dead, he exerts an influence these kids

feel every day of their lives. He made the kids rich, for one thing. Often, he made the kids famous, too. Oil portraits of the great man burden the walls where the rich kids grew up; visions of him pester their dreams. Sometimes they live in his house. And they dutifully gather biographies and leatherbound editions of collected letters on their shelves in a kind of shrine.

The rich kids' money inevitably leads them back to their family. In one case, it used to do so literally. Helen Strauss's family company so dominated her hometown's economy in the nineteenth century that the family minted its own bills and coins. Usually the intermingling of family and money in family money is only figurative, but it is still compelling.

The rich kids' peers in the workaday world have to leave home to seek their fortunes, trotting off to take jobs in business or law. But for the rich kids to seek their fortune, they look back up to the august family founder. Among the recipients of Great-Granddad's largesse within the family, this shared financial heritage reinforces the natural ties of blood. In the immediate family, it turns brothers and sisters, economically speaking, into identical twins. But it also tightens the bonds with distant cousins, great-aunts, half-brothers, thereby transforming the greater family of descendants into something that more closely resembles a tribe or, even, an ethnicity. Rich kids are Rockefellers or Mellons or Pulitzers the way the common-born Americans are Irish or Greek or Lithuanian: they have a shared heritage that goes beyond their individual identities to unite them.

When a rich kid thinks of his family, he doesn't think of Mom and Pop and Bub and Sis. His family reaches back generations to Great-Great-Great-Grandfather and spans outward to fourth cousins. He sees his family as a long and ever-widening line of nobility, of which his immediate family is just one speck. In family genealogies, the whole business is usually pictured as a tree, with the founding ancestor as the sturdy trunk at the bottom and the descendants branching out above. But the rich kid himself views it the other way up—with the illustrious ancestor far above him, huge and imposing, like a Greek god, forever out of reach, and the kid himself down on the bottom.

And, in keeping with this view of himself as having come from a royal lineage, the rich kid always knows from what "house" he issues. The Rockefeller descendant I've called Terry, the one who is still waiting for his full inheritance to rain down upon him, has gone through life explaining that he isn't a John D. Rockefeller but a William, as though that settled something important about his character. In his case, the "house" is manifested quite literally as the fenced-in family compound in Greenwich, Connecticut. He grew up there with his extended family, all of the members linked by their descent from their Founder, William Rockefeller. Terry counted twenty-five cousins in his age group in the neighborhood; five of them ended up in his elementary-school class.

In the case of brand-name heirs, their "house" is more metaphorical—it is a matter for them of whether they are one of *the* Fords, *the* du Ponts, or *the* Pillsburys. George Pillsbury reported that he was plagued by the question when he was growing up in Minneapolis. "But when I told them I was," he said, "they never had much of a response. They seemed to wonder why they had asked the question."

The money reinforces the familial line, partly by drawing attention to it. The family money is like the wire connecting the Christmas tree lights: it makes all the bulbs light up. That can even catch some of the family members by surprise, as it did the Paine Webber heir Roger Elkin. Amazed as he was to discover his own fortune at twenty-one, he was even more taken aback a year or so into his daughter's life when he tried to establish a trust fund for her; he found out that his dead grandfather had already beaten him to it, endowing her handsomely from the moment of her birth by a provision of his will. She was a Paine as soon as she was an Elkin.

There are other ancestral links in a family, but the money line is the one that counts. Often, the wealthy families themselves believe that a special nobility has been conferred upon that particular strain of the family lineage that bears the money, and arrange their genealogies with that in mind. Michael Pratt was disturbed enough when he saw what effect the monied Pratts had on Amherst College; he was appalled when he saw their effect on the family tree. "The guy who made the money in our family is my great-great-great-grandfather Charles Bradley Pratt," he said. "He was a senior partner at Standard Oil, and he made his money running the country for a few years with Rockefeller. He is called the Founder. Of course, his father Ezra Pratt was a very good carpenter in Watertown, Massachusetts. Why shouldn't he be the Founder? Well, he's not. Charles Bradley is the Founder."

And the Pratts gather regularly to pay homage. When they assemble they all wear coded badges to show how they are related to the Founder. Michael found it amusing. "I was C1 something," he said, "but I can't remember exactly how it goes. I went with my girl friend, and they gave her my number with a plus sign beside it to designate 'paramour.' I asked what would happen if someone showed up with a gay lover. Would they get a minus? No one was amused by that."

Other families have better senses of humor. Roger Elkin says that at one recent reunion, hundreds of descendants of William A. Paine, one of the original partners of Paine Webber, stood up and raised a glass to themselves as "*real* Paines."

In the extended Wynne family of Texas, including Jimmy and Shannon, the gang has split into rival factions called the Snakes and the Mongooses depending on whether or not they are in direct line of the money. The Snakes are all descended from the wealthy lawyer Buck Wynne and are so named because of those Tiffany-designed gold rings of bejeweled serpents of the Nile that Jimmy and Shannon wear so proudly. They are copies of one awarded to Buck by a client grateful for the way he disposed of a major lawsuit. The Mongooses were formed by a cousin who married into the family and are so named because, of course, mongooses eat snakes—and gobble up their inheritances in this case. But instead of going at it like natural enemies, the Snakes and Mongooses gather peaceably every year at one of the Six Flags parks built by Shannon Wynne's father Angus, where they have a kind of hootenanny, including a fashion show for the Snakes and initiation rites for that year's crop of Mongooses.

It's natural that rich kids should attend a lot of reunions of the whole clan, for the money has a way of reaching out beyond the nuclear family to pull distant relatives into the family fold. The true father here is the Family Founder, and all his descendants are his children. Consequently, in these rich families, cousins often feel as close as siblings. Charlie Chiara, the grandson of financier John Loeb, grew up with his cousins, the Bronfmans of Seagram's Liquors; their houses stood side by side on common property in Westchester County, New York. Charlie's mother's sister had married Edgar Bronfman but had obviously been unwilling to leave her Loeb family too far behind. "There were ten of us children as you drove up the property," said Charlie. "Our house was first and theirs second. It was a big party all the time." Although the Bronfmans eventually divorced, severing lucrative business ties between Seagram's and what was then Shearson Loeb Rhoades, the family bonds remained intact. One of the cousins remains Charlie's best friend. Charlie was best man at his wedding, and his picture hangs over Charlie's desk at his little production company in Hollywood.

With their control of the family purse strings, the grandparents act more like Mom and Dad. That can get a little strange. Barbara Behn, now in her thirties, recalled that when she was a small child, her grandfather Sosthenes Behn, the "Prince of Telephones" and founder of ITT, absolutely doted on her, carrying on as if he had sired her himself. Accustomed to material pleasures himself—for an office, he occupied a salon done in the style of Louis XIV—he would take her to F.A.O. Schwartz and, she said, "nearly buy out the store," then round out the occasion by asking her, although she was only four or five, to have luncheon (no mere lunch, of course) with him every Saturday at his corner table at La Côte Basque. And every year until he died when she was six, he celebrated her birthday in the penthouse suite of the corporation's thirty-three-story Gothic skyscraper on Manhattan's Broad Street. There he would summon the directors to a long boardroom table, put Barbara's chair—bolstered by the Manhattan phone book—in the place of honor, and, as the company's French chef wheeled out a huge birthday cake, lead all the executives in singing Happy Birthday.

And that wasn't all. There were other distinguished relatives on her well-fertilized family tree. Barbara used to pass her summers in Newport in a modest place, by local standards, called Stonybrook. But her great-uncle was Edward Julius Berwind, the coal king, who built for himself a château to rival the Vanderbilts' monument to conspicuous consumption, The Breakers. His was the Elms, inspired by France's Château Daniel; and Barbara's great-aunt, then in her nineties and confined to a wheelchair, used to invite Barbara and her sister to come over to play there every Sunday as children. They had a wonderful time climbing on the statues in the garden. "We were so small," said Barbara, "we'd ride them like horses." They'd visit the extensive greenhouses with the gardener. And they would watch delightedly as their great-aunt summoned the butler, Benson, to feed their dog. "Benson was more of a snob than my great-aunt was," said Barbara. With great ceremony, Benson would serve the animal roast beef off a silver platter. On rainy days Mrs. Berwind would invite them to bring their games inside. "The house had a huge ballroom," said Barbara, "and my aunt would take us kids into the ballroom and get a ball and say, 'Come on, let's play. That's what ballrooms are for.' So we'd go inside, her in her wheelchair, my sister and me, and we'd play catch."

But these grand old ladies in the rich kids' past were not always so charmingly eccentric. As in Oz, there was a wicked witch for every good one, and their existence served to remind the kids that money does not necessarily make people good. It just makes them rich.

I tracked Julia Pierrepont-Stromsted down through a screenwriter friend of mine. Despite her formidably double-barreled name, she was a spunky, tousle-haired free spirit of twenty-four, who mixed in some leftist political organizing with her main line of carpentry work. Jules, as she is called, talked to me in a Manhattan apartment while baby-sitting three toddlers left in her care by her current carpentry customer. Easygoing, she was perfectly comfortable with the threesome tugging at her arms and legs as we conversed.

In her family, however, the elders were not always so accepting of the younger generation. Her grandmother was a Pierrepont, as in John Pierpont Morgan (the J.P. branch dropped the original Norman spelling), and she never let young Jules forget the heavy responsibilities that such a background entailed. "She was a pillar of iron and really grim," said Jules. "Whatever she thought was right was right. She had a preconceived notion of what people had to be like to fit the mold, and it just wasn't me." It wasn't anybody Jules knew either. For her grandmother had some pretty farfetched ideas of propriety. When Grandmother was visiting, the girls were not allowed to leave the house unless they were wearing white gloves. Nor could they use public telephones, to say nothing of public rest rooms, which were sure to be "diseased." Jules was not to go out on a date unless chaperoned. In fact, she was not to speak to anyone unless she had been properly introduced. "All the old sort of Vanderbilt manners that you read in the how-to etiquette books were a religion for her," said Jules. "It was like it was still fifty years ago!" Most of these rules were harmless enough, except for a couple that created some unforgettable scenes.

The first arose out of Mrs. Pierrepont's belief that a young lady should finish everything on her plate. Jules knew enough to do her grandmother's bidding, but on one visit to her grandmother's Connecticut estate her thirteen-year-old sister was less careful. She chose to slice the fat off her roast beef and leave it. "Eat that," said Grandmother, pointing to the fat. "Eat everything on your plate."

"But it's fat!" replied the sister. "I can't eat that. It'll make me sick!"

"Young lady," insisted the redoubtable Mrs. Pierrepont, "you will eat what you are told to eat." And when the sister still wouldn't give in, Mrs. Pierrepont sprang out of her chair, swept the fat up off her plate with her hand, and shoved it down the girl's throat.

She swallowed it, but only for a moment. True to her word, she then proceeded to be sick on the dining-room floor, an extraordinary spectacle that roused even the servants from their professional detachment and sent the rest of the family scrambling to the girl's assistance. If they hadn't intervened, Jules firmly believed, old Mrs. Pierrepont might have made her eat it back up again. "It was unbelievable," said Jules, "complete madness and bedlam. It was totally perverse on

Grandmother's part, but that's the way she was. Everybody was afraid to cross her because what she said was always right. And that's the kind of thing she did all the time."

On another occasion, such firmness of character on the part of Mrs. Pierrepont almost killed her granddaughter. That was during a visit to the lady's Charleston property when the two of them went driving with an aged admiral, one of Mrs. Pierrepont's many admirers, at the helm. As Jules recalls, the gentleman was "a little shaky" at the wheel, and as they were crossing a bridge going into the city, the car suddenly swung to the bridge's edge, struck the guardrail, and bounced back. The admiral continued jauntily along as though nothing had happened. Jules was horrified. "Grandmother!" she yelled, tugging at her grandmother's sleeve. "He's going to drive us off the bridge! He doesn't know what he's doing!" But Mrs. Pierrepont showed no more concern than the admiral, just stared stonily forward.

Jules was panic-stricken. "We've got to tell him to pull over!" she screamed. "I'll drive, or you'll drive, anything. But we've got to get him to stop!"

Finally the old lady turned to her and replied firmly: "There are some things you just do not do."

"But I don't want to die!"

"You will if you have to," answered Mrs. Pierrepont, and turned her head forward once more, as if to meet her fate.

Jules survived the trip but has never been able to keep her Pierrepont ancestry in quite the proper perspective since.

If Jules's grandmother had just left Jules to wander about the marble halls of her estate, she might have been able to get her point across more effectively. Nothing, as a rule, quite brings home the grandeur, sturdiness, and glory of the family tree as a trip out to the grandparents' house. It is here that rich kids gain their first sense of that august lineage stretching back behind them nearly to infinity. Spacious as their own homes may be, the grandparents' place is usually big enough to have fathered it. And, if it has survived the wreckers' ball, the great-grandparents' mansion is even more stupendous. The whole progression of family real estate back in time, each mansion more monstrous than the last, is like an endless series of Chinese boxes, with the rich kid the tiny prize at the center.

But the grandparents' house is impressive enough—invariably palatial; surrounded by acres of woods, fields, or just limitless green grass; bustling with servants; the walls laden with oil paintings of the family pantheon of ancestors; and the driveway jammed with so many glossy Rollses and stretch limos, it seems as though there must be a funeral going on.

Michael Pratt's grandparents' house was a Long Island estate, one of six that his great-grandfather Frederic Pratt—called "Pooty"—built for his children. (Pooty's place was even bigger, of course.) The grandparents' mansion was a towering affair made of white-painted brick, with a series of steps leading up to the front door that Michael still finds exhausting. Out back there was a grape arbor that the family gardener had grown from cuttings he had received personally from the gardener to the king of Spain. But on his first visit at the age of ten none of that impressed Michael so much as the fact that the halls were so spacious he could ride his bicycle down them, and nobody seemed to mind. On the big social occasions of Thanksgiving and Christmas, however, he recalled that such freedoms were curtailed. He was forced to display what were termed "Grandma manners" and banished with the other young fry to eat by themselves at a special table adorned with the family crest.

The grandparents of a steel heir I'll call Hugh lived three blocks away from him in Chicago in a heavy baronial-style house full of medieval tapestries and dark furniture in more rooms than Hugh could count. About the only modern thing in it was a spiral staircase made entirely of stainless steel in celebration of the family business. Outside, beside a croquet lawn and a bowling green, the house was surrounded by glorious English gardens shaded with weeping willows. And inside, a library of botanical books had sprouted two stories high, ringed by a balcony, with stacks behind that were nearly as extensive as the gardens themselves. Hugh used to play hide-and-seek in the stacks and around the upper floors with his cousins, and he took pleasure in conducting military maneuvers with his toy soldiers on the library floor. Sometimes he would wander over to the house to be alone. But even though there were always fourteen servants on call to answer his every request, he didn't feel quite right being there by himself. "The house scared me," he said. The place is smaller now, since an aunt inherited the property and brought the wrecker's ball to it—all except for the library, the steel staircase, and a carved-marble vestibule. She rebuilt the entire thing in steel, a move that won her the admiration of the *Architectural Record,* although a little less from Hugh. "I think the facade is kind of ugly," he said, "but the inside is nice."

"Growing up, I had a far greater awareness of family than of money," said the Rockefeller, Terry. Most rich kids shared the sentiment. The money itself is tucked away quietly in these families—like their genes. And, as with the genes, only the money's consequences show—in the swank neighborhoods, the polo ponies, the best schools, and, of course, those elaborate and expensive family reunions.

Sometimes, though, the family life-style doesn't give the game away, particularly in the Northeast, where the frugal Yankee mentality takes hold. Although she grew up in a Long Island mansion, the rich kid I've called Helen Strauss always felt like a pauper. Partly this was because she had some megarich Whitneys, Mellons, and Vanderbilts for neighbors. But her misapprehension was compounded by the fact that she and her siblings were raised by a grandmother who had a pronounced case of poverty chic that drove her to such extremes as patching worn bedsheets together to avoid the expense of replacing them with new ones. Helen will never forget the sensation of sleeping on sheets with a hem. Even more confusing, the grandmother's only indulgence was her collection of primitive American furniture. Although priceless, the ancient stools and chairs were so nicked and scraped with age that to her granddaughter they looked like hand-me-down junk. To cap it all off, the grandmother used to take pleasure in inviting her well-oiled neighbors over for dinner and serving them, instead of filet mignon and champagne, sandwiches off paper plates and milk in grape-jelly glasses.

The cash itself, which might have clarified matters, was

rarely displayed around the house, regardless of its social style. Monetary affairs were taken care of by an army of professionals in distant downtown office buildings. Middle-class kids learn early about the significance of a weekly paycheck. Rich kids never know where the money comes from, or, for that matter, where it goes. One heiress told me that she was freely indulged with lavish presents, pleasure cruises, and cars when she was growing up. When she turned eighteen, she found out from her trust officer where this munificence had come from: her own trust fund. These were gifts, in other words, that she had unknowingly bestowed on herself.

If the money is a mystery to rich kids in their youth, the purchases are something of a puzzle, too. The houses were often full of the latest electronic gadgets, as if to make up electrically what these kids lacked in personal human contact. A rich kid from a Dallas oil family remembered that at her parents' house, which was done in the style of Frank Lloyd Wright, everything seemed to operate at a touch of a button. Drapes opened and shut electronically; the TVs appeared from behind panels; and the bar popped out from behind a wall-sized painting. But you had to pour your drink yourself.

But the biggest surprise was how big these houses were— high, wide, deep, they indulged themselves shamelessly in every dimension, especially that fourth dimension of time. The best of these places were old, a century at least, the better to reflect the age of the money that maintained them. That's why so many of the homes of the rich kids were castles, which perfectly combined the twin imperatives of history (or at least pseudo-history) and bulk. Then, the whole business was set off in comfortable seclusion by acre upon acre of grass or forest or some happy combination of the two.

For these kids growing up, it must have seemed that their houses and surrounding grounds were designed for a race of giants. On a practical level, the jumbo size meant that it often involved quite a hike to go play with the neighbors. But inside, these houses gave them their first taste of the isolation that would prove to be their lot as they grew older. The black millionairess Shiela Waters, normally giggly, grew quiet as she recalled her childhood in a big house by a park in

RICH KIDS

Washington. "No matter how many people were in it," she said, "our house always felt empty." In her loneliness, she came to think of the half-dozen servants in the house—from the "official housekeeper" on down to the cook—as her jailers. "I remember looking out the window one day into the street and thinking, 'My God! I'm imprisoned here! Nobody knows I'm here!' I mean, it's all very lovely, but it's nothing more than a lovely prison."

Others felt the same way. In the greater scheme of the family, the money might pull everybody together; within any individual family, the money pushed everybody apart. In their vastness, the houses were often sectioned off, so that all the children had, at the very least, their own rooms, and often their own play area, complete with their own nanny to oversee them.

Few rich kids grew up in close contact with their parents; instead they had maids to bring them up. In more high-toned families she was called the nanny or governess; in the less, the baby-sitter. Either way, these women ended up mothering these rich kids well into adolescence, when the kids went off to boarding school.

Heartless as this arrangement may seem, the children almost universally liked it. As Cary Ridder, a cheery heiress to the Knight-Ridder newspaper fortune, blurted out: "I wasn't raised by my parents—thank God!" She explained that her mother was far too busy with her political career and her packed social schedule to keep track of such petty details as picking her children up from school.

While a certain coldness creeps into most of the rich kids' recollections of life with Father and Mother, their hearts leap up as they recall their nannies. Sometimes the objects of their adoration are so unlikely, it seems that some primitive psychological force must be at work akin to the imprinting that allows baby ducklings to fall in love with cardboard boxes. Terry Hunt, an heir to the Alcoa aluminum fortune now working as a psychologist in Boston, has spent many an hour contemplating the rapture he felt for a deaf, arthritic eighty-five-year-old Czechoslovakian woman named Apola. Strictly speaking, she was the family cook, but she ended up giving so much quality time to Terry she might as well have been his nanny. Terry had, in fact, developed strong feelings for the woman who really was his nanny, but he was squeezed out of her affections when his younger sister came along. So he turned with love in his heart to Apola. "I had a very intimate relationship with her," he told me. "It was very intimate, very secret, and very special. She was a woman who could hardly walk, but she and I together were like a pair of teenagers in love. I'd say things like, 'I can't wait for my parents to leave so Apola and I can be together.' " Unfortunately, Terry's mother found such sentiments alarming and sent Apola packing. "Ostensibly that was because Apola couldn't get along with the rest of the help, and she would turn off her hearing aid when she wanted to tune people out," Terry explained. "But I knew the real reason." Terry was crushed, and, like a tiny Romeo, he pursued his love to her new place of employment, where, with tears streaming down his cheeks, he pleaded with her to come back. Unfortunately, Apola's new mistress wouldn't let her go. So his first great love passed out of his life. Terry was all of five years old.

These maids were all strange objects of affection, coming from backgrounds so different from the rich kids' own. They were poor, for one thing, and they were usually foreign, frequently French or German. Michael Pratt's family went for a series of Nordic blondes. Now, he said, "portions of my childhood are scattered all through Scandinavia." And there were, as with Annie Owen's beloved Goldie, a good number of southern black women as well.

But in the very difference lay these women's strength. They supplied some basic human values, a kind of reality principle, to lives that might otherwise have floated away entirely in the ether of financial freedom.

Elizabeth Meyer, the self-professed "porpoise in the sea," believed she might have gone under if it hadn't been for her Lil. She was a savvy black woman who, even if she had herself grown up as one of eighteen children in a sharecropper's family, had a special insight into how to handle her princely charges. She paid them to be good, laying out cash for making their beds and taking baths.

And she had a no-nonsense approach to high society as well. She went along one time on a family visit to Elizabeth's grandparents' house in Westchester County. Although it was a spectacular 750-acre estate designed by Charles Platt, the family always referred to the place as "the farm." Since Lil herself had grown up on a real one, she knew a farm when she saw it. She took one look at the marble front steps and turned to Elizabeth's father in shock. "Dr. Meyer," she exclaimed, "this ain't no farm!"

To her utter consternation, Lil was then waited on by the various liveried attendants inside as though she were one of the rich kids herself. She didn't go for that at all. "Poor Lil would get hysterical," Elizabeth recalls. "She'd be horrified by these ghostly white butlers who'd appear out of nowhere and say in a deep voice, 'Yes, madam?' She'd go into the kitchen and they wouldn't let her cook. The place would look like a hotel kitchen and it would be full of French chefs with their Escoffier hats. That really set her off. 'Boy,' she'd say. 'I could sure cook up a storm in that kitchen.'"

Despite all the solicitations of her grandfather, to say nothing of the attentions of her own parents, Barbara Behn still regarded her nanny as the one who shaped her life. Dadu, as she was called, first came into the Behn household at nineteen to minister to Barbara's mother when she was a child. Her mother's first husband, a Norwegian ambassador to Germany in Munich, was looking for someone to take care of his children and happened to ask the man in charge of winding the embassy clocks. The clockwinder recommended his daughter, and she served the family from the age of nineteen until she died at seventy-six, with an intermission in her thirties to get married. "If I were to write a book about anyone," said Barbara, "it would be about Dadu. Everybody in the family had quirks except her. She was rock steady. She knew more than just changing diapers, too. She served for a time in the secret service in Munich—she wasn't a spy, but she handled secret papers. She gave me a sense of good and bad, and showed me that all men are created equal. But she had an interesting aristocratic streak. She always said: 'It's better to die with a silver spoon in your mouth than to be a traitor to who you really are by going to live in a dump.' I loved her enormously. She'd punish me by threatening to leave. I called her a witch once, and she locked herself in her room and claimed she was packing a suitcase. I'd leave notes under her door saying, 'Please don't go! Please don't go!' She never left, thank God. I don't know what I would have done if she had, I loved her so."

When the kids finally do grow up and leave the house, they often maintain relations with their nannies as if there were indeed a blood tie. Having received so much from them in their youth, they try to give something back as adults, and frequently send them money and take care of them if they get sick in old age. One New York heiress flies down south once a month to see the black nanny she calls "my Mamie," even though Mamie last took care of her when she was four. "I also see that her needs are met," says the heiress, "and I give five-thousand dollars a year to her church." Terry Hunt flew to Czechoslovakia to get back in touch with his heartthrob Apola and discovered that the love still burned even though she was then pushing a hundred. "Our relationship still had an erotic basis to it," he said. "It was beautiful!"

And Elizabeth Meyer was so absorbed in her wonderful Lil that she wrote her senior thesis in college on her. She flew down to Baltimore, where Lil was then living, for a series of interviews. It was a very moving time, for Lil was ailing, and she died just after Elizabeth finished. "I was blown out of the water by that," said Elizabeth. But Lil's spirit lived on, for Elizabeth still felt an unexpected kinship with older black women—and a special sense of comfort in their presence. "Whenever I am with them," she said, "I feel I have gone home."

As an adjunct to his psychological services, Terry Hunt has developed a line of isolation tanks, otherwise known as sensory deprivation chambers, which clients use to aid their therapy or for simple relaxation. He designed his first tank in the shape of a coffin. His latest, however, looks like a small Porsche. The user climbs in through its flip-up front hood. Inside, he or she lies naked in a saline solution at body temperature in the darkness, perhaps indulging in such extras as stereo or Jacuzzi bubbles, the mind filling with whatever lovely phantasms it can bring forth.

It's an appropriate interest for a rich kid like Terry to develop after a childhood spent sealed off in a "lovely prison" cell. In his isolation, the mind of a rich kid naturally fills with private fantasies. The sharpest consequence of being in a family that was so big in so many ways was simply that the rich kid got lost in it. As a result, he often ended up wandering off into his own solitary world. As if to encourage the children's flight of fantasy, their rooms were often stocked with toys and games and fabulous slimy creatures. Elizabeth Meyer had a room full of lizards that she played with for hours on end. Michael Pulitzer had a vast train set that overran a pool table. Annie Owen had her menagerie of chickens and guinea fowl, Sonia Belahovski her horse and "little hideaway places" in the barn.

Even though Amanda Holladay, the Hillsborough heiress, grew up in a castle with, she said, "stained-glass windows and turrets and lots of secret rooms," she still turned inward to her own imagination to fill out her days. She spent hours by a single tree in front of her house elaborating on a fantasy involving invisible souls she called the "flea people." "They were no bigger than fleas, so you couldn't see them," she told me straightforwardly at our interview. "But I could. I represented them with little glass beads. They looked very well, I must say. I gave them names that were subtle variants on the names of everybody in my family. But they were much better in every way. They were very attractive. They lived in villas and had a great time. They had helicopter pads and all the accouterments of wealth I could think of." Mostly, they had fun. Amanda herself, by contrast, had the same access to all these material pleasures in the real world preferred her fantasies of wealth to the real kind.

She also devised another set of magic characters from the chivalric era, the "flower people." These she represented with flowers from her mother's garden. She placed the flowers on fallen leaves, which indicated their palaces, and devised "endless country intrigues and secret rendezvous and battles" to occupy them. And so she would while away the hours, oblivious to the reality of great wealth under the turrets of her parents' house, as she dreamed her own dreams under the trees out front.

George Pillsbury's sister Sarah, a slender blonde who had moved on from Liberty Hill to develop her own production company in Hollywood, recalls that she developed her first interest in theater to fill the time during which she was left by herself. And she had so much time alone, it turned out, for the simple reason that she was a Pillsbury. The common methods of absorbing free time, like watching TV, were banned in their house, or at least severely restricted, as inappropriate for children of their elevation. "All of us kids would whine that all the other kids could watch as much as they wanted," she said. "And our parents would say to that, 'Why do you want to be like all the other kids?'" The Pillsbury children couldn't exactly say. "There was the sense," Sarah concludes, "that the standard was set by the Pillsbury family, not by you as an individual."

Sarah says that other prohibitions were somewhat more pernicious, such as the way she was discouraged from developing friendships first with the gardener's kids and later with her public-school classmates, since her parents felt that she would soon be going off to private school anyway and didn't want her to be tied down to old friends. She felt particularly deprived that she was never allowed to be a Brownie. Surprisingly, such separatism didn't stop Sarah from repeatedly being elected class president in her public elementary school; it just left her feeling lonely. Nevertheless, in her private moments, she recognized her own special star quality and explored it. She spent much of her free time up in her room listening to Barbra Streisand musicals. She even choreographed them so she could sing and dance the lead parts all around the living room, imagining herself a Broadway star, with Gower Champion her choreographer and Harold Prince her director. And at the big Presbyterian church, before her family switched to the Episcopal one, she dreamed, as she sang the hymns in her frail soprano, that "someday my voice would be heard alone above all others." If any of her movies ever hit the silver screen, someday, in a way, it will be.

Just as Amanda and Sarah's imaginings took off from their family life, these private fantasies of the rich kids often mingle with the facts of their illustrious lineage to produce dreams that are steeped in the ancestral tradition. The kids see the big houses of their ancestors, they hear the history, and, secretly, they start to swell with it all. While these musings can be as benign as, for example, a Kennedy's ambition to be a congressman or senator, they can also have a slightly discomfiting quality as the kids strain to square the supposed greatness of their family with the often rather gloomy circumstances they actually find themselves in. Just as the money itself will, when they come into it, provide an unnerving point of comparison as they try to place a value on their own selves, so the family's heroic past sometimes contrasts unpleasantly with their own present. The tots dream of being titans.

The Houstonian Emily Montgomery dropped the name of Alice Kleberg Reynolds Tatum to me on one of her wonderful postcards (she had to squeeze to fit it all on one line), and we met at teatime one afternoon in a Dallas fern bar called the Stoneleigh P. Alice wore so much of that family jewelry, the Biwa pearl and all, she jingled faintly when she walked in. Like many rich young women, I was discovering, Alice had the kind of skin that belongs in a soap commercial, also a pair of dewy blue eyes, brown hair that was swept up in a bun, and a firm squared-off jaw that made me take the rest of her face more seriously.

To Alice, the Kleberg family history—replete with government service in Congress, agricultural innovation, and shrewd real-estate purchases—had become a kind of religion, and it stirred within her feelings of longing and obligation that she didn't quite know how to satisfy. "I used to be afraid and hidden about who I was as a Kleberg and what I stand for," she said. "It embarrassed me because I wasn't normal. I was always taught to be normal. I went through a very dowdy phase, when I didn't wear anything that would symbolize who I was. Now I understand who my ancestors are and the quality they represent, and I don't ever have to be ashamed of them again."

Alice attributed much of her early uncertainty about her identity as a Kleberg to her non-Kleberg father Dick Reynolds, who managed both to exalt and impugn his wife's family name. He was, said Alice, a "John Wayne type" who charmed everyone except his immediate family. Although Reynolds himself came from what Alice felt, with only the slightest touch of patronization, was a perfectly respectable background in the men's clothing business, Alice sensed that he felt overshadowed by his wife's Kleberg ancestry. Determined to rope his wife in, he insisted the family live entirely on his salary; the Kleberg money could go only to charity. He took over the management of his wife's finances and demanded she cut back on her career as an arts patron to stay home and take care of the children without benefit of maids or baby-sitters. Reynolds himself was not the most affectionate father, and Alice distinctly remembered his rebukes to his children. "People like us don't do that," he'd say. But he never made clear what they did do, and Alice grew up ashamed of herself for being "abnormal." She had to live up to a different standard but never knew what it was. She only knew what it wasn't. She felt lost.

Her parents divorced when Alice was twelve, and that took some of the pressure off. It also led to a firsthand understanding of what, concretely, the Kleberg name stood for. To console herself, Alice's mother took her on a trip to look over the family holdings. The jaunt took them to six countries on four continents.

Much of Alice's life since had been spent trying to come to terms with her history. While many heiresses had trouble mastering the details of their families' past, finding them the oppressively masculine recounting of one swindle after another, Alice had taken her family history to heart as if it somehow contained her own life story. She noted, for example, that she was but one of about a dozen Alices in the family genealogy—of whom five were still living when I spoke to her. She believed there were traditional Alice traits that shed light on her own character, particularly altruism and a tendency to be "mother to her mother," something that had been true for Alice since her parents' divorce.

On the face of it, however, the history of the King Ranch,

which the Klebergs married into around the turn of the century, does not seem to be one of overwhelming generosity. Aside from a few stints of public service and some impressive agricultural innovations, the essential spirit of the King Ranch story is contained in the injunction that Captain King picked up from his friend Robert E. Lee, to "buy land and never sell." Richard King had come by ship to South Texas from New York City as a stowaway at age eleven and become a steamboat captain on the Rio Grande. But in 1853 he took Lee's advice and started buying up the properties of Spanish families fleeing the state during the Mexican War. By the time of his wife Henrietta's death in 1925, the King Ranch had grown to 1.2 million acres, an area bigger than the state of Rhode Island, and eventually included 10 million more acres in Australia, as well as an odd million here and there in Brazil, Venezuela, Morocco, and Spain.

Yet in the tale Alice discerns "a great selflessness" on the part of the captain and his wife Henrietta. She noted that Henrietta used to cover the diamond earrings the captain had given her with black enamel so they wouldn't attract attention. Since Henrietta's death, under the Kleberg regime, the ranch has developed a new breed of sturdy cattle, the Santa Gertrudis, as well as a strain of grass to feed them. And it has also funded various philanthropic organizations. "We have an incredible ability to provide for other people, giving them food and education," Alice declared, her voice swelling with the faith like a minister's.

Alice's own altruism emerged during her teens when she tired of the high-society aspects of her inherited "whiskypalian" faith and branched out with a radical priest to become, she said, a "Holy Roller." With a band of like-minded youngsters, she went around to orphanages, hospitals, and retirement homes to do "pilgrimage work." "We felt we were helping God's children," she said, "giving them some hope for life, some happiness."

She had phased that out now, but much of the religious fervor had been transferred to her effort to bring the family history in line with what she saw as its original principles. "I've lived with a lot of pessimists in my family and some real myopic people," she confided. "And there's just too much to offer people. We're given too goddamn much to be so selfish!"

She felt that many of these unfortunate tendencies were evident in the family manse, the famous King Ranch house that Alice's friend had compared to Fantasy Island. Alice still visited there occasionally and was sorry to see how the place had changed. It had fallen from grace. "My fondest memories of the house are of the cool tile floors," she said. The house was built around a center court and designed to be air cooled. Originally, the floors had been covered with throw rugs of saddle blankets that were woven on the ranch. The bedrooms had had simple rustic four-poster and two-poster beds. All the furniture had been made of raw wood, the boards lashed together with rawhide and covered with leather. But now the only rooms that held to the original spare design were the ones belonging to the "elders." All the porches had been enclosed for air conditioning, and all the bedrooms done over into what Alice called "little hotel rooms with pinstriped wallpaper and shag rugs." Each one had its own motif. And the cabinets were jammed with horse-racing trophies won by the King Ranch's distinguished line of thoroughbreds like Assault and Man o' War and oil paintings of them, along with pictures of the cattle that sired their original herd. "It's all much more commercial than I'd like," said Alice, "but then we are in the twentieth century, aren't we?"

Despite the attention that she had given to her family history, Alice claimed that it had come as a big surprise on her twenty-first birthday to discover a trust fund that, when it became fully her own at age thirty-five, would leave her set for life. And it gave her a new angle on the responsibilities of being a King Rancher. "It is so *big*!" she exclaimed. She was a student of landscape architecture at Cornell at the time, but when she saw how much money was headed her way she decided that she had better "lay the foundation" for it by learning about high finance. She got a job at Citicorp, which put her through a couple of whirlwind training courses and then set her up in Houston as a corporate loan officer. And then she said, "My body gave way with two ovarian cysts. It was like, time out! You're a little young, yes?" By the time the complications were resolved, she had spent two months in bed, lost one ovary, and suffered so much scar tissue on the other she doubted she would ever be able to bear children.

She was married now to a "self-made man" and noted real estate developer named John Tatum. The ceremony had been conducted in a small chapel in San Antonio, with few relatives invited. She hadn't quite settled into married life yet, since she was still shuttling between her old apartment in Houston and the new one she shared with her husband. She and John were planning to buy a new home in a former power-generating building in Dallas. "We want," she said, "to have a house that is ours together."

So for her the future was still forming. She said that her favorite possession was her glass collection, which had been somewhat reduced in size because of all the damage it had received in various moves. But her most prized piece was still intact. Mulberry-colored below turning into pale green above, the sculpture had the shape of an inverted heart, except the two points didn't come together at the notch. "To me," she said, "the piece represents a convergence, of ends meeting but not quite touching, It's a dilemma, but it's a whole, since it is all one piece. I suppose that's my life, But I hope I never find what I really want, because then I'll stop fighting."

In middle-class families, the time of greatest closeness between parents and children and between brothers and sisters comes when the kids are still young. The family still lives together in the same house, some of the siblings possibly sharing the same room. The children wear hand-me-downs from their elders, attend the same local schools, go to the same hangouts, perhaps share the same friends. How different this is from the childhoods of the rich kids, so isolated from their parents and from their brothers and sisters inside their vast houses. But they do catch up eventually. For them, the time of greatest family feeling comes after they have grown up and left home.

Their inheritances, surprisingly, bring them together. The money pays for long-distance calls and regular visits, of course.

But more importantly, it provides a shared and extremely private bond. When a rich kid finds out about his own trust fund, he also finds out about the holdings of his brothers and sisters, and, often, gets a pretty good idea about those of his parents' as well. In uncovering something so intimate, it is as if he has seen their private diaries. On becoming adults, all the members of the family learn something about each other that no one else will possibly ever know. By sharing such a secret, the family members develop a rare and solid form of trust that is not so different from love. All rich kids feel that, deep down, only their families really understand.

Sometimes the siblings act on their money identically, in the way that Sarah Pillsbury founded Liberty Hill shortly after her brother George founded Haymarket. And in those families where the children all go off in separate directions, as is more often the case, the money in some way keeps them connected. While Ando Hixon, for example, is a professional investor, his brother is a spiritual-talk-show host; while the woman I've called Marie, who lost much of her money through some improvident investments, is in a seminary, her brother is a rancher; Elizabeth Meyer is a real-estate developer and yachting enthusiast, her sister a Jehovah's Witness. But running through these different personalities is the same money, and it unites them. In Elizabeth's case, and in others, there is a practical aspect to the shared wealth, since she has to join her siblings on a regular basis in a conference call to decide how to manage their joint holdings. As she says, "We're all caught up together in the spiderweb of *Washington Post* stock."

And this unifying principle applies between children and parents as well. When rich kids come into their money, they see life from their parents' perspective in ways that the non-wealthy will probably never manage. When the middle-class kid turns twenty-one, his father has finally become well established in his profession and in his life. That's not necessarily true for the fathers of the rich kids, for, at least in the old-money families, they are living off their own inheritances from *their* fathers, so they are rich kids, too, just older ones. In these wealthy families, there is only one true father, the Family Founder who made all the money. All his heirs are his children, regardless of their age. That awareness, while it can upset the power balance, can also breed a special intimacy between parents and children. Sonia Belahovski confided that she likes to sleep with her mother in her double bed when she goes home to visit. Other relationships are nearly as close.

Michael Pratt's father, Charles, has died, but Michael believes that, while he lived, his father lived completely for him; he grappled with the money so that Michael didn't have to. And that has paved the way for Michael to go into his chosen profession of community organizing for such causes as fighting price hikes on New York City's subway fares and curtailing the price-gouging practices of certain inner-city grocery stores. The two looked remarkably alike, except for the ruddy beard that Michael now sports to make himself look older. "My father grew one once," he says, "but my grandmother had a conniption fit. 'How can you have a beard, my beautiful baby?' she told him. So he shaved it off. He thought he would grow one after she died, but he never did."

Like Michael, Chotch, as his father was called, had a strong social conscience from an early age. It first came out at sixteen when he tried to organize the maids in his parents' house, the one where Michael later rode his bike down the halls. That move went over only a little better with the maids than with his parents. Although he never joined the Communist Party, Chotch became enough of a social activist that the House Un-American Activities Committee saw fit to ask him some questions. Later he branched out into the arts to become a fairly well-known photographer, and to marry an actress and fill his house with such show business stars as Mike Nichols and Elaine May. He also took son Michael on his first political demonstration, an antiwar march at age eleven, in which Michael climbed up into the nooks of St. Patrick's Cathedral in New York to get a better view.

"My father was an extraordinarily moral, strong man," says Michael. "He changed lives because of his passion, his caring. There were times when I didn't see how I could live with the privilege along with my political ideas. I'd feel the pull of that contradiction. He lived with it with a grace that I seek to emulate. He went through hard times, sure. I think my salvation is that my father went through the trauma for me. He went through twenty years of hell so that I could be happy."

Yet the principle of improved relations between the generations best applies to the families of old money; where the lucre is of more recent vintage, generated by the father, it can seriously disrupt the family harmony. It is one thing to hold one's ancestors in awe for creating the family wealth; it is quite another to see one's father that way. There is probably always going to be some strife in any family as children grow up and prepare to displace their parents. But the matter is drastically complicated where the father is a self-made tycoon, and that can stifle the children in any number of ways. The young man I've called Edward, the one who has made an occupation out of renovating his house, is the son of a Scandinavian who slipped out of Norway to escape the Nazi occupation in the Second World War. With three friends, the father sailed across stormy winter seas in a twenty-nine-foot yacht, navigating by handheld compass, to reach America. He arrived with just eleven dollars' worth of Norwegian currency in his pocket. Yet within ten years, he had built one of the largest shipping fleets in the country and become a millionaire many times over.

Edward, however, had little of his father's drive. While he described his father as harsh and distant, he is mild and friendly. Edward once went into business importing hammocks from the Yucatán, but even though the profits were rolling in, he tired of the life and sold out to his partner. His greatest accomplishment was playing on the winning team in the national Ultimate Frisbee championship. Because of his father's seagoing experience, Edward decided not long ago he should attempt something similar, so he joined a crew of three to deliver a forty-nine-foot yacht from North Carolina to the Caribbean.

It was an unfortunate idea. The first day out, the boat got caught in a massive storm that ripped the mainsail to shreds before the crew could get it down. But the winds were so fierce that, sailing downwind, they were able to "surf" just on a jib. Edward was terrified, and he stayed that way even after the winds subsided. "I thought about death regularly on the boat," he said. "At night I worried about getting run over by tankers that didn't shine their running lights. And I was afraid of pirates, too. There are lots of pirates in the Caribbean. They shoot you and throw your corpse overboard, and then they take your boat for smuggling pot. I had an evacuation plan all worked out, so I could sneak out of my bunk and hide in the steering well in case the pirates came. They never did, but I decided—the open ocean, man, you can have it."

6

Can't Buy Me Love

Amanda Holladay, the ethereal Hillsborough heiress who spent so much of her childhood playing with the "flea people" on her front lawn, didn't think of herself as being on the make when she flew to Barcelona. A woman of proper East Coast manners despite her West Coast upbringing, she recoiled at the very *idea*, arching her plucked eyebrows in horror as we sat together over lunch in that fashionable San Francisco restaurant overlooking the Pacific. But, as subsequent events showed, she was certainly in the mood.

We only got onto the subject by accident. She started to clam up as I quizzed her about the price of various pieces of jewelry she had about her person. "Well then," I kidded her, "let's talk about your sex life instead."

"That would be easier," she replied airily. "It's so vulgar to talk about how much things cost." Then, to my surprise, she brightened. "Sure, let's talk about my sex life," she said. "What do you want to know?"

"Does money make sex better?" I asked, a little embarrassed to be so straightforward.

"What do you mean, money strewn around the bed?"

"Not exactly," I said.

"I never isolated money as a factor." She batted her eyelashes. "I never saw the green stuff when I was looking at the taffeta pillows."

"But at least it improves the location," I said. "On some exotic beach, say, with the sun going down . . ."

"But think about it," she replied. "All that sun and the sand and the fleas. You've got to remember the harsh realities." She added that she had once spent a night of frustration with a boyfriend in a situation that should have been romantically ideal. The two were sailing in a sixty-foot cabin cruiser so big it towed a yacht behind it instead of the usual dinghy. "That was dreadful," Amanda said. For one thing, her friend's parents were aboard—they owned the boat, after all. And the cruiser was crawling with so many crewmen the two lovebirds could never be assured of any privacy.

No, all her fantasies were perfectly chaste, she assured me. The closest she came to any romantic preoccupation involved old Fred Astaire and Ginger Rogers movies. "I've watched those over and over and over again," she said with a sigh.

"No sexual fantasies?" I pressed. "None at all?"

"Well, I guess I do have a weakness for the artist in the garret. I've seen a lot of plays about that, even acted in a couple of them, and I've been to tons of operas, too. But if you're talking about making love to a stranger, I can assure you I'm not interested. I've always been wary of strangers ever since I was a child. I saw all those vultures come down on Father just because he had money. I can only do it with people I've been introduced to. I tell you, I'm very shy. Plus, I'm choosy. I don't like men who wear jewelry or are overly groomed." Then she thought for a moment. "But I suppose there is Ezio Pinza and Mary Martin in *South Pacific* . . ."

With that, a big smile came over her face and she remembered her vacation in Barcelona. "Well, I guess there was one time . . ." she began.

As with so many love stories, this one started with a failed romance. Amanda had fled to Europe to put some space between her and her old boyfriend whom I'll call Paul. He had, in fact, been the very artist-in-the-garret type she went for. Nice as the idea seemed in the theater, it didn't work out so well in real life. Paul was a struggling painter who had been, she said, "set adrift" by his parents on his majority instead of being set up the way Amanda had been by hers. But the seas into which he floated proved too heavy, and Paul soon jettisoned his painting career and headed to law school. He relied on Amanda to support him.

She let him move in without paying a share of her rent, and she bought all the food. Rather than show much in the way of appreciation, he responded by disparaging her dead father whenever he had the chance. Considering the circumstances, said Amanda, "that seemed rather inappropriate and hypocritical."

Worse than the way he treated her father, though, was the way he treated her Jaguar, a particularly sensitive issue since it had been her father's favorite car. "He was always grinding the gears," she said. "I guess it was his way of taking out his anger against me and the family. I took a lot of the hostility for a long time. I felt that I had money and he didn't, so I should share."

Her feelings for her Jaguar finally won out. "He was so hateful that finally one day I just told him, Paul, if you grind the gears one more time, that's it. Well, sure enough not long after, he did indeed grind the gears again, and I said, 'Paul, pull over and get out.' He did, and I got behind the wheel and never let him drive my car again."

She pushed him out of her life shortly thereafter. And, as rich kids often do when love turns bitter, she thought she would take a trip to try to recover from the whole miserable affair. She wanted to go to an English-speaking country and considered flying to Scotland, but this was the end of January, and she decided that would be too cold. Then she remembered that she had some Spanish friends from graduate school at Berkeley where she was studying Japanese, and she booked a reservation to pay them a visit in Barcelona.

The friends being well-to-do, they made her a temporary member of the Barcelona Country Club for the duration of her stay, and that's where she met the young man she called her "dark-eyed stranger" and I'll call Juan. She was sitting by herself in the club dining room having some tea and catching up on her Japanese homework when, as she put it, "into my peripheral vision wandered this god."

"I don't know what caught my attention exactly," she went on. "He just looked *interesting*—you know, intense, intelligent. He had dark eyes and dark hair and not terribly dark skin. He was having lunch with his family. I saw him across a crowded room, just like in the song.

"We noticed each other, but I'm shy about eye contact. That's too forward for me. I tried to look at him when he wouldn't see me. I found him so intriguing! I had a crush on him immediately. I often get crushes on men I have had no contact with. I never expected to speak to him. I figured that would be a let-down and spoil the fun."

To Amanda's astonishment, when the dark-eyed stranger's lunch was over, he did not walk off into the sunset but instead ambled gracefully over to her table and introduced himself.

"He addressed me in English," she said. "That was good, I figured he couldn't be a complete idiot. And he said something sweet and not oily, not smooth. It was completely unthreatening, and I was totally smitten."

Despite her normal caution with strangers, she gave him the telephone number of the house where she was staying. He called shortly afterward to invite her out. She was favorably inclined but first had to clear it with her hosts, the parents of one of her college friends. She described the couple as "paranoid" types given to installing bulletproof glass in all the windows and requiring the family chauffeur to carry a concealed handgun. Fortunately they knew Juan's parents, so they gave their blessing. "He wanted me to go riding at a nearby stable," she said. "I know how to ride, so I said fine. I said fine to just about everything he asked. Except one. About that I was quite reluctant."

They rode through the forest for hours, winding from one bridle path into another. Amanda remembered that the occasion was "fabulous" but had no recollection of any details except Juan himself. "I don't remember what kind of horses," she said, "I don't remember what kind of trees. I didn't see any of the trees. I have no idea what was in the forest. I was completely preoccupied."

When the ride was over, Juan got just as busy, calling often to ask her out. Eventually he arranged to meet her at his parents' house one weekend when they were away and no one was around except the caretaker.

"The house was very beautiful," she recalled. "It was near a botanical garden in a town sort of like Beverly Hills, if you can imagine that in Spain. The house itself was terribly fashionable, quite contemporary, with lots of wonderful modern art. It had clean lines, white-and-turquoise walls, and a vaguely Moroccan motif. It was beautiful! It looked out on a fabulous garden, and it had a deep, deep lawn all around, with a forest behind it."

In Amanda's eyes, Juan looked no less inviting. "He had excellent manners," she said, "and he was brilliant, handsome, charming. His only fault was that he paid little attention to dress, which appalled me. But otherwise he was splendid. He was so bright. He'd read a lot of English and American fiction, and we talked about that. I forget what else, though, I was so gaga."

True to his Spanish blood, Juan made "endless efforts" to seduce her, but she resisted them because, as she said, "she wanted to keep things orderly." Even though she had left Paul back in San Francisco, she still felt that it wasn't right to take up with anybody else. And it was hard to put Paul entirely out of her mind because he called her every night. All the more upsetting, he used her phone, since he was still living in her apartment, so she was paying for the calls. Yet she said that if she had been totally unencumbered, she would have been all the more "shy," because she would have had no excuses to fall back on.

Nevertheless, one morning when she came to visit and, as was now becoming customary, the parents were away, Juan leaned over to her for a kiss, and this time she did not pull back. She couldn't help herself. "I just became overcome with passion," she said. Casting about for a place to consummate the attachment, the two settled down on the cool marble floor of the vestibule. "You have to understand that I'd resisted him for so long that we were both rather . . . highly . . . *aroused*. It wasn't violent. It was impassioned. And it was intensely erotic. Marble may be one of the hardest substances known to man, but we had young bodies. What can I say?"

Actually, the two lovers just began the festivities on this altar. They then proceeded to go through every room in the house anointing the territory with their commingled love scents like a pair of priests sprinkling holy water.

The affair was luscious while it lasted, but, like most youthful enthusiasms, it came to an end a week later when Amanda had to return to the U.S. She recognized that, in retrospect, it was probably just as well. For all his dark-eyed charm, Juan was self-centered, and she could see problems lurking in his relationship with his father, who had a towering ego of his own. "The fantasy had to end," she said sadly. "The worm always turns."

Ah, love! For all the difficulties that it poses for the average Joe and Jane, it seems to offer nothing but trouble for their more moneyed peers. This tryst of Amanda Holladay and her dark-eyed stranger, brief and fantasy-filled as it was, stands at the high point among the romances I heard about. For the most part, money tends to be an impediment to love.

It's not for any lack of desire. As was true of Amanda, rich girls have often developed a powerful fantasy life in their youth, and it comes with a full complement of romantic urges. But, bred in isolation, the kids don't always know how to act on their desires. Like money, sex was not a fit topic of conversation around the house. In the heavy Victorian atmosphere that so often pervaded the homes of the rich, it was a matter of some shame and embarrassment. So the rich girls tended their thoughts of love like a secret garden. As it proved to be for Amanda, it was full of the most luxuriant flowers, but only for themselves to enjoy.

As the rich kids grew older, difficulties arose in finding

suitable objects for their affection. It was in the quest for love that they first sensed the strains of class conflict—both with others and, more complicatedly, within themselves. Few rich kids sought out lovers from their own lofty station in life. They were eager to break out of the gilded cages of their youth; and, in the antiestablishment late sixties and early seventies when most of them came of age, their tastes in people mirrored the general public's. They didn't like rich kids either.

And the trend has continued. While about a third of the rich kids I interviewed were married, and another quarter were involved in long-term relationships, none of them had selected a partner from their own privileged ranks. Few of them had come anywhere close. Far and away, the tendency was to select a lover from a more mainstream background. Some of this, of course, is mere practicality: most of these heirs would be hard pressed to find a mate fully as rich as they. In fact, for this reason one heiress, Sonia Belahovski, who had gone for the "shaggy kids" over the "rich kids" in her youth, called her secret wish to marry a man who could match her fortune a "fantasy," as if she herself were no more than a lowly Jane Eyre hoping to land Mr. Rochester.

But this downward mobility in romance must be due at least partly to the decline of high-society festivities—the whole panoply of country clubs and balls and coming-out parties that were havens for matchmaking among the well-to-do. Nowadays, rich kids are thrown back on the same tracks for finding someone compatible as everyone else: college classmates; office colleagues; and people they meet by chance in bars, on airplanes, and at cocktail parties.

And that can be upsetting for some of these well-bred young ladies and gentlemen. The proper Houstonian Emily Montgomery was taken aback by one man's advances at such a gathering with the unwashed. "This fellow latched onto me," she said with a laugh, "and to try and seduce me he pulled out this letter that had been written to him by a woman he'd slept with three weeks before. 'Dear Mark,' it said, 'I thought I was dreaming when I thought back over what you did to me last night. . . .' And she went on about how wonderful the whole experience had been. And he handed it to me to read! I said, 'Is this supposed to be some sort of sexual reference? I'm sorry,' I said, 'but I don't accept them.' That was *weird*!"

Yet the obvious consequence of the rich kids' social plunge is a marked disparity of wealth between the two halves of the happy couple. And that can cause trouble between the have and the have-not. In the more dramatic cases, all the tensions that naturally exist between the leisure and the working classes are condensed in the romantic union, so that whatever love may be felt between the two lovers is imperiled on both sides—on the bottom by envy and greed, on the top by suspicion and protectiveness. As Amanda told me, summing up her problems with Paul and other struggling artists she had been drawn to, "My money has always been a problem. The guy either tries to profit from it, or he resents it. Now I'm quick to spot the hostility, and as soon as I do, I drop them. I back off." All the way to Barcelona, where she can have a fling free from the economic consequences.

It is said that a woman can never be too rich or too thin, but neither is true. Both qualities are bound to attract unwanted attention. Like physical beauty, the money draws attention to exterior characteristics in a way that can be frustrating to the woman locked inside. It can be alienating to discover what a boyfriend really likes a rich girl for.

Alice Tatum experienced this discomfort with a boyfriend at Cornell, where she was studying landscape architecture in the seventies. Frank, as I'll call him, was a potential NHL hockey player who was, she thought, sufficiently talented and secure, despite his own middle-class background, not to be rocked by her wealth. Since Frank came from upstate New York, he soon took the opportunity to drive her home and show off his parents' place, a modest two-story house in the suburbs. Alice felt obliged to reciprocate by inviting him down to see her father's 14,000-acre ranch in Austin. Frank had never seen such a spread. Thinking it important to show him the full scope of what lay behind her, Alice then took him on down to the family homestead, the King Ranch, whose million acres made Alice's father's place look like a tot lot.

Frank, of course, was stupefied. "He was in awe," said Alice.

"He had never seen that much wildlife, or that great an expanse of land. It was unreal to him." Real or unreal, the spectacle went to his head, and he started acting strangely when the two returned to Cornell. "He got more and more possessive of me," she went on. "I couldn't even see my girl friends, he got so jealous. I grew very tired of that." Failing to pick up on Alice's distress signals, Frank sought to make their relationship permanent by proposing marriage. Alice delicately responded that she was too young for such a commitment. She needed time to grow. And she suggested that she might start by spending more time apart from him. Frank, however, was enraged by the idea.

"That's just not fair!" he screamed. "Here you go and show me everything you have to offer, and then you take it away. You can't do that to someone!"

"Well, I'm just glad I saw your true colors," Alice replied.

That should have been the end of it, but it wasn't. Frank couldn't let her go. Alice came home to her apartment late one night a few weeks later, closed the door behind her and was hanging up her coat when someone grabbed her from behind and threw her on the bed. It was Frank, and he was laughing hysterically. "I almost shot him," says Alice, "I really did. I had a gun in my apartment."

It turned out that he had been watching the place at night. Since Alice happened to rent from his uncle, Frank had been able to obtain a key and let himself in. Alice told him to go away and stay away.

But he didn't. She took the next semester off in order to be a debutante in Texas and thought that she had left her troubles with Frank far behind. But one day when she was traveling through Bryan, Texas, she spotted his car, with its New York license plates, on the campus of Texas A&M. She shot out of there without making inquiries, but she could only assume that he'd transferred there to be nearby in case she ever changed her mind about him. "I guess he just hoped that someday I would come back," said Alice. She never did.

Alice is not the only rich girl whose money has attracted such flies; nor was she the only one to come to such a swift and painful discovery about her lover's true intentions. The documentary filmmaker I've called Helen Strauss, whose grandmother had misled her so utterly about her class standing, fell abruptly out of love with her rock musician boyfriend when he tried to put the touch on her for a $20,000 synthesizer. "You don't need the money," he said, "and I do." She threw him out.

Yet such sudden revelations are rare. More often, there is simply a dreary dwindling away of love. In affairs of the heart, the truth is often complicated: while the money plays a role in the man's attraction for the woman, there are other factors, too. The question is precisely how much the money has preoccupied him, and that can be difficult to determine. "I consider myself very acute at reading people," Elizabeth Meyer told me, "but you can't divine someone's subconscious. You never know what someone likes you for. You never know if it's your money or your beautiful blue eyes."

Preferring to believe that it's their eyes, many heiresses are remarkably slow to give their men the boot. One called a halt to her yearlong love affair with a destitute Italian sculptor who had been taking advantage of her only when she tired of having to chauffeur him everywhere. He had never gotten around to securing an American driver's license. She didn't mind that he never contributed to household expenses; he claimed, with remarkable regularity, that the bank had closed before he could get cash. "Generally," she said, "I took care of him. And eventually, he just became dependent on me. Finally it got so that I was driving him around, and it just got on my nerves. He was pathetic, and I felt sorry for him. But you just don't respect anybody then."

It's easy for these relationships to get started, since rich young women never lack for admirers—for some good reasons. To judge from the two dozen I talked to, they all have a variant on the glowing qualities that attracted me to Annie Owen—a peppy conversational style, good looks, wide-ranging experiences, an insider's acquaintance with the rich and powerful. The problems come up if the love should ever falter, for the relationships often drag on regardless. That's because, at least from the man's point of view, the affair has something else to feed on.

When we spoke, Elizabeth Meyer was just coming off a long-term relationship with a sometime carpenter I'll call Bill. At least, she *thought* she was coming off it. "Ostensibly," she said, "we've broken up." But the affair had lingered on like a case of mononucleosis, and matters had devolved to the point where Bill was less a lover than merely a nonpaying resident in Elizabeth's house. And he had come to enjoy the arrangement. "Essentially, I give him room, board, and utilities," she said. That, apparently, was inducement enough. "He is kind of a strange person," said Elizabeth. "He is pretty much a loner, and he lives very frugally. He can live on six-thousand dollars a year." Like the hosts in *The Man Who Came to Dinner,* Elizabeth couldn't bring herself to show her guest the door. As with the heiress-turned-chauffeur above, she found herself being taken for a ride—before she realized she was driving. "My problems with Bill are interesting," said Elizabeth, taking the detached and scholarly tone she often adopted in discussing the problems of wealth. "He'd say that the problems between us lie with my money, in his inability to live on my level and mine to live on his. My feeling is that he's freeloading on me."

Elizabeth claimed not to mind his taking advantage of her, since she felt there was plenty of money to go around. She was more disturbed by the effect her money had had on him: she worried it was turning Bill into the sort of aimless lout— a stereotypical rich kid, one might say—that Elizabeth had herself spent a lifetime fighting against becoming. "Bill just doesn't *do* anything," she said. "If he had an occupation, a way to identify himself, he'd be better off. My wealth keeps him from finding an occupation. I told him long ago, look, you've got to go establish yourself. I'm very kindhearted and I get a lot out of him. I use him for snuggling. But I'm pushing him out now. Eventually, he'll go to California. He's been talking about that for ages."

Yet another reason that Bill had been able to hang on had to be Elizabeth's difficulties in finding a replacement. Even though she had many attractive qualities besides her stock portfolio, she declared that "men won't go to bed with me." While they were drawn to her wealth, once they got up close and reached the wooing point, they backed off, intimidated. In Elizabeth's view, the problem wasn't that men were attracted to her money, although they may have been; the problem was that at some fundamental level they were repelled by it. Her wealth ran counter to the natural power lines of romance in which men assume that they are in charge. Yet a vast fortune like Elizabeth's empowered her to a far greater extent than most men can ever hope to reach, and in Elizabeth's view the result was, for her, a prescription for celibacy.

"I've thought about this a lot," she said. "I don't think a woman with money can get involved with a man who doesn't have as much or more money. If the man ever thinks that his wife or his lover is powerful—unfairly powerful—it will drive him crazy. I've found this out in my relationships. Whether or not I actually wield my money as a weapon against the man I'm with, I don't know. I probably do. But much less than they think I do. And even if I didn't, I'm considered just as dangerous, because I can do what I want. I think that a lot of men want to keep women financially helpless, because otherwise the women won't need them. Women with money don't need men. They really don't. That's an incredible release for me, but it's also an incredible burden."

For men, the problems aren't so bad, largely because the power of their money plays along the conventional lines. Consequently, none spoke of love troubles with the degree of anguish that the women did. But their money didn't make their romances trouble-free, either.

Men, too, had to grapple with the disparity of wealth, since they were just as inclined as women to fall in love with people who had less—often considerably less—money than they. Yet while women tended to view their men either as charity cases or ingrates, the men saw their women as financial advisers of a sort. These free-floating millionaires relied on their women to give them a basic, down-to-earth understanding of the value of a dollar. Far from being the frivolous baubles of thirties films, chattering in lower-class accents as they hang on their men strolling Park Avenue, these women are equal partners.

They might even hold the upper hand because, having come up through life the hard way, they have a grasp of economic reality that their lovers lack.

In part because of this professional overtone to the male view of courtship—in which he is less falling in love with a woman than hiring one—men tend to be considerably shrewder than women about sniffing out gold diggers in their midst. One man has even gone so far as to devise a quick test to determine a woman's true intentions. "I always check a new woman over," says this heir. "I watch her very closely. And I test her. It comes down to whether she can look me straight in the eye and talk openly about herself and her life-style when we're getting to know each other. I'm in no hurry. I can afford to sit back and wait. If she seems at all evasive, she fails."

This need for scrutiny increases for the brand-name heirs who are passing along the family name as well as the family money. Rich women can be less circumspect on this point, since they lose their last name when they gain their mate; indeed, that can give marriage an added appeal. But for men, the question can bring in the family to pass judgment on a potential spouse. Even though our Rockefeller, Terry, does not have Rockefeller for a last name, the ancestral aura is so powerful that he might as well possess it; and the family acts to protect the name's integrity as though he has it. "Because of our history," Terry explained, "the family tends to look closely at people who want to marry into it or get involved with it. I'm very aware of potential family censure in my choice of a wife." Perhaps not coincidentally, he is still a bachelor at twenty-nine.

After they do marry, this approach can lead the men and women to change the traditional roles of husband and wife, so that the women commute to their jobs in the city and the men stay home to do the dishes and take care of the baby. Several men whom I interviewed freely described themselves as househusbands this way. Paine Webber's Roger Elkin, for example, put his career as a film producer on hold after the birth of his daughter, yet his wife continued to commute to her job as a TV producer. He was happy with the arrangement. "We decided on the basis of need and demand—the squeaky-wheel principle," he said. "For the first year of my daughter's life we didn't have any day care. Now we have a woman who comes in. But I knew it was going to be an incredible bonding experience for my daughter as well as for myself. I had the time. I figured I should do it."

More often, though, the parental roles aren't switched, just the responsibilities. In most relationships where inherited wealth is not a factor, women usually have considerable say over the household budget. One might think that when the man holds all the money, he would exert more influence over what to spend it on. Actually, he often exerts less. Since rich kids haven't worked for their money, they are grateful to trusted outsiders who can tell them how to value it. The wife acts as a counterweight to the husband's instincts—often to the point of neutralizing them. Where the husband is inclined to be tight, the wife often loosens him up, shelling out for the luxury he would regard as a wasteful extravagance. Where the husband is inclined to be too lavish, the wife reins him in, giving a more "sensible" cast to the couple's fiscal policy.

The San Francisco counselor of wife-beaters, Daniel Griswold, may have reduced himself to the austere circumstances of a monk, but if it weren't for his girl friend Laura, he might have stopped buying things altogether. Because of his frugal streak, she served a vital function in his life. While Daniel could do elaborate comparison shopping, he could never bring himself to shell out the cash, while Laura had the opposite problem. So at least on that score the relationship has been ideal. "For the first couple of years we were together, we talked a lot about how to spend money," he said. "Now it's as if I lived on her salary as a schoolteacher. Before, it was as if I made a lot less." For example, even though he recognized he badly needed a car to get around, Daniel said that he might still be consulting car dealers, taking test drives and then returning home on foot, if it weren't for Laura. "Once she got involved in the purchase," he said, "she wanted to end up with a car. So we got one." In fact, they got one from the first dealer they went to and drove away in a Dodge Colt. "If we had gone to a different dealer that first time," he said, "we would have gotten a different car."

Michael Pratt's live-in girl friend tried to spruce him up a bit and get him out of the blue jeans and flannel shirts he had favored in his effort to avoid, as he said, "giving messages that I'm an upper-class guy.

"I'm dressing up more now," he said. "That's Ginger's work. She's such a good dresser." But he also recognized that other aspects of his life-style, such as the condominium they just bought near the Hudson in New York, can be hard on a girl from a modest background. That kept him from aiming too high with his purchases. "The money is tough on Ginger," he said. "It's wonderful, but it's weird. Ginger has trouble knowing that we can have whatever we want right now, without working years for it. What will we want when we're fifty?"

The AMP heir Ando Hixon credits his wife for giving him the stability he never would have found as a rich kid flying solo. Now a reformed hippie working as an investment banker, he had passed several years in a Boston-based band called The Duke and the Drivers, playing saxophone and percussion in his stage persona of Rhinestone Mudflaps. He had settled into the rock 'n' roll heaven of drugs, booze, and groupies on a seemingly perpetual tour of beer halls and college towns when his girl friend put her foot down and made him choose between the band and her. He gulped twice and chose her. "If I hadn't met her," he says, "I'd have rocked on forever."

And he has come to appreciate the way that she rules the roost. "When we had our first baby," he says, "we didn't look at each other and say, 'We're making a baby, I love you.' She turned to me one day and said, 'Ando, I'm pregnant.' I went out and looked at the stars and didn't know *what* to think. But she took command, and thank God for that."

Where there is this disparity in wealth between the rich and not-rich half of the couple, the two have to decide what level of society they want to live at. Unlike most people, whose social rank is determined by this year's salary, heirs can choose; they can live well or poorly, as they wish. The presence of a less wealthy Significant Other throws another factor into the equation—the twosome can pick his or hers. Do they go for the high style of the rich kid and buy the biggest house on the block, go out to dinner every night, drive a Mercedes, and hire a maid for the kids? Or do they select something that the poorer half might prefer, or at least be more used to, and live like other young couples in a rented apartment decorated with secondhand furniture—the hardwood floors, good light, and odd heirloom the only concession to their hoarded capital—and make all their major purchases on time?

It's a big decision, and most couples face it the way all newlyweds and live-ins would: by working out a compromise. As one midwestern duo manage it, the household expenses have pretty much dropped to what he, the unendowed one, can afford. They decided on the principle of fairness—since he couldn't rise, but she could fall, they both drifted down to the level where he could contribute his fair share. That means they split the mortgage payment down the middle, along with everything else. And that necessarily limits their shopping sprees. Yet, the wealthy wife has made an exception for certain necessary heavy expenditures that would otherwise send her husband into debt. "I paid to insulate the house last year," she says. "I had the money, and it made sense to do it, so I picked up the tab." She finds that this spending approach has improved their purchases. "Just because we can buy something," she says, "it doesn't mean we should. I give more thought to my purchases this way."

The Mellon descendant I've called Heather had likewise pitched her life-style to her boyfriend's minuscule salary as a drummer in a rock band, but then occasionally nudged it back up again with a heavy outlay of her own. Consequently, the two of them seesawed in a way more typical of rich men and their women. "I can spend money," she said, "but he won't. He'll go for weeks without spending a penny. I pull him up from that, and he pulls me down. So we hit a middle ground." But it's an uneasy middle ground, more like a no-man's-land between two armies. Heather told me she had trouble being the one with all the money.

The two met at an eastern college, where Tom attended on scholarship. He grew up in a small midwestern town. "His parents fought all their lives for what they have, and they struggled day to day with finances," said Heather. "For Tom, what he has in his checkbook is what he has." Heather, of course, had it much easier—private school, summer place, all the extras. Since Mellon is not Heather's last name, Tom didn't even know that Heather's background was anything special until a friend clued him in one day at college. It didn't seem to matter. "The money was incomprehensible to him," said Heather.

The sofa in their little Georgetown apartment summed up their arrangement—and her discomfort. It was handmade. He built the frame out of two-by-fours, and she sewed the slipcovers for the cushions. And she agonized over the material. In a whisper, she confided that the $300 she spent on it was the most she'd ever laid out for any one thing except for a plane ticket to her parents' place in the Bahamas. And it was agony! As it happened, Tom's sister was staying with them when Heather went to the fabric store, and she insisted on tagging along. "That really made me uncomfortable," said Heather. "I had pretty much decided what I wanted, and before I went to buy it, I told Tom that I was nervous about buying anything with his sister. He told her how I felt. At the store, she was very understanding about what I was doing. It seemed to me that she was *too* understanding. She kept saying, 'Don't feel nervous, don't worry about it.' I felt she could have done nothing, or she could have been understanding, or she could have been *overly* understanding. And that's what she was."

The money discrepancy nagged at her more directly, too, affecting her relationship with Tom. Heather had tried to dodge the money question—as she said, to "block out the trust fund"—by living cheaply. She had become a vegetarian in part because it cut the grocery bill. Yet, as with water, one might use very little money, but no one can use none. Despite Heather's determinedly low-key style, the money did creep in, such as with the $10,000 check Heather found under the Christmas tree from her parents every year. From his parents, Tom got $25. Despite her antimaterialism, she enjoyed the windfall. "It's nice," she said, "really nice, because you can do things, have things, go places." Unfortunately, one of the places that Heather most liked to go to was her parents' house in the Bahamas, and Tom couldn't afford to come with her. "I would pay for him," she said. "But he won't take it."

Such gifts were a big issue. Heather fretted for some time about what to give Tom for Christmas the year I saw her. Since she released herself from the no-spending requirement on the question of clothes, she thought she might do the same for Tom and buy him a suede jacket. She even took him down to the store to try one on, but he couldn't bring himself to take it home. "He said he'd feel uncomfortable wearing anything so nice," she reported. So they left the coat on the rack; she ended up giving him a membership to a racquetball club.

For his part, Tom had an even worse time buying presents for Heather. "One of the issues he has to deal with," she said, "is that he will never be able to give me anything that I can't buy myself." Except his love.

"In a relationship where the woman has the money and the man doesn't," Heather concluded, "that's hard. I don't think it would matter so much in reverse. It is hard from both sides. I would love to be taken care of by a man and have everything paid for by my husband, just as he would like to be able to do that for his wife or girl friend. But for me, that will probably never be. As much as you want to say we're all liberated and it's a modern world and all of that, still you get down to the basics of the man providing for the woman. I don't think anything is going to change that."

This is not to say that money can't add a certain sparkle to a budding romance, even if it does weigh the love down later. Winston Goodfellow, the Italian car enthusiast who had roared through his inheritance in Ferraris, would not have had half as much fun in his love pursuits if he hadn't had a little money to lay out for the occasion. Take, for example, the time that he pursued a bunny from the San Francisco Playboy Club. "She was—ohhhhhh!" said Winston, when I asked him to describe her looks. "I loved her personality, too. And I found her an enigma—that was another challenge." And so he set out to woo and win her.

He asked her out, and she said yes. That was a miracle right there, but then the bunny was in for a surprise of her own. Winston had waxed up his current Ferrari for the occasion till it gleamed like polished silver. He opened the door for her gallantly, climbed in, and took off. After she had gotten accustomed to the thrill of driving in a "purebred racing machine," she asked him timidly where they were going. Winston said he knew of a great greasy spoon across town where they could get a terrific hamburger and smiled inwardly as her face fell. He loves surprises.

Actually, he had another plan in mind that had been the result of many hours of almost Napoleonic preparation. "I broke my ass to make sure she had a good time," he told me. He took her out the beach road but then started driving about the surrounding countryside in an apparently aimless pattern. When the bunny asked where on earth he was going, he replied, "Just a minute, hang on. I haven't found it yet." In truth Winston had, with some distress, spotted his "cohort"—on whom he was relying to set up the fabulous occasion while Winston gathered in his prey—hurrying to the prearranged spot, obviously behind schedule. Winston had to go into a holding pattern but maintained his sleek calm. Finally, all was ready.

Winston pulled up the car by some dunes near the Pacific shore and let his lady out. He took her hand and led her out over the desolate drifts of sand. But then, just when she must have thought that Winston was a psychopath and that her next breath would be her last, the two came to the top of a rise and lo, in a romantic hollow between the dunes, they spotted—a picnic spread for two. Laid out on a red-checkered tablecloth was everything one could possibly want for a lunch by the sea: wine in a silver cooler, crystal glasses, roast beef, assorted cheeses, shrimp. . . .

Love flashed in the Playboy bunny's eyes, but it was only temporary. While she thoroughly enjoyed the feast and eagerly agreed to another date, Winston never did progress as far with her sexually as he desired. "She just didn't want to," he said sadly.

But things have worked out better. He never stoked the fires of a girl friend's passion to such a white heat as he did for a girl I'll call Lisa. It was her birthday, and to celebrate it properly, he asked her where in the whole state of California she would most like to spend the night with him. She said the Pebble Beach Hotel, and the words were hardly out of her mouth before the two of them were in Winston's Ferrari heading south from San Francisco. They reached the Pebble Beach by nightfall, booked a room by the eighteenth hole of the adjoining golf course, had dinner, and then retired for the evening. "When I took that girl inside our bedroom door—boom!" Winston exclaimed. "Man, she almost jumped right on top of me. And she was just so utterly, utterly in love at that time that she couldn't stand it. So she just ripped off all my clothes and it was . . . Well, her nickname was 'Heaven Two,' and she certainly was that night. She went nuts! The place cost me a hundred a night, but I would say that was money very effectively spent."

So pleased was he by the success of this birthday present that Winston quickly started thinking about the next one. He had the plans all set. "I was going to go down and pick her up in a limo. All she knew was that we were going out for a night on the town. But I don't say which town. So *boom!* the limo would take us out to the airport and *pow!* we'd catch a flight to L.A. Then *boom!* a Rolls-Royce would meet us at the airport, and *bang!*, we'd drive up to this intimate restaurant I know there called the Fine Affair. Our menus would be set in advance. As soon as we came in, *brrrrm!* the food would come out. And for dessert, the waiter would bring her a necklace on a tray. Afterward *boom!* we'd catch a flight back up to San Francisco. Then *bang!* we'd go out for some dancing at a nightclub. I'd take her to one of the clubs that's high up on a hill with those beautiful low lights—nice and quiet and intimate. And then *boom!* we'd go to the Mark Hopkins. You don't get a room for cheap, let me tell you. And there we would screw the night away."

Vivid, but all hypothetical. That perfect date never came to pass. When I asked why, Winston said simply, "We broke up," and did not elaborate. *Boom!*

Oh, well. He had already put the past behind him. There would be other girls, he knew, and other nights of love.

7

Friends and Other Strangers

Terry, the Rockefeller I talked to, and I took a cab together downtown after our interview, he to catch the Rangers-Islanders game, I to meet some friends. There is always an awkward transition when a formal interview concludes and gives way to the looser give-and-take of general conversation. But as often happened after my interviews with rich kids, Terry did not slip back into his original demeanor as one of the guys. Although he still wore his khakis and faded flannel shirt, he had given up his cover and emerged as a rich kid. We returned to the subjects I had raised in the interview, and I asked him if there were any questions I should be sure to ask other rich kids. He gave me a penetrating look and said yes, there was one: "How do you know who to trust?"

RICH KIDS

With that, I reached my corner and we couldn't pursue the issue, but I was struck by the remark. It suddenly occurred to me that rich kids were like foreigners caught behind enemy lines. Because the knowledge of their true identities as scions of the rich is so explosive, they have to stay on their guard and scrutinize everyone they meet. Huge as their past looms in their lives, they feel they must keep it a secret from others. They can't trust strangers with the information. A rich kid can't risk being transformed in the other person's eyes from an average person into a kind of god—omnipotent with all his money and connections, and possibly available for personal favors. For all their supposed power, the rich kids can never feel secure.

Like most outsiders, they do their best to blend into what they perceive as the mainstream. They watch what they wear, many of them consciously dressing down because, as one of them put it, "I don't want to be alienated from everyone by my wealth." Or, as Michael Pratt said, "I don't want to give any messages that I'm an upper-class guy." Sometimes they deliberately coarsen their educated accents, dropping the final *g*'s on their participles, turning *th* to *d*. Like Candace Hooper, who had visited Skorpios, they have to restrict their knowing references to the wealthy and powerful, and, for that matter, limit discussion of their travels and spending sprees. Most rich kids exercise caution, even, in describing where they went to school, since boarding schools are always a big tipoff, particularly if they are located abroad. By this means, ironically, rich kids often succeed in concealing their identities from fellow rich kids as well, since it is only by such clues that rich kids themselves can identify other rich kids in their midst.

In the case of the descendants of famously rich families, the rich kids tend to keep quiet about their ancestors. Terry confided he didn't like to tell people he was a Rockefeller. "There is always a moment of decision when you meet someone," he said. "It's almost like being in a confessional. Do you tell them there is Rockefeller in you? If they don't know, then they don't know much about you. But once you tell them, then you have to face their expectations." And by those expectations, Terry was referring to the line of reasoning that goes:

if he's a Rockefeller, he must be loaded; if he's loaded, he must be happy; if he's so happy, he should do something for *me*. To tell about the Rockefeller, therefore, automatically incurred an unstated sense of obligation—one that Terry couldn't always fulfill even if he wanted to, since he hadn't yet come into his full Rockefeller inheritance. For instance, it meant that, at restaurants, the people he went out with were always passing him the check. That had happened again a few weeks before we met, and he was still irked about it. He'd gone out to dinner with a woman he described as being "of some wealth," a fact he had determined by the presence of a John Singer Sargent painting on her apartment wall. At the restaurant, when the bill came, Terry's date blithely passed it to him with the words, "You have more money than I. You pick it up." Terry did indeed pick up the check, but he dropped her.

Similarly, the Mellon descendant Heather worried about her status in the world at large pretty much the same way she fussed over her relationship with her musician boyfriend Tom. She didn't want her background and fortune as a Mellon to get in the way. So she kept quiet about it. For her, the question was: to whom could she reveal that her middle name was Mellon? Actually, she once slipped—she said it was an accident—and had her full name printed out on her bank checks, which were drawn on the Mellon National Bank, thereby compounding the problem. But in general she left the Mellon part of her as a mysterious middle initial. "I think it's a secret and that's funny," she told me. Funny meaning peculiar that she should feel the need to conceal her identity from the world; this is no laughing matter. "I have to keep it inside of me. A few close friends know, but *very* few." It distressed her when people found out. Normally as placid as her limpid blue eyes, Heather was angered one summer when the identity she thought she had left behind in the status-conscious East caught up with her in her refuge at an art gallery in Santa Fe. An older busybody colleague came up to her at a party and blew her cover by loudly exclaiming, "Oh, you're a Mellon, aren't you?" Much as she would have liked to right then, Heather couldn't deny it.

"She said I looked like one," Heather told me, her voice

full of scorn. "That's bull! Nobody looks like a Mellon. She found out by snooping through my correspondence or reading my résumé.

"It made me uncomfortable in front of everybody," she went on, "because I know that to them the name means only one thing—big bucks."

It is an open question, of course, whether that really is what the Mellon name stands for in the popular mind. But it's significant that Heather thought it was, and that her extraordinary heritage in the end boiled down to the money. Seeing themselves as one big bank vault, many rich kids naturally strive to remain inconspicuous. But that keeps them hidden from strangers and friends alike. Rich kids feel embarrassed to be who they are.

Just as money can't buy love, it can't buy friendship either. Nonetheless, many rich kids do lay their money out for their friends, even if they hold it back from strangers. Since they are not bound by the usual constraints of money and time, they can prove wonderfully loyal friends, regularly making the thoughtful gesture that makes friendship sweet. They provide the "special" gift for Christmas or a birthday that is sure to be remembered; they think nothing of long-distance, even intercontinental, phone calls; they are quick with the invitation to their country house; they don't mind jetting over for a weekend; they lay out lavish dinners; even in city quarters, they maintain a spare bedroom for visitors.

Steve Graham of the *Washington Post* family had tried for a time to work this special leverage to his advantage. With a long interest in theater that gave his manner a pleasant archness and a kind of style that seemed to require a cigarette holder to complete it, he had developed a successful career as a Broadway producer, with the long-running off-Broadway show *The Middle Ages* among his credits. For a while, though, all his money gave him was an act that put him up onstage and placed everyone else in the audience.

Steve started in on the high life rather abruptly in his junior year at Harvard. He had previously subscribed to his parents' attitudes about the crass vulgarity of the rich and attempted to conceal his fortune. In high school he had scrupulously avoided the madras-pants set and fallen in, he said, with the "disaffected, hip, drug-using crowd." But that all changed at Harvard when a friend managed to squeeze him into a private social club, the Fly. Instead of the predictable tattered look of his antiwar peers, now he began to affect the sartorial style of Noel Coward: the crisp white suits and dinner jackets, and, inevitably, some of the social attitudes that went with them. "Suddenly," he said, "I began to live rather well. I would hire Lear jets to take trips with my friends. We'd go to Jamaica and other places. I traveled to Europe and stayed in the best hotels and ate at the most expensive restaurants. I spent potsful of money." So much money, in fact, that he alarmed his trust officer, who announced that if he kept it up all the money would soon be gone. Steve ignored him. "I kind of flipped out of one era into another, passed out of the guilty sixties into the conspicuous-consumption seventies."

In the process, he attracted quite a following among the less well financed who were no doubt interested to see what this golden boy would do next. "None of my friends from the Fly were all that rich," he said. "I had one or two friends from extremely rich families. My closest friend was English and from a not at all wealthy family, although he did have a kind of upper-class pretension."

He realized, looking back, that he may have developed his flamboyance with an eye toward winning them over. "I've always been eager for attention," he admitted. "As a kid, I was frequently uncomfortable dealing with one person, but I loved to have a group focused on me. I suppose that's why people become performers. I never seriously tried to become an actor, but I did acquire this sense of public display as a way of being noticed." At Harvard, he began to carry this mark of distinction rather far. He drove a BMW, for example, but his had a spectacularly crumpled door. "The door had never closed all the way," he said, "and one day as I was backing down a street in Cambridge quite rapidly, it caught on a parked car. There was just the worst noise you ever heard. The door crunched up like a tin can, and glass went flying everywhere. There was a girl in the front seat who was extremely shaken but not injured. I never did get the door fixed. I was never able to do practical things like that. So I drove it around with the smashed door that was tied on to the car with a T-shirt."

His greatest adventure occurred the night that he decided to steal a page from F. Scott Fitzgerald's semiautobiographical novel *This Side of Paradise* by inviting some of his friends out to a restaurant and then sneaking out without paying. "It sounded amusing," said Steve. "I figured if Fitzgerald could do it, so can I." And there must have been the added pleasure of being able to pay but simply choosing not to. So Steve gathered three of his friends and drove down to a place called Hugo's Lighthouse in the South Shore fishing town of Cohasset one evening to try it out. As Fitzgerald had recommended, Steve led the group in ordering the most expensive items on the menu, washed them down with French champagne, and then—before the bill came, but when the repast was complete and Steve was swelling with what he termed "drunken bravado"—he aimed his cohorts toward the door.

They got out all right, and they reached their cars safely, but they'd barely made it out of the parking lot before the Cohasset police loomed up behind them, lights flashing, pulled them over, and arrested them all for drunk driving. The police had been alerted to their condition by the restaurant owners, who had watched them stagger to their cars. Surprisingly, the police were quite pleasant about the whole thing, offering the group cigarettes and making conversation, but they threw them all in jail anyway and then set bail so high that Steve had to call his friends in Cambridge to get up a collection to spring them. Later, because he needed to enlist the services of the family lawyer, Steve had to tell his mother, Katharine Graham, about their glorious adventure. "She didn't seem pleased," said Steve. Fortunately, the story never made the papers—"We're not a high-profile family," he said—but the event convinced Steve how dangerous it can be to live by fiction.

But while the money may help convert strangers into friends, it can also make their friends into strangers. Rich kids have to worry about what their lovers *really* like them for. So with their friends. Is it, as Elizabeth Meyer put it, the money or the blue eyes they go for? Do the friends see them as good buddies, or as free theater tickets, unlimited fresh salmon, all-expense-paid world cruises, a bottomless heap of cocaine, a source of business capital, or, as with Steve, an automatic good time?

Obviously, there should be an element of sharing in any friendship. And if rich kids have more to share, so much the better. Still, there does come a point where they are overdoing it. But where? This matter of giving money to friends is so knotty that the Vanguard Public Foundation's alternative guidebook for the young rich, *Robin Hood Was Right*, devotes a whole chapter to it. The book mentions an intriguing case in which a woman deposited $500 every month directly into the bank account of her best friend, but concludes that it is nearly impossible to keep such payoffs from upsetting the balance of a friendship. The donor feels unfairly powerful, the donee too deeply obligated. The book ends up recommending that any gift be made in as detached a manner as possible (by guaranteeing a bank loan, for example) and for a clear and urgent purpose—like emergency car repair or lifesaving surgery.

Even loans can be problematical, since they call attention to the uncomfortable fact that one party has more money than it needs, the other less. And, more philosophically, they also remind the rich kids that all interpersonal relationships involve financial details, for everything costs money. It is the common background to everyone's lives. Michael Pratt, the Amherst graduate who went on to do community-organizing work in Queens, got himself into serious trouble once when he lent a co-worker $500 to pay his rent so he wouldn't be evicted. The co-worker, however, was a towering black man whose previous address, it turned out, had been the federal penitentiary for attempted murder. He took it badly when Michael tried to collect later. "We were at the office," Michael remembered. "He wanted to step outside and settle this in the street." Michael sensibly declined the offer and wrote the loan off as a total loss. Now, he said, "I hardly lend people a dollar."

He preferred to make his handouts more discreetly, by

laying on fabulous dinner parties. "We entertain here a lot," he said about his new apartment on the Hudson. "I'm lavish, with nice wines and everything, and I get enormous pleasure out of that. That's how I spread it around."

He had learned, however, to restrain his generosity when he dines out. "I've gotten into trouble with that," he said. "If I take a friend out to dinner, I don't want that friend to think Mike can take me out to dinner *forever*. So I generally don't do that, unless it's an impulsive thing. Or unless a friend can afford to take me out to dinner the next time, which is *lots* of fun."

The young man I'll call Alex Trammel, a Los Angeles resident who allowed himself to be identified only as an heir to a sizable robber baron fortune, maintained a steely self-assurance in most things. He had, for example, abruptly terminated his career in investment banking one day when he determined that his "growth curve had flattened." In fact, he resigned from the working world altogether to spend his days in splendid isolation in a fabulous apartment on Wilshire Boulevard, venturing out only to talk to passersby on the sidewalk.

On the subject of spreading his wealth around to his friends, Alex was predictably assertive. He made it a rule that whenever he went out to dinner with anyone he should pay the check. "I'm a grown person," he declared, "and it's impossible for anybody to take advantage of me." Yet even he admitted that he did once have a problem when a certain nameless European came for an extended visit at Alex's glorious apartment. Although the European wanted to leave the timing of his departure open, Alex pressed him to state a "definite termination date" before he came. He said in a month; Alex said fine. When he appeared, said Alex, "I helped him here in the U.S. legally. I extended him the privileges of the house, laundry, food, and everything. He took all that and then left a personal phone bill for over four-hundred dollars, including calls to Japan, the East Coast, and Europe. I consider that abusive. I paid the bill. I wasn't interested in making him pay, because I am interested in refining my life"—one of those high-sounding phrases that dot Alex's conversation; here, he meant he hated hassles. "But he was abusive. He didn't ask or even tell me. I was more than generous. He was less than appreciative. The appreciation was the thing. I decided right then—this relationship ends."

With some irony, Elizabeth Meyer called her purchasing power the "money wand"—wave it and problems vanish. But she was reluctant to wave it in other people's direction. She had, in truth, been known to treat one friend to an all-day New York shopping spree and to pay for the scholarship of another, but she always screened the recipients of her largesse and set conditions. She made her shopping proposition to a woman who she was sure would take it in the right what-the-hey spirit, and she gave the scholarship to a man on the grounds that the two of them never speak of it again. But in general she was leery of handouts. "How do I know what's good for another person?" she said. "It's tempting to play God. Your heart goes out to someone, and it appears that their problems are money problems. But all you do is delay the money problems, which is their inability to live within their means, or make them worse. Say someone's car breaks down. You say, 'Here's money for a new car.' But then they can't get gas for it. They can't repair it. They basically can't afford the car in the first place. No, gifts like that almost never come out right." In her view, the money came to her, and it should stay with her. Money was hard enough for those who spent a lifetime learning to manage it. For those who weren't prepared, it would be impossible.

Beyond the question of granting friends access to their bank accounts, there is a more disturbing issue: that a friend, like a lover, would be so blinded by the lucre that he or she would forever see the rich kid as nothing more than rich. The rich kids might have looked out at the world through green-tinted glasses growing up; once they are grown they can themselves be seen through a green lens by which every aspect of their character takes on the unmistakable hue of money. So a rich kid inevitably has to size all strangers up: how would they react if they knew he was loaded? Can he trust them to continue to treat him like a regular person? While scholars may debate Fitzgerald's comment about the rich being "different from you and me," in their hearts all rich kids know it's true. They are different. They are marked by their money.

Helen Strauss, the documentary filmmaker who was raised by her penny-pinching grandmother to believe she was a pauper, nevertheless had a keen awareness of the gap between her and everyone around her when we spoke. She came into her money even more precipitate than most—ascending from what she thought was total poverty to the ranks of multimillionaires while she was still in college. As we sat together having brunch at a SoHo coffee shop, she discussed her unique position in terms that went even further than the idea of being a foreigner in her own country. She felt her money transported her to another plane of existence altogether.

Like other rich kids, she grew mystical as she talked about her strange circumstances. "There is a reality that I do not participate in," she said. "I have to keep judging that reality, and I keep getting it wrong. It means I inevitably step on people's toes, because I can't actually see where the boundary is. It's as though other people are wearing a pair of glasses, and I can't see. It sometimes makes me feel as though I was completely without substance."

I wouldn't have known quite what she was talking about if I hadn't seen her try for the past hour to exercise her hypersensitivity on me. Frustrated by the limitations of the five senses, she seemed to try to go beyond them to pick up some invisible aura or vibration that would tell her the truth about me—and the "real" world I belonged in. She was like a deer sniffing the air for the smell of hunters, her ears pricked for their tread, some dewy morning in the forest.

The reality of the everyday world—economic reality—is, of course, entered into by the average person as soon as he gets his first paycheck and tries to stretch it to cover his first bills. Helen was a stranger to all that. Hers was a wonderful freedom, and she loved it, but it separated her as though she alone could fly. And she always had to concentrate to take the full measure of those ordinary folk who lacked her powers. As we spoke, she reacted not just to my words but to my inflections and tone of voice, even my body language, and I could sense her computing all this information before she framed her responses. And I saw this quality in all the rich kids I interviewed: part anxiety, part uncertainty, part caution, part neurosis. Everyone trying to gauge the gulf that separated him from this stranger before them. All of them wondered the same thing: where is he coming from? What does he want? Does he understand? Can I trust him?

Rich kids have probably always been set apart, but this generation of heirs is the first to feel so uncomfortable with its towering status. It makes them feel lonely. Previous generations at least had the comfort of knowing that, although they might be different from the average, they weren't unique. They had their set. These rich kids' parents, for example, could gather for cocktails on the lawn of the Palm Beach Polo and Country Club and speak confidently of "people like us." Today's rich kids aren't too sure that there really *are* people like them. That is why the Haymarket-Vanguard network for alternative philanthropy is so popular: it provides one of the few ways for rich kids to meet "people like us."

The conventions of affluence have largely disappeared, and rich kids head out into the world pretending that they are no more than solidly middle class. They hold jobs, even if they don't, strictly speaking, need them. They avoid the private clubs their parents enjoyed, thinking them old-fashioned and undemocratic. They pride themselves in their egalitarianism. Long gone are the days when a rich kid could put down on his marriage license, under Occupation, "Gentleman," as Reginald Vanderbilt did in 1902. Few heiresses celebrate their emergence into womanhood with a debutante ball of any sort, let alone one in the style of Barbara Hutton's famous debut of 1934. While the rest of the country suffered through the Great Depression, she and her guests danced the night away amid silver birch trees and eucalyptus to the sounds of Rudy Vallee's orchestra and three others, all flown in to New York from California for the occasion.

Only one of the rich girls I spoke to had come out, and that was King Rancher Alice Tatum. Her debut, curiously, played on her general ambivalence about the value of money itself. More a kooky frat party than a proper debut, the affair took place at a casino in Austin. Using play money, all the guests worked the crap tables, then took their winnings to a mock auction that followed, in which such prize items as a flea-bitten mink cape were auctioned off to the highest bidder. At midnight, everyone chucked the multicolored bills in the air like so much confetti. "It was raining money," said Alice. And that was only appropriate.

If rich kids indulge in social events that were once the whole fun of being rich, nowadays they do so in a new spirit of disaffection. A young Texan named Richard Potter whose way into Dallas high society had been lubricated by his family's oil money exemplified this trend. With his long hair, beard, embroidered boots, and raffish manner, he didn't cut the expected figure out on the ballroom floor. Still, he attended about as many formal events as anyone I talked to.

He and his equally hang-loose business partner Jimmy Wynne—one of the "Snake" Wynnes—did the whole scene right. "Jimmy and I do that formal stuff a few times a year," said Richard in his ol'-buddy Texas accent. "We put on our tails and get dolled up and go partying at the balls. I go to have fun, not to be uncomfortable in a stiff outfit. I see a whole lot of my friends. We party and dance and play around. I usually hire a limo and driver for the occasion. To me, that makes sense from a number of standpoints. First, it's kind of fun to ride in the back. But you're probably not going to come home until three or four in the morning after drinking all night. Who can drive then? It may cost two-hundred dollars for the night, but heck, you can spend fifteen-hundred dollars if you're caught driving under the influence. So I figure a limo pays for itself."

The robber baron heir Alex Trammel was likewise highly sociable, just not in the traditional sense. Short and slightly paunchy, with the soft features of those upon whom life has made little impression, his feet in slippers the afternoon we spoke, he displayed all the trappings of a thoroughly upper-class creature, but his social behavior was of a far different stripe. Because of his occasional forays out to the sidewalks of Los Angeles, he called himself a "street person," and the milieu seemed to give him the sort of sustenance and identity that aristocrats of a previous era might have gained in the ranks of the Four Hundred. A short while after his divorce a few years back (he sent his ex-wife a wedding present on her remarriage addressed to Mrs. Trammel), he fell in love with a homosexual man he met in West L.A. while they watched the filming of a *Colombo* episode. As abrupt a departure as that may appear, Alex himself found it unremarkable. "I have never made sexual distinctions between people," he said. And he partied a lot at various city discos—chiefly the Roxy and the Lingerie. But few could keep up with his furious dancing pace any better than they could keep up with the flights of his fancy. He often ended up twirling alone.

In fact, the only person to speak well of conventional society—meaning lace, afternoon tea, and proper conversation—was the giggly black millionairess and Jane Austen enthusiast Shiela Waters. And she did so from considerable experience, having attended no fewer than thirty-six parties, some primarily for whites, some for blacks, and some evenly mixed, in her current hometown of Washington the Christmas before we spoke. And, aided by the godmother of a close white friend, she had broken into one of the world's tighter and higher social enclaves, the du Pont circle of Wilmington, Delaware, run by a gang of petticoated *grandes dames* so powerful they are referred to as the Syndicate.

"I adore Wilmington," Shiela told me. "I visit my friend's godmother whenever I can, and I always go to all the parties, the summer engagement parties, the luncheon and dinner parties, all year round. Once I got past a couple of social arbiters, I was all set. My friend's godmother has a pool that covers several acres, and we have picnics there. Picnicking in Wilmington is a big thing. Whenever I get fed up with the world, Wilmington is where I go."

It is an index of the topsy-turvy world of the rich kids that it should be a black woman who most sought out the innermost groves of polite society. So many things in their lives stand upside down: heights and depths, freedom and confinement, rich and poor, black and white.

But the rich kids came of age in a strange time: the sixties.

RICH KIDS

The society that might have harbored them from the political firestorm itself went radical chic in those years. When the news hit of the ghetto riots, persistent poverty, the Vietnam War, and all the assassinations, the customary ceremonies of initiation—the debutante balls, the clubbing, the champagne breakfasts, the whole Rodgers and Hart routine—suddenly seemed terribly antiquated and, to use a sixties word, irrelevant. Some rich kids went to extremes to express their dismay. A prominent example was Diana Oughton, a descendant of the founder of the Boy Scouts, who accidentally blew herself up while trying, along with other disaffected rich kids, to make a bomb for the Weathermen in a Greenwich Village townhouse.

Far from welcoming the call to serve their country in battle as had previous generations of aristocrats, the male rich kids of the sixties felt it was their duty to dodge the draft for the Vietnam War. Of the dozen draftable men I interviewed, none had served, all of them making use of such upper-class loopholes as college deferments and sports injuries to escape induction. One enterprising soul told me he slathered peanut butter on his rear end and replaced his customary boxer shorts with his girl friend's panties for his appearance at the induction center. It worked: He was pronounced unfit to serve.

But rich kids everywhere grew up alienated from their class. They went into hiding, and many have yet to reemerge. Helen Strauss had only recently rocketed into her millions in her college years in the early seventies, but she knew better than to make a display of her good fortune. "I always dressed the same as other people back in those days," she told me, "the usual Levi's, you know. I never wore jewelry. And I remember a friend of mine screaming at me one day for being an upper-class woman. I looked down at my jeans and my hiking boots and my T-shirt, and I remember thinking—'How can he tell? What gave me away?' "

The suggestion back in those days that one was a member of the upper class invariably sounded like an accusation. While the rich kids may have been disposed to feel sensitive about their position at the top of the heap, the not-rich kids also exercised a new freedom in making them feel bad about it.

Spunky Jules Pierrepont-Stromsted, who had her own
grievances with the upper class (at least as manifested by her
redoubtable grandmother's savage sense of etiquette), was living incognito in the mid-seventies in a rambling, Victorian
commune and commuting to Ithaca College in upstate New
York when she came under unexpected attack from one of
her fellow communards. After Jules's white-gloves childhood,
the commune was heaven—"clunking around," as she said,
"in work boots and utilitarian shorts," growing vegetables,
fixing ten-speeds, and rapping about life. After a year, she
came to think of the ten-member commune as her family,
one far better than her original one, and she became fast·
friends with the only other woman there, a flower child I'll
call Annette. The two spent a lot of time together working
on such political causes as antinuke rallies in town. To Annette,
however, Jules was nothing more than Jules Stromsted. At
that point, Jules said, she "hadn't been feminist enough to
hyphenate my mother's name. Besides, Jules Stromsted
sounded so nice in the region, so wholesome and down-to-
earth." The Pierrepont part was in her name as it was in
herself—right there in the middle, but hidden. "My Pierrepont past had never come up at the commune," she said,
"or maybe I deliberately never let it come up. When I left
my family, I left my whole environment and all the money.
I made my own money."

One day, however, Annette was driving Jules back from
town in "some jalopy, a Plymouth or something," and she
happened to bring up the subject of her family's origins. "She
was telling me how her folks had come over on the boat and
stuff, and just built themselves up by running a shop or something like that, and it was really . . . She was so *proud* of it.
Then she asked me, 'What did your family do?'

"I was vague about it," Jules continued, "and she said,
'What are the names?' I was reluctant to say, but I guess at
that point it didn't mean anything to me. So I told her, pretty
casually, 'Oh, well they're Pierreponts and they . . .'

"But the moment I said the word Pierrepont, it was like
the end. Annette slammed on the brakes and she turned and
just looked at me. And she said, *'What?'*

" 'Come on,' I said, 'that's them, you know. That's not me.'

"And she said, 'The Pierreponts! That's fucking J. P. Morgan!'

"I said, 'Well, yeah, but . . .'

"And she said, 'That's the *fucking ruling class!*' I'll never forget it. And then she said, 'Get out of the car.' "

Jules meekly did as she was told. "My world was shattered, completely shattered," she said. She trudged back to the commune, packed her bags, and left for England, without telling anyone. She wanted to make such a clean break with the past, in fact, that she didn't even tell her parents. It was nearly a year before they found out where she was. But one thing that she *did* do, practically as soon as she reached the British Isles, was put Pierrepont back into her name, hyphenated to the Stromsted, as it is still.

Because of the hyphenation, she is sometimes called Pierrepont for short. Otherwise, the name can be a mouthful. "Lots of people tell me, 'Oh, what a long name. It sounds like a sneeze!' " she said. She did it partly out of feminism, "but also because I was going to make damn sure that if anybody was going to fuck around with me they were going to do it right from the beginning. It's like—OK, anything else you want to know? It's right here."

The heavy politicization of the late sixties and early seventies weighed on rich kids. It raised the specter of their own complicity in the many tragedies of the era, opening them up to the blame of others. But during this time, another related event made them even more uneasy about their blessings, and that was the heavily publicized kidnapping of their kindred rich kid, Patty Hearst. If ever a single deed could embody their latent fears, that was it: that a band of anonymous revolutionaries should seize them and hold them for ransom for a worthy cause. It showed that the money that was beginning to confine their lives as they grew from rich kids to rich adults might do worse. It might *end* their lives.

A lot of rich kids still worried about being kidnapped when I spoke to them, and their fears probably stemmed from this one incident, for statistically such crimes are rare. Ransom kidnapping—kidnapping for money, that is—has historically been so infrequent that no federal agency keeps statistics on it. A book called *Ransom Kidnapping in America 1874–1974: The Creation of a Capital Crime* by sociologist Ernest Kahlar Alix goes some way toward correcting this oversight. According to Alix's survey of newspaper accounts, there have been just 236 reported cases of ransom kidnapping in the hundred years from the first reported case in 1874 when, after an outbreak of child stealing, a pair of criminals in Germantown, Pennsylvania, made off with a child and then demanded $20,000 for his return. However, because of the publicity, any individual case is likely to take on far greater significance than the statistics might warrant. Since the crime combines wealth and danger so dramatically, it invariably commands the nation's attention. What's more, when the more sensational cases do occur, they are likely to provoke a wave of copycat kidnappings by criminals impressed by such an apparently easy way to make money. So the crime snowballs. In this century there have been two clusters of ransom kidnappings—one centering on the disappearance of the Lindbergh baby in 1933, and the other centering on the snatching of Patty Hearst in 1974.

Rich kids themselves are terrified by such tales, since they see in them confirmation of their fear that the people who envy them for their money are going to make them pay. One heir is still so frightened by the Hearst case that he wouldn't allow me to divulge any identifying details beyond the fact that he had once lived on the West Coast. "I was in Berkeley around the time Patty was kidnapped," he told me, "and the whole thing made me very, very nervous. Patty didn't have a life-style that attracted that kind of thing. God, I was in the public eye more than she was." This heir kindly sent a letter to Patty in her jail cell expressing sympathy and support for her in her plight. Patty replied by form letter. "The Patty Hearst case still makes me nervous sometimes," he concluded, "but I can't live my life like that. I just hope that people don't find out I'm rich. I think I have good taste in people. And you can bet I have a damn good security system in my house. . . ."

RICH KIDS

Yet in some cases the lingering worries are legitimate, for crazy things can happen to people in the spotlight. Coke Anne Murchison, daughter of the Dallas Cowboys' former owner Clint Murchison, said that a man once charged into the family's office building in Dallas claiming that he was Coke Anne's husband and demanding to see her father. Stopped by the receptionist, who knew Coke Anne wasn't married, he smashed a vase on the floor before he was carried off by a policeman and prosecuted for creating a nuisance. "He was a friend of a friend I'd met a long, long time ago," said Coke Anne. "He was just nuts." Other rich kids said their families had received kidnapping threats, but they had been warned by the FBI not to discuss them publicly. And some individuals had had scary encounters with strangers and never found out what provoked them.

King Rancher Alice Tatum had one of those and was glad she had a .38 caliber Colt pistol handy to keep it from turning into anything worse. That took place in Ithaca, when she was going to architecture school at Cornell. She was driving back from a gay men's bar in town where she had been having drinks with some of her student friends. She climbed into her Audi around two-thirty in the morning and headed for home. But she soon noticed that no matter which way she turned she kept seeing the same headlights in her rearview mirror. She stepped on the gas and made a few quick evasive maneuvers—"They used to call me Maria Andretti," she told me—and thought she had lost her pursuer, so she slowed down and headed quietly back to her house. But as she was rounding the corner to turn into her driveway, she was suddenly panicked to see the same car again. Before she knew it, the car pulled into the driveway right beside her, a door opened, and a man came straight for her. Alice kept her wits, though, and reached down under the seat for her Colt .38. When the other driver—"an average-looking, shrimpy guy"—reached her car, Alice lowered the window, poked the gun out, and aimed it at his head. "May I help you?" she asked.

Alice recalled that the whites of the man's eyes "got real big" at the sight of the gun. "No, thank you," he replied, disturbed to see the tables turned on him so quickly. He turned on his heel, hurried back to his car, and drove off.

Alice made a note of his license-plate number and passed it on to the police, along with an account of what happened, but nothing ever came of it. The man never bothered her again. "I have no idea what he wanted," she said. "There are a lot of weirdos in college towns. Maybe it was because I had just returned from that gay bar. Who knows?" That's just the problem: you never know.

Such problems, both of dangerous encounters and nasty politics, are bound to arise from the rich kids' attempt to integrate themselves with the world at large, to mingle freely as though they were just regular guys and gals. But, in truth, they are different, and they have to behave differently. There are classes in America, unfashionable as it is to admit it, and the rich can only truly be safe—and comfortable, for that matter—among their own kind.

It is really no surprise that the black millionairess Shiela Waters should be the one to seek out the innermost circle of polite society among the du Ponts of Wilmington. As significant as it is to be black in America, it is even more significant to be rich. Wealth defines the rich kid, and it separates him more deeply than the color of his skin.

Shiela had come to this conclusion herself. With her bubbly charm and quaking laugh, she acted fully at ease as we sat together over brunch in a French café in Georgetown. But that was just a pose, a tentative philosophical position. As she said, "I'm afraid of the world, but I'm still open to it." She remembered that as a baby being wheeled down the sidewalk in her pram in one of Detroit's better neighborhoods, she would look out at all the strangers around her, white and black, and "feel that they loved me." She was not so sure about that now.

The older she had grown, the more she realized how unique her position was. Her grandparents had given up some rice fields in the deep South the family had held since the Civil War to chase the dream of racial equality in Detroit. There, her father managed to parlay a small dry-cleaning business into a prosperous career in real estate. "My family always believed in property," said Shiela. "My earliest memory is being taken to see *my property*. That still continues. And I still own it." But the transition from southern farmers to northern landowners had not been easy. In a move that the family believed was racially motivated, her father and uncle's company was hit in the thirties by a $100,000 IRS overtax. Under the strain of fighting it, Shiela's uncle suffered a heart attack. Worse, the first hospital the family drove him to refused to take him in because he was black. He died before he could get to another one. "My father never felt at peace with that until he saw me graduate from Yale," she said. "He came all week, and he seemed to mellow before my eyes."

So successful had her father become by the time Shiela was born, however, that her birth was heralded with an announcement in the Detroit newspapers. Her childhood governess was so well qualified she later became a prominent judge. Admitted by a special vote of the trustees, Shiela was the first black in her kindergarten.

Rich as her father was, though, when Shiela was seven her mother remarried a white Texan who, with his gas holdings and consulting firm, was richer still, and she moved to a higher financial league in the East. "My toys were houses," she said. "And I had a real sailboat, a small yacht." She attended exclusive prep schools and then went on to the Ivy League.

When we spoke, she was working in a high-society philanthropic organization and, in her spare time, composing rhythm-and-blues songs at the piano, some of them exploring the poor black's life that she never had to know. One lyric, interestingly, came to her while walking up Beacon Street on Boston's Beacon Hill when she was suddenly overcome, she says, by the "dullness" of the world. It depicts the bleak existence of a middle-aged black couple in Detroit. She's depressed to find she's "fatter and flatter/Than I thought I'd ever be" and he, beaten down by his job on an automobile assembly line, turns to her with a frightening mixture of rage and lust. In lines that neatly convey his desire for sex and murder, he sings, "But if I close your eyes/And take your breath away/I can make it through another day."

Shiela had explored her blackness chiefly in her imagination. In every other respect she was just another rich kid. Having made a trip to Paris by herself at sixteen, and then spent a year at England's School of Archaeology after prep school, she was considered at Yale one of the otherwise pearly white "Eurofags," an elite group of young cosmopolitans. She had memorized poetry by the yard, Emily Dickinson's verses being her favorite. " 'Standing as a beggar before the eyes of God,' " she said, quoting. "That's a posture I understand." Intellectually, that is.

With all this behind her, it is only natural that she should single out her wealth as her defining characteristic. It has made the world her bauble. "My basic experience of power and confidence is very different from the majority of blacks in this country, even wealthy ones," she told me. "That is what alienates me the most. It's almost impossible for me to feel a victim of the world. My basic feeling toward the world is practically narcissistic. I still feel that it loves me, just as I did as a child. That fundamentally is what alienates me from the black experience in America of the dispossessed. Those, of course, are very valid experiences. They're true. Mine is untrue. But what I have come to realize is that mine is true for me. That is what happened." Other rich kids could say the same.

And, like a lot of rich kids, Shiela had spent considerable time in psychoanalysis trying to come to terms with the contradictions of her life. But she had had trouble getting the most out of therapy because she had found that black therapists disapproved of her interest in white society. And white ones simply didn't understand her.

She faced a similar problem in her relationships outside of the therapist's office. While she had never been short of friends, she felt she had never found anyone in whom she could completely confide. It was not for lack of trying. She had spent seventy dollars a month in long-distance calls as a teenager and continued to maintain faraway friendships, calling a "Eurofag" friend in London, for example, once a week. But she had had trouble with ones closer to home. Through high school she had never dated a black—"I didn't know any!" she said. Recently, after a determined search, she had been out with three black men, but none of them proved satisfactory. "Their inner life is not similar to mine," she said, referring to her taste in literature as much as to any more soulful qualities. She had enjoyed a long-standing friendship with a black woman she met back in prep school. Diane, as I'll call her, is the daughter of a prominent black family with a strong literary and political bent. But Shiela found herself cut off when Diane's politics veered sharply to the left, away from the white society that Shiela found so appealing.

Things came to a head one night in New York. Shiela was going out with a fairly genteel white lawyer I'll call Franklin. The plan was for the two of them to attend the opening of a new Neil Simon play on Broadway and then to head to Diane's place near Columbia University, where she was living with a black man named Jammer. This was Diane's first romance with a black, and she wanted Shiela to meet him. Knowing that Jammer was "a really street guy," Shiela was not looking forward to the evening. "The last thing I wanted to do was to be *exposed* to Jammer," she said, more than a trace of class prejudice showing.

Predictably, then, Shiela and Franklin dawdled over dinner after the play, and by the time they could steel themselves for the trek up to Columbia it was well after midnight. At that hour, they couldn't find a taxi, so they decided in what Shiela called "total craziness" to take the subway. The two of them had such limited experience with subways, they boarded the wrong one and soon found themselves in the thick of Harlem at 3:00 A.M. That was scary.

"We got off the train," said Shiela, "and there were these three black guys, and one of them right away threatened me with physical violence. I got hysterical. I didn't figure it out at the time, but I think they took me for a prostitute. Why else, they figured, would I be dressed up and out with a white guy? 'Why would you want to do this?' one of them said. I didn't know *what* he was talking about.

"I was sure that I was going to be killed in the middle of the night in Harlem, and my parents would never understand. My mother wouldn't know why I was there, wouldn't know about me and Diane and Jammer."

She didn't spend too much time pondering the situation. "I ran out of the subway station in hysterics," she said. "I ran upstairs to the street, and I found a white taxi driver.

He was weird. Even though this was the dead of winter, all he had on was a pair of pants and a rolled-up T-shirt. He had a gun on the front seat. I found out later that he drove Harlem for the thrill of it. Can you imagine? I screamed at him, 'I'll pay you anything you want, anything! Just get me out of here!'

"He said OK. But first I told him he had to get Franklin out of the subway. He went back down the stairs with a gun to rescue him while I stayed in the cab. Franklin said the scariest part of the whole thing was when this huge man came down after him with a gun. He thought it was all over for him.

"We made it out of there safely, but that was one of the most traumatic things in my life. I could not even *repeat* to you the things some of them said to me. The hatred they felt! They hated me because I was black. They hated Franklin because he was white. That was my most complete exposure to racism in my life. It totally scared me. I'm still nervous about being in New York. I'll never take the subway again."

She met Jammer later. "I couldn't stand him," she said. "He was really street—mean, hard, indifferent. I like gentlemen. Diane finally broke up with him. Now she's going out with someone who's Jewish."

And Shiela resolved to confine her social adventures to those delightful poolside picnics with the Syndicate in Wilmington, Delaware.

The friendships, like the loves, went best with those of shared backgrounds. Between such intimates, money was not an issue, and nothing needed to be explained. The best friends were those of longest standing, so that there was not only a shared background but a shared history. To outsiders, their kind of goofing around may seem slight or inconsequential. But it was at least honest and, for those involved, fun. Ironically, such friendships marked a return of a sort to the social atmospheres of their families. There, too, the money that made everything possible was nowhere to be seen. Only in a relaxed atmosphere could the participants enjoy all of the easy familiarity on which a solid friendship depends.

That at least seemed to be the case with the quartet of

friends, all heirs, with whom I spent an evening in Pasadena, California. This was near the arroyo at Jerry's house, a small stucco cottage, perfect for newlyweds, although he lived there alone. Bought only in the last few months, he had not yet gotten around to furnishing the place. The stereo was still stationed on the floor, and there were just a few chairs scattered around, and no pictures on the white walls.

Jerry was entertaining his older brother Henry, their friend Alden, and Alden's girl friend Louisa. (I've changed their names at their request.) While the interrelationships seem clear enough to me now, they were completely mystifying at the time—a point that cannot entirely be explained by the quantity of Bordeaux consumed along with Jerry's artichokes and Delmonico steaks. All the introductions were remarkably casual, and none of the connections were detailed. To judge by appearances, the foursome had as many possible interconnections as a Lego set; the strict terms of brother, friend, even lover didn't seem to apply. All of them showed about the same degree of jocular affection for each other. Indeed, although Louisa was now Alden's official girl friend, she had once been Jerry's, a fact that didn't seem to disturb anyone.

And the four were mutually interchangeable in other ways. They completed each other's sentences; enjoyed private jokes; kidded each other constantly; dressed the same (except for Louisa, who wore a simple flowery dress) in frayed, open shirts, casual pants, and running shoes. And, prep-school graduates all, they shared a penchant for the preppy version of the good life—irony, athletics, and seclusion.

While none of the four had to work, they all held jobs, and the four seemed to regard them as a pleasant way to fill up the day and augment their trust funds. Alden, for example, marketed gasoline to gas stations in the L.A. area, and Henry worked the night shift in a train yard. But both arranged their hours to leave plenty of time for fun. When Alden tried to claim that he put in eight-hour days, Jerry pointed out, "It takes some people eight hours, it takes others four hours." And then Louisa chimed in, "And it takes Alden two." Everybody laughed at that.

While Alden did enjoy such solo pleasures as a day spent snow skiing in the morning and body surfing in the afternoon, they all agreed that the best times are shared, preferably with all four of them. They all used to get together with a fifth friend on his yacht to sail out to Catalina Island for the day, but that ended in acrimony after the friend stole away Henry's girl friend. "You're only sore about it because she had big boobs," said Alden when Henry recited the grim story. Some thefts, apparently, were unforgivable.

The conversation turned the way their lives do—to pleasant diversions. "We have four or five absolutely unique types of weekend activities," Alden observed. One was to take one of the two planes owned by Henry and Jerry's father and fly off to "pump quarters and catch the shows" at Las Vegas. Another was to "do our Sierra operation" and drop down on some desolate mountaintop to camp for the weekend.

But their favorite getaway vacation was to take off to Punta, "the point," halfway down Mexico's Baja peninsula on the Gulf side. A six-hour car ride down a dirt road from the nearest highway, the place was virtually inaccessible except by plane, so they had it to themselves, except for a few professional pilots who occasionally dropped in.

"It's pretty much out in the middle of nowhere," said Alden between pulls on a postprandial cigarette. "But there's a beautiful crescent beach a mile and a half long, about six thatched huts, and then a small hotel. It caters to American pilots and to occasional visitors like ourselves. You don't have to be rich, but I suppose you do have to have a certain amount of wealth to get there. It's as pretty a place as any in the world. We've all traveled a lot, to Europe several times and just about everywhere else, and this is our first choice of where we want to go. It is absolutely exquisite. It's completely rustic and untamed, and there is no one around for sixty miles. We go down there, the four of us, for long weekends about three times a year. Sometimes we go tandem with another group of friends who have a plane. But we just go for P and Q. That's peace and quiet . . ."

"No, we go for fun and games," interrupted Jerry.

"And getting away from civilization," said his brother Henry.

"And waking up every morning with a hangover," said Louisa.

"We lie on the beach there," continued Alden, undaunted.

"There's great fishing!" exclaimed Louisa. "And scuba diving!"

"We fish," agreed Alden. "We bring down all our scuba gear and go scuba diving."

"And we go clam digging," proclaimed Henry.

"Yes," said Alden. "We whip out our clam rakes."

"We play cards!" noted Louisa.

"And we drink!" added Jerry. "We drink a *lot.*"

"And we party very heavily," said Alden.

"Yeah," said Louisa. "We bring a lot of liquor down with us. We drink a lot." Then she brightened, "It's our own little bit of heaven." On that point, they all agree.

PART IV

Work

8

The Pursuit of Happiness

Who are you?

Most people, when asked that question, give their names and, if pressed for a fuller account, give their jobs. They are bankers, or accountants, or computer programmers. An occupation does help place people, establishing their interests and their accomplishments. If they add a title—the assistant branch manager of the New World Bank in Elmira, New York—that pins them down quite exactly. You can tell exactly what rung they're on, and what ladder.

Ask that same question of a rich kid, and you never get such a tidy response. "There is no way to sum up the totality of who I am, or what I do," huffed the iconoclastic robber baron heir Alex Trammel, fixing me with his customary hard stare. "There is a truth, but it's a process. It can't be explained as an event." He then proceeded to list his daily activities. "I eat, I dress, I have lunch with people, I go to movies. I love to drive. I have a house in the mountains and I go there. I garden. . . ."

Alex is a bit of an extremist in this, as in other things. But the point is made. There is no fixing a rich kid by his occupation.

When I decided to define rich kids as people who had enough money so that they didn't have to work, I had only intended it as a way of establishing who was rich. Yet inadvertently I stumbled onto the key difference in their lives. Sure, the rich kid has more money than the average person. When he figures that out, on his eighteenth or twenty-first birthday, that marks his First Great Awakening. But, more important, because of the money, he doesn't have to work. That discovery, which generally lags some years behind the other, marks the rich kid's Second Great Awakening. It means the daily grind that absorbs so much time and energy of so much of the rest of the American population can remain unknown to him. The rich kid might as well live on a different planet. He never learns what it is to slave over a résumé, to *have* to get up in the morning, to do someone else's bidding, to sweat, to scramble for a promotion, to worry about being fired.

Rich kids may indeed end up taking jobs, but if they do, their attitude toward them is different. Other people, at bottom, are wage slaves. They need the money. Rich kids have the money. So at work, they seek something else, and if they don't find it, they can always leave and look elsewhere.

Actually, many rich kids only enter the work force accidentally. Everybody else has a job, and the idea that one should work for a living is deeply ingrained in the national psyche. So rich kids naturally think they should work, too. Consequently, after graduating from college, many of them head to a downtown firm, and, once their fathers have put in a good word for them at the personnel office, they land a position, often a rather plain one in business or banking. They wear the gray flannel business suits, carry the monogrammed briefcases, and read the paper on the subway in to work. And they may even go along for a few years without ever questioning what on earth they are doing. Of course you work! Doesn't everybody? But then, one fine morning, the idea comes hurtling up at them out of the darkness like a freight train, a distant low rumble at first, then gaining speed, and growing louder and louder, and then, finally, they think—wait a second! I don't have to do this! I'm rich!

That's pretty much what happened to the rich kid I'll call Matt Trenton in San Francisco. Thirty-nine when we spoke in the spring of 1983, he was a twenty-four-year old stockbroker when this realization hit him. Ever since, he had been trying to figure out what to do with his life. And that had been an occupation all of its own.

A West Coast relative put me in touch with him out there. She had encountered him in the new-wave psychological circles Matt traveled in his continuing quest to make sense of his money.

We met in a modest seafood place by the harbor. Matt was tall and lean, with a smooth, angular face, stunning blue eyes, and a laid-back manner. With his blue jeans, western-style shirt, and healthy good looks, he seemed like a Hollywood version of a cowboy before the days of cinema vérité. He was, actually, dabbling in the movie business when we met. He had just been burned in a deal that he was working on with a distinguished movie producer—I recognized the name—developing a revolutionary device for special effects. Matt had put a fair amount of his money into the project and also enlisted several members of his family to the cause. He'd handed over nearly two million altogether. Now the enterprise had gone down the chute, and Matt was trying to get his money back. "Did it put a hole in your finances?" I asked.

"Not a hole," he said, "but a fairly large dent."

Matt still wasn't starving by any means. He wanted to recoup his losses largely to salvage his pride. That's typical with rich kids, I was discovering: they always have some special reason for wanting to make money.

When not playing the movie mogul, Matt was by his own description a househusband. He looked after his baby daughter while his wife, a writer, worked upstairs. But that arrangement was another way station on the long, nearly two-decade journey in search of meaningful employment that began early one morning at age twenty-four.

He was married to his first wife at the time, but she'd kicked him out of the house, so he was living by himself in an apartment in downtown Boston and working as a stockbroker. He was miserable. He hated the work; it was so regimented and stifling. And he was doing badly at it, losing money for all his clients. He was entitled to "draw" a salary to meet his needs, but he couldn't bring himself to do it. Matt, who had been president of his college class, not to mention rich from an electronics fortune, felt he was destined for better things. "At twenty-four," he griped, "I must have been the youngest guy on the train with a briefcase and a *Wall Street Journal*. Eventually, I just went berserk." He had already become an alcoholic, which had accelerated his departure from his marriage. But it hadn't occurred to him that there was a more sweeping remedy to his plight until that fine morning when he woke up with a start. There was a voice screaming at him from inside his head, he told me, and it was yelling two words at him over and over: *"Go sailing! Go sailing! Go sailing!"*

So he did. He quit his job, bid his estranged wife goodbye, and left Boston for the West Indies, where he bought a thirty-eight-foot gaff-rigged ketch named *Pegasus* for $25,000. Although he had done a stint in the Navy, Matt had no idea how to sail the damn thing, so for several weeks he sat belowdecks in the harbor reading how-to books. Finally, he screwed up his courage, lifted a finger to the breeze, hoisted the mainsail, and sailed on out.

He went with the winds for a year and a half. He cruised to St. Croix, St. Thomas, all the Virgins, down to the Leewards, St. Bart's, Montserrat, Grenada. He picked up a few nautical hitchhikers along the way—one ex-con from South Africa, a male model from New York. As a gesture of solidarity, the three of them had their ears pierced in St. Croix. Matt wore a tiny golden ball most of the time, occasionally a fishhook. "The three of us had a great time," he said. "They were a couple of guys totally out of my reality."

I asked him if that was part of the appeal. Did he feel he was reaching a deeper reality by facing a bracing wind as he tossed about the Caribbean with these unlikely mates?

"That's a great point," said Matt. "I never thought about that, but I suppose it's true. All I wanted to do was get as far away from Boston as I could. I figured this was about the furthest I could go."

While it may seem that Matt had freed himself from the cares of the workaday world entirely as he scooted about the Caribbean on the good ship *Pegasus*, that is not the way he viewed it. To him, this was work, real work. It was work to raise the sail, work to keep from running aground on the nasty barrier reefs, work to locate the right anchorages, work to stay on an even keel. And, for this work, he was even receiving a kind of payment. Not money, of course, but then money had never mattered much anyway. His financial needs were taken care of by his trust officer, who arranged a checking account he could draw on at various ports in the Caribbean. No, his payment was more individual, and it went to the heart of his unusual enterprise.

A nine-to-five job takes the average worker out into the marketplace to make a contribution others value and pay money for. Matt's took him away from the marketplace altogether, where, operating independently, he had only himself to please. Naturally, the reward was personal, too. It couldn't be measured in the universal tender.

He had elevated himself from the status of individual worker practically to the ranks of a corporate entity himself. He was Matthew Trenton, Inc., whose product, reward, and whole reason for being was his personal growth. He was developing a new, improved self. And, when he weighed the experience later, it was in terms of his growth that he tallied up the results on the ledger sheet. He had gained: some useful sailing techniques; some important social skills; the ability to take care of precious equipment; a new faith in himself in facing stormy seas; and, most important of all, a deeper understanding, out in the wide and blustery ocean, of who he really was.

"Everybody thinks, 'Oh, isn't it wonderful to sail around the Caribbean,' " he told me. "But for me, it was really the growth of taking something I knew nothing about and really mastering it. I've been called irresponsible, but, actually, that was as responsible as I've ever been. It would have been irresponsible to go sailing out into reef-laden waters without knowing anything about how to sail. That's irresponsible. People have done that, and they have lost their boats. Hell, some of them have lost their lives. No, for me, that year of sailing was the greatest. It was outside the parameters of everything that had ever been expected of me. I had been on a perfectly good track, but this . . . wow."

Matt's happiest moment that year was taking his disbelieving parents out on *Pegasus* when they came for a visit at Christmas. It was like showing off a glowing company balance sheet to the stockholders. Matt confidently headed *Pegasus* out of its anchorage into a stiff breeze. The sea was thrashing, but he held the tiller steady and faced down the wind. "Everybody was just hanging on," he told me, "but I was a pig in heaven. It was a statement, and everybody saw."

Yet there is still an important difference between this kind of "work" and the genuine paid variety. In the marketplace, real work takes place within set boundaries. It is orderly and measured. If it goes well, it is rewarded by pay raises and promotions; if it goes poorly, there are threats and, ultimately, firings. Taking place so much within his own mind, the work of a rich kid like Matthew, by comparison, is nebulous. There are no objective standards by which to measure his progress. Without cash payment for his efforts, there is no clear way to discern their value. His work doesn't have to sell, so there is no distinction between success and failure. Either way, the experience contributes to his personal growth.

These questions became more pronounced on his next adventure, which was to round Cape Horn aboard an oceangoing tugboat operated by the Chilean Navy. His natural father—as opposed to the stepfather who had raised him—suggested it and arranged the adventure through the Chilean Embassy in Washington. As the rich often do in justifying their vacation sprees, Matt passed this one off on professional grounds. The whole experience would be filmed. This was not a junket. This was a documentary.

Unfortunately, the only cinematic episode to the entire

escapade never made it into the film. That occurred when Matt and George, as I'll call his father, accompanied the crew of the tugboat in delivering some supplies by longboat to a tiny navy outpost on a small island located in treacherous waters off the Cape. The boat was swamped by a wave and the men had to swim ashore, where they crowded into a two-man hut for two weeks before a passing ship could rescue them. The island was a kind of magical paradise. "You could reach out and pluck birds out of the air," Matt said. "They'd hardly ever seen people before. We weren't in their reality." The whole crew survived by eating some sheep grazing on the island and mussels that they gathered on the shore. "It was the experience of our lives," said Matt. Unfortunately, they hadn't thought to bring the camera along to record it. "We were just going to be ashore for five minutes," said Matt with a sigh. "We had no idea we'd be marooned."

The movie fell victim to other oversights as well. While it was edited fairly professionally, it never reached any commercial theater screens. "It just failed in the marketing," he said. "We never really got that together." So, like his Caribbean cruising, the documentary trip ended up being judged solely in personal terms. "Let's just say that the film was one of the more expensive home movies ever made," he told me.

Since then, Matt had moved to California, where he could be free of the weighty associations of his past. He had sampled many of the growth therapies that California had to offer and, in a burst of inspiration, had even set up his own, one exclusively for heirs and heiresses to large fortunes. Once again, this was personal business.

He sent out engraved invitations to every rich person he knew, even flew out to their gentleman's farms to recruit them, then rounded them up for a series of seminars at a variety of fancy San Francisco hotels. While he had trouble drawing as many rich kids as he wanted, he had no problem attracting the attention of the national media. An interview with the *San Francisco Chronicle* was syndicated across the country, and that brought offers to appear on the *Today Show* and the *NBC Nightly News,* and to write his life story for Harper and Row. Matt turned them all down.

He concentrated on the seminars and was amazed to see

the parade of sad sacks come out of ratty cars and through the polished doors of the Fairmont Hotel. "The whole thrust of the seminars was to get these people to take responsibility for their wealth," said Matt. "So many of them were in awe of it, or afraid of it. There was a lot of grief in the room, a *lot* of grief. One guy broke down when he talked about his father, who had died when the guy was only six months old, leaving him only with this legacy. Everybody cried a whole lot. But this was the seventies. It was a time to cry." Each seminar culminated in a moving moment when the students were supposed to step up to a blackboard and write down their financial net worth on one side and their annual spending on the other. It was amazing to see the discrepancy. "They'd put down assets in the millions," Matt said, "and then they'd list their living expenses at ten or fifteen thousand a year."

When the seminar was over, Matt was pleased to hear that a few inheritors went out and spent some money on themselves and bought a new car or a fur coat. Matt himself had taken something different away from the seminars. He recognized that one of his own most critical assets was the money itself. And it was being dreadfully underutilized. "I concluded that I just wasn't exercising my ownership. The money was there, there was no point pretending I didn't have it. I had to take responsibility for it. I had to invest myself in it."

But that meant that instead of buying things as his students were doing, he would buy activities. It wasn't *having* that he wanted; it was *doing*. It was "work"—an occupation that he did on his own terms, for his own pleasure, that others might have trouble distinguishing from play.

"I want to do something just for the joy of doing it," he said. "That's what the money has given me an opportunity to do. Because of my money, I can do something just because I like to do it. Not because I should do it, or I have to do it, or because I'm expected to do it. Like, it's OK for me to stay home and take care of my wife and son and support my wife in doing what she wants to do, and make sure the house is clean. It's OK for me to do that for a while. To take trips, to explore and not 'do' anything, quote-unquote. It's OK as long as it is fun."

* * *

Fun. One might wonder why it took Matt nearly twenty years to realize that he wanted to have fun with his money. But the money doesn't seem to have been made for his fun. It is serious stuff, created by sweat and daring, managed and maintained by those cheerless souls at the trust company—and the object of such earnest striving everywhere Matt looked, it felt like a desecration just to go off and have a good time with it. Sure, you could go off on an occasional spending spree, that was fine. But take the Family Founder's hard-earned and just burn it all up in frolic? No way.

So it takes a while for the rich kids to get, as it were, from the grim grayness on the front of their hundred-dollar bills into the lovely green on the far side.

In his rich Wilshire Boulevard lair, his feet encased in slippers, his neck warmed by a silk ascot, the robber baron heir Alex Trammel could hardly be more different from the hang-loose cowboy Matt Trenton. But the "professional" paths that they have taken with their riches have been nearly identical. They both started climbing up the ladder of the professional world after college, and both jumped off it to ascend another ladder of their own making—one that they hoped led to a greater understanding of their innermost selves. For both, this quest brought them the same discovery: like golden seeds inside a golden apple, their souls were full of money. Who were they? They were rich.

When I asked Alex how he grew up, he responded without a trace of irony "straight up and six feet tall." Then, in case I had misunderstood, he added, "I am trying to communicate with you in a nontrivial way." When I rephrased my question, he described a multinational upbringing as his father swung about the globe to manage the large and sprawling family corporation. Alex was born in St. Louis, then passed stretches of his life in Baltimore and Houston before the family relocated to Paris, where he commuted to a private school for expatriate Americans; then he pushed on to a preprep boarding school in America at thirteen, Exeter at fifteen, Princeton at eighteen, and the Stanford Business School at twenty-two. Upon graduating at twenty-four, he did what everyone viewed as the only sensible thing and took a job in Los Angeles as an investment banker. Alex was even reasonably happy at it, and a good deal more successful than Matt Trenton; but then the years slipped past and he hit thirty, the time of many a drastic reconsideration, and he heard the faraway whistle of that freight train rumbling up the tracks. So, just when his fellow young bankers were polishing their acts in their effort to make partner, Alex abruptly handed in his resignation, cleaned out his desk, and quit.

"My growth curve had flattened," he explained. "I went to learn finance. I was interested in the actual function of money, and I thought that I-banking would be the best place to find out about that. Mine was a generalist firm. I got to work in a number of industries, a number of companies, on a number of problems. But investment firms were consolidating then at a rapid rate. The firms were getting larger and larger, and the larger they got, the less entrepreneurial and individualistic they became." In other words, he realized that he was losing his freedom, and that made him question whether he'd ever had any at the job in the first place.

But, viewed another way, Alex was delving down through the various layers of his existence. As with all rich kids, his life was moneyed to the core. He started out by examining the family money, the distant stuff that grew out of the family business and then expanded by provident investment to provide the architecture of his life. But as time went by he was getting into his personal assets, first his own trust fund, and then the paycheck. He was curious to see how it would feel to be linked up to the vast money exchange between banks and corporations, bosses and workers, buyers and sellers. But the salary he received had no effect on him at all, and he quickly grew to resent the dreary bosses and dronelike colleagues that came along with it.

"I never went into investment banking to work for other people," he said. "In the long run it doesn't make sense for me—either financially or personally. I just went to see how money worked. And once I'd found out, I could leave, because I could afford to. But there was a personal aspect, too. I finally got bored to death by the people there. The problem for me was that in I-banking, people talk nothing but I-banking and are interested in nothing but I-banking. It's totally time-consuming. And I'm much too broad-spirited a person to put up with that."

Alex claimed to have been inner-directed since the age of six, when he first started bossing his governess around. "It was never a burden having her there," he said. "If I wanted to go to the park, I'd go to the park and make sure we got home. I was on the street by myself by age ten." But despite this early independence, he sensed he was still vulnerable to a syndrome that pervades the working world—the equation of performance and self-worth. "Through school," he said, "I was good at performing tasks, so I was perceived as good."

And it was the same story at the investment firm. "But gradually," he went on, "I realized that while I cared about fulfilling my responsibility, I didn't care about deriving worth from it. That's probably where wealth comes in. I don't have to care whether I'm good at it. I happen to be good, but that makes no difference to me. I don't care. In our society, it is supposed to be good to work thirty years to become president of a corporation, and to postpone your gratification all those years. To me, that's crazy. I've had my own sense of self-worth since my teens. In our society people derive their worth from what they do, which is why they work. If you take away this avenue, they're lost. They lose touch with the world. If you meet people and they ask you what you do, tell them you don't work and just look at the reaction. They think you must be kidding. But that didn't matter to me."

So Alex quit the firm, and he went back to his apartment on Wilshire Boulevard to spend the next six years, by his own account, "thinking." "I needed to answer one question," he said. "And that question was—was it just money that made me perceive the world the way I do, or was it something else? So I had to find out how other people perceived the world, and why." To conduct his research, Alex went out into the streets of Los Angeles and held conversations with friends and passersby. "I'm a street person," he said. "I choose not to study things, because I believe that knowledge is a synthesis of events. And I want to synthesize for myself. I don't trust other people to synthesize for me." In other words, once again, Alex preferred to be his own boss. He was duplicating Matt Trenton's flight to sea aboard *Pegasus*. Both journeys took the rich kids out alone into an alien world to find themselves.

But Alex might as well have sought answers from the whistling wind, for, aside from discovering his own homosexuality in his encounter with a gay man during that *Colombo* episode, he didn't end up gleaning much useful information from L.A.'s street people. "I have concluded that basically other people do not want to think," said Alex dejectedly. "And that's because once you start, you can't stop until you've reached some conclusions. For some reason, people find that difficult. They prefer to believe that they are only pawns in a great chess game that is played by deities never seen." Maybe that's because they have to work for a living, which would answer Alex's initial question. Was it the money that made him perceive the world the way he does? Yes.

So Alex decided to relax on that front and, instead of examining his position, started to make use of it. He had gotten down to the center of himself and found the money there. "Because of my money, I can do many, many things," he said. "People tend to stick to narrow bands of their potential. If a circle is three hundred and sixty degrees, I have filled out most of it in my own explorations. If I wanted to be a rock 'n' roll singer, I could be. I can afford to make it happen. I've just chosen not to."

Recently he had emerged from this self-imposed exile from the working world to start a small design firm with a few employees. But he only worked there two hours a week, and he was leery of defining his occupation too narrowly. That was when he told me it was impossible to summarize "the totality" of who he was and what he did. "I still spend most of my time thinking," he added, "thinking about why people do things. I'm very interested in perception, beliefs, and human motivation." But he didn't worry the subject any more. He preferred to enjoy himself; that was work enough. He had gotten heavily into the dancing scene at the Roxy and had started to laugh a little more—at some unlikely jokes, like the slogan he saw on a T-shirt, "God: she shaves"—and, in general, to have "fun."

I asked him what was fun.

"Everything," he replied with a smile. "I only do things that are fun."

And what are those things?

He considered that for a moment. "Fun would be instances where there was very little stress," he said.

But what's the most fun of all?

"Life," he said. "You know, I heard a great definition of life the other day," he added. "It was—'not death.' I thought to myself, the person who thought that up had done a lot of thinking."

Fun. Nearly all the rich kids were hooked on it. Unlike Matt and Alex, however, most managed to find an occupation that at least took them out of the house. Yet their commitment to fun dictated an unconventional notion of work. Remember Henry, of the fun-loving Pasadena quartet? He worked the midnight shift directing trains at a train yard. When I asked him why, he turned ecstatic. "There's so much lore!" he exclaimed. "Look at the West. How did the West get built? By the trains! And there's the whole thing about the way they ran their empire. The *power!*" Not to mention the thrill of playing with a life-sized train set. Recall Winston Goodfellow and his Italian cars, and the music he heard in the roar of the engines. Shannon Wynne, of the "Snake" Wynnes, had put together a string of successful restaurants around Dallas, starting with the 8.0 and continuing through Nostromo and Tango, all of the names concluding in the little oh! of ecstasy. Elizabeth Meyer raced *Matinicus* for a cup, undaunted by the fact that everyone who entered received one. And many others, like Roger Elkin and Sarah Pillsbury, had been drawn to the biggest fantasy land of them all, Hollywood.

Like a diamond, their glittering fun on the job had many facets—escape, fantasy, thrills, freedom. But fun, unlike a diamond, is not forever. To the rich kids' frustration, it so often proved momentary, leaving the rich kids to hurry on to the next thing. No individual job ever lasted very long. Their résumés, consequently, would run for pages, if they bothered to type them out. The perfect job proved as elusive as the perfect lover—the kids never worked at one long enough for it to blossom into a commitment.

And the pursuit of happiness often took them, like Alex Trammel and his 360 degrees of experience, around in circles. In the usual kind of work, one job leads to another in a reasonably straight line—up. But fun work is random. The rich kids hop about from job to job like frogs in a pond, with little reason for going from one spot to the next, except that it looks like fun.

And the moves are generally lateral—from one top spot to another. Born at the top, a rich kid prefers to stay there in his job. So, like Matt Trenton on the S.S. *Pegasus,* the rich kid tends to take his place at the helm, running his own company, even if it consists of only one employee, himself. It's a rare kid who has the confidence that he has made the right career decision to put in the time it takes to rise in a larger corporation. And, himself the son or grandson of a corporate mogul, he is too impatient to start in the mailroom. A more brazen kid might buy into a company and install themself at the top. The less brazen one will go off by himself in a solo occupation like writing, architecture, or independent producing.

But the very pleasure of these self-invented jobs often keeps them from proving satisfying. "Sometimes I feel as if everything I've done in my life has been a hobby," laments one of the rich kids quoted in the alternative guidebook *Robin Hood Was Right.* Many rich kids' occupations have that breezy quality of a pastime. They do them because they are fun, but precisely because they are fun, the rich kids haven't put in the kind of sweat equity to build them into anything more— bigger and more lasting. That's too much like work. Plus, there's no pressure on rich kids to buckle down. The fear of the unemployment line that keeps everyone else going when a job turns tough is no threat to them. One rich kid whose job as a theatrical producer incidentally netted him a salary as well as good times often forgot to cash his paychecks. The oversight only bothered him because he felt his co-workers would like him less if they discovered his true social standing. He didn't need the money. The interest from his trust fund kept rolling in.

After graduating from Harvard, Steve Graham had a notion that he would write a book about the bordellos of Europe. Unlike most other would-be writers, Steve had the wherewithal to do extensive research without any commitment from a publisher and conducted thorough firsthand investigations from Barcelona all the way north to Amsterdam. The research was the fun part; he never got around to the hard part, writing it all down. And even the research proved a little wearing, since he caught hepatitis and mononucleosis simultaneously somewhere mid-continent. "It was a bogus mission," he admitted.

Candace Hooper, the heiress who'd been to Skorpios, also had a book in the making. Hers was about ESP, and was born of many a dinner party's chatter about occult experiences. Strange tales of beds rocking back and forth, the recognition of strangers from a previous life, etc. All reasonably captivating after a glass or two, but of dubious literary merit. That wasn't what appealed to her. In fact, the book itself was more party talk than project. Candace was likely to bow out as soon as it became work.

Used to getting their way, most heirs are unacquainted with the hard realities of the commercial world; they rarely develop the traits that draw rewards in the marketplace, namely the sterner qualities of discipline and determination. It is not, as is often said, that rich kids lack ambition; they lack the grit to attain it. As Annie Owen put it in describing her first mission to New York to work for a dress designer, "I just wanted to have a hoot in New York." So it was for Candace and the others. They didn't need money, couldn't define success, already had fame. They just wanted a hoot.

While many of these hoots, like the yachting and the whoring, occur outside the realm of conventional work, a fair number take place inside it, without too much of a difference in their essential character. They are still hoots.

Ando Hixon's hoots had involved conventional work and

unconventional work, and he still wasn't too clear about the difference, since he didn't have to make money either way. He had known that from an early age. Growing up in Pasadena, he was forbidden by his parents to hold a paying job. "They felt there were other people out there who needed the money," he said. While his friends had paper routes and mowed lawns, he was reduced to "hospital work and old-nanny work visiting old folks." Except for a stint in the United Nations, stationed in Ghana and Western Samoa, his father had never held a paying job either. In a sense, his father let his money do the work for him. The original AMP investment—in a company that produces the plastic clip in the back of the telephone—was still reaping plentiful rewards.

Uninterested in charity work, Ando was free to indulge himself in his favorite pastimes, and he turned first to rock 'n' roll music. At Boston University, he joined a band called Duke and the Drivers. He couldn't play any instrument, but that didn't matter. (Actually, he had taken several years of piano lessons from a Russian countess as a child back in Pasadena but had always been able to sidetrack her away from music by chatting her up in French, one of her favorite languages.) He had become friends with the lead guitarist of the Drivers, who soon invited him to join up. To be sure, Ando looked the part of a rock 'n' roller, with his then long, wavy hair, high spirits, and husky, cigarette-thickened voice, and that may have won him the spot. It could also be that Ando's net worth played a role in the guitarist's calculations, for Ando soon found himself paired with another wealthy band member as the group's main financial supporters.

Ando thought nothing of this at the time, though. He just hurried out to buy a saxophone. "I bought a top-of-the-line tenor," he said. "That way I'd only have to buy one." The guitarist taught Ando everything he needed to know. "He taught me my licks, as they say, my techniques, my riffs, my showmanship." But Ando had a natural talent for what it took to make it in rock 'n' roll. "I can bullshit beautifully," he said. "The first night I picked up a saxophone, I blew a four-note break on it. I thought I was John Coltrane. My veins stood out on my forehead just right."

Out onstage, he adopted the suitably tinseled name of Rhinestone Mudflaps, but he disdained the blue jeans, spangled capes, and rainbow-colored costumes of his colleagues. He wore a business suit in what he saw as a kinship with the rhythm-and-blues kings of old. More importantly, he said, "That's what guys go to work in."

At first the group played small clubs, but gradually some national attention came its way and the Drivers garnered a "multihundred-thousand-dollar" two-record contract from ABC Records. To promote themselves, they took off on a national tour. Because of his personal experience with high finance, Ando was put in charge of maintaining order after the money hit. That was hard. "When the ABC contract came in," said Ando, "I looked around at all the guys and tried to figure out who was going to crumble and who was going to hold up. Well, the guys I took to hang in there, they were the ones in their hotel rooms all day screwing around and ordering escargots."

Ando also had to work out the logistics of the tour. Despite the money from the contract, there were still serious constraints. The band had to get around in one large station wagon, trailed by a U-haul truck bearing all their musical gear. It was not a happy time. "I'm lucky to be alive," he said. "We were rock 'n' rollers. We didn't just act the part. We were in there, did it all—all the drugs, all the booze, the whole thing. But the glamour wore off fast. You find yourself on the road with all its temptations. So much of the life is just lonely and sad. Eventually I just got bored with the whole routine."

And, after four years, he'd had enough. His girl friend, later his wife, encouraged Ando to settle down, but he was beginning to realize for himself that he couldn't rock on forever. He was haunted by the vision of one of the many who tried. The Drivers had come into Jimi Hendrix's New York recording studio—"the Holy Grail of rock 'n' rollers," he called it—one evening to try out some songs. Eric Clapton and the Rolling Stones would be in later for a late-night session, but when Ando arrived with the Drivers only one man was in the studio. "He was a grizzled older guy with a silver Kenny

RICH KIDS

Rogers beard and he had these big saddlebags under his eyes. He looked beat! We talked. We all thought he was a janitor, or a hanger-on, or some gofer. But you know who he was? He was the guy who wrote 'Sea Cruise.' You know 'Sea Cruise'? 'Baby, won't you send me on a *sea cruise.* Sea cruise!' " Ando grunted it out, emphasizing the triple-time rhythms. "And there he was," he went on. "Without any real . . ." His voice trailed off.

Ando wanted to avoid that fate. But how? He took some time off to think things over and went back to Pasadena. And it was in California that he had his new vision, the one he still pursued when we met in the winter of '83. He had been lying on a beach outside Los Angeles, he remembered, when suddenly in the distance he heard a gentle noise coming down from the sky. "I was keeping my head empty," he said, "trying not to worry about things, and then I heard this hum come down the coastline. I didn't pay any attention, but then I could feel a shadow come over my whole body. The whole sun went out for a moment. I opened my eyes and there it was." It was a Goodyear blimp—big and fat and, to Ando at least, beautiful, just hanging there in the air. It was a natural object—and symbol—of a rich kid's aspirations: up there high in the sky, buffeted by the raw winds, immense, casting a huge shadow. Yet it was operated by just one man alone. It attracted Ando powerfully.

"I could see the pilot," said Ando, "and I got him in eye-to-eye contact. I had a strong feeling of brotherhood with him. He was alone and smiling. He gave me the thumbs-up sign. I gave him one back. He made a big loop out to the ocean, and then he came right up over me. I just felt so excited! It was so very long. The mass of the thing! The structure, the sound. It was so quiet, just a whirring noise. It was like this big ship flying in the air."

Like a kid in a toy store, Ando wanted one.

At first, he thought only of piloting the big balloon. "I could do anything I wanted to do," he said, "so I was going to learn how to fly one of those things." But then he decided to try to get a blimp off the ground in another way altogether. Thus was born Ando's second career, as a builder of blimps, and he was not yet thirty.

Ando went down to the library to do some research on the history of blimps, then checked out contemporary efforts. He visited the sites of five dirigible projects and selected one, "the real maverick," to buy into. That one was developed by Frederick Ferguson, an engineer operating out of a garage in Vancouver, Canada. He may have represented Ando's alter ego. "All this guy had when I met him was a cocktail napkin with a sketch of his blimp on it," said Ando. But Ando had something else—money. Because Ferguson was just getting started, Ando could purchase a considerable slice of the company for a fairly small sum, but he preferred not to discuss "hard figures."

By 1983, thanks in large part to Ando's infusion of funds, they had a working twenty-foot model. A big glossy photo propped up in the corner of Ando's Boston office showed it off. At first glance, it looked like a poster for a sci-fi movie: the scene is a vast, brightly lit hangar, with a crew of men in jumpsuits gazing up at an enormous white bubble that is floating up toward the roof. A cabin, or "gondola," is slung underneath the big ball; attached to a central axis, it hangs from the balloon like a Santa Claus beard.

"That's my baby," said Ando proudly, "the LTA 20-1"— LTA for Lighter Than Air. Ando expected the final product to run 200 feet across. He envisioned a market for it in the transportation of heavy materials, such as timber or oil derricks, in remote areas, either wilderness areas where there are no roads or out at sea. Helicopters now do the work, he said, but they cost a hundred times as much per ton-mile.

Of course, the LTA 20-1 will not come cheap. He expected that it would cost $300 million to get it into production, although much of the outlay would be offset by prepaid orders for the blimp. While Ando had been willing to put some of his own money into the project, he knew that he would not be able to go it entirely alone.

To get backers he had eased himself into pinstripes once again. This time, though, his stage was the top floor of a Boston highrise in the offices of the investment firm of Foster, Dykema, Cabot and Company. The arrangement was strangely similar to the deal with Duke and the Drivers. Once again, he came to the job without experience. While all his colleagues at Foster Dykema had MBA's, many years in the field, and narrow specialties in bonds, stocks, or growth companies, Ando had never been to business school, never held a job in investment banking—not counting his efforts with his own portfolio, of course—and had no particular expertise in blimp design, manufacture, or marketing. Nevertheless, here he was, installed in a glorious office, his blimp pictures on one wall, a big picture window with a view of the Boston skyline on the other wall. The glass turns into a mirror, the better to reflect on his good fortune, perhaps, when the sun goes down.

Ando had been using the firm as his own private business-school program. "I'm in training here," he said. "They're baby-sitting me, filling me in on some of the aspects of business I'd let slip by the wayside because of my rock-and-roll days. I do grunt work. I'll go off to the government library of the Harvard Business School if somebody here needs to know something." And he tried out some of his own ideas on his colleagues. "I pick their brains. I go to other people in the office with my ideas, and they tell me whether it is realistic. But these days, I have only one business drive, one product, one passion. And I find myself unable to commit to anything else. And I've picked a real doozie.

"If you looked at the blimp stacked up against any of the other thirty or so business deals on a desk in three months and compared them, you'd have to think this one is crazy! There are a lot of other business deals out there that are more controllable, the future is more foreseeable, and where there's a framework to make the analysis. Blimps haven't been in production since the end of the zeppelin era in the thirties. This is a fresh page. This is the high frontier, the leading edge. It's a radically different concept from every other flying machine that's ever been devised. There are no precedents. Maybe that's what attracts me. I'll tell you one thing, though. I'd rather sink some dollars into this and see it fail than redo some condos on Beacon Hill and make three-hundred-thousand dollars."

We looked at the blimp picture again. Dimpled to reduce drag, the bag of air looked like a huge golf ball. Quite an image, I said. He told me that he enjoyed its lovely rounded-ness, its respect for nature in saving so many trees from being blasted for roads. And, for himself, he liked the quixotic aspects of bringing blimps into the world. "If we make it, the airship is a good symbol for me," he said. "If it doesn't, it's still a good symbol. At least I've tried." It's OK either way. Ando had other careers ahead of him. "I could see the UN in my future," he said. "I could see trout farms in Alaska. I'm still way up in the air."

Ando's blimp may rise indeed. Sometimes, the search for fun leads a rich kid to a worthwhile, practical project. Or it may lure him on to some fuller commitment by tantalizing him with the deeper satisfaction of seeing a project through to successful completion.

When rich kids did commit themselves to a job or a project, it most often occurred in the arts, which provided means for the critical element of self-expression. Writing, painting, acting, singing, sculpting—all of these often proved fulfilling. But, in the end, the most satisfactory branch of the arts was the most expensive one—producing movies. That had everything going for it. As movie moguls, rich kids could rub elbows with the stars, which was certainly fun. They could take advantage of their own personal golden rule—he who has the gold rules—so they could run the show. In the screenplays they developed, they could freely indulge all the fantasies of their childhood years of isolation. And, since they held so much cash, they could get past the chief barrier to entry into the field. The job was tailor-made.

Charlie Chiara, the grandson of financier John Loeb and nephew of Seagram's chief Edgar Bronfman, answered the call in 1981 and bought a chunk of a small production company in Hollywood called Selluloid that operated out of a small, creaky bungalow in West L.A. Selluloid made and distributed video cassettes and was—much to Charlie's excitement—getting into the magic area of feature films. "You know what my job was a while ago?" he told me excitedly. "My job was to go through casting books and make up lists of prospective cast members with names like Jeff Bridges and Peter Strauss and Kurt Russell and Nastassja Kinski and Valerie Perrine. These are not hard things to do! OK?"

Only twenty-three, Charlie had a lot of youthful enthusiasm

that came out in a restless manner and an unabashed delight in the glory and glitter of tinseltown. Round-faced, with a child's soft features, he was growing a mustache to temper his youthful appearance. "We're not exactly on the lot yet," said Charlie, using Hollywoodese to mean the company was not fully established. "But we have a place of business and some business to do. And that's two steps up from where I was before."

Where he was before wasn't so bad, either. He'd been a sales representative for Seagram's, a company whose chairman of the board was his uncle Edgar Bronfman. Charlie had started there in trade research—"basically going to bars and liquor stores all day and getting people to fill out questionnaires," he said. He hadn't been embarrassed to use pull to get that position. When he graduated from Marlboro College, he went straight to Uncle Edgar and asked if he could have a job. Edgar said fine, but Charlie then wanted to appease his conscience by going through the usual employment channels "like everybody else." Well, not quite. Charlie played it safe. At the end of his first interview, when the personnel director asked if Charlie had any further questions, Charlie said he had only one. "Do you know that my uncle is chairman of the board?"

He got the job, but, after a year, life as a Seagram's salesman began to pale, and Charlie started looking around for more exciting opportunities. Like many young companies, Selluloid needed an injection of cash, and the fact that it was coming from a youngster who was completely inexperienced in the field didn't bother the original partners. They figured Charlie's Seagram's connection might play to their advantage. Seagram's, after all, had recently put up some money for the Jack Nicholson film, The Border. Possibly, if Charlie asked Seagram's nicely, Selluloid could extract some more. So the deal was struck: Charlie would buy 25 percent of the company; the company would sign Charlie on as a partner.

The possibility of taking advantage of Seagram's, however, evaporated quite quickly—practically as soon as Charlie approached them for his first deal. He thought it was a natural. Charlie was trying to produce a how-to video cassette called

Dean Martin's Bartending Guide. He wanted Seagram's to put up the money for it in exchange for copious references to Seagram's in the program. The problem was that, in order to at least appear impartial, Charlie was going to refer to other liquors as well. "I was sure I could pull it off," said Charlie. "I had Dean Martin. I was sure I could get sponsoring from Seagram's. I got Dino for seventy-five thousand dollars, but I didn't have to pay until I had the seventy-five thousand dollars. I was going to have Seagram's all over it, but I felt I should mention at least *some* others, like Smirnoff's vodka, but the Seagram's guys saw Smirnoff and went 'Red flag! Red flag!' I said, 'Come on! You can't be that one-sided!' But they said no. I approached it as a business decision. Maybe I should have approached it as a favor."

Despite his best efforts, the money was not yet flowing into the company, but Charlie was confident that it would, and in the meantime it was compensation enough to get a chance to hobnob with the stars. And in this, he had found considerable reward in his contacts with the cast of *Hill Street Blues.* Charlie had been hooked on the show since it started back in his Seagram's days, before he came to Hollywood. He'd used his VCR, given to him by his parents on graduating from high school, to record almost every episode. "I'm not a fan," he said. "I'm a freak!"

When he came to L.A., he used a friend's in with the show's assistant director to visit the set. That was a thrill right there. In chatting with the assistant director, Charlie mentioned that he possessed a nearly complete set of recordings of the show, and Rich, the AD, was dazzled. The show's makers didn't even have a set themselves. Could he borrow it to make a few copies? Charlie named his price—a *Hill Street Blues* satin jacket "like the heavies have," and an invitation to watch them film a show. Rich said he had a deal.

Slow and repetitive as they were, the eight days he spent on the set watching his favorite actors record his favorite TV show were blissful. "Who'd ever guess that I'd get to meet the whole cast of *Hill Street Blues?*" he asked, still amazed at his luck. At the end of it, the cast and crew presented him with the *Hill Street* jacket—signed by all of them. Rich promised to send him scripts to future shows. "I love it!" Charlie exclaimed. To show his gratitude, Charlie invited them all down to his beachhouse for a party. Miraculously, many of them came.

"I'm a groupie," Charlie admitted. "That's what one of my partners here, Peter, calls me. He says, 'You're just a groupie.' But they'll get mileage out of it, too, because I go to all the parties now. Sure, I'm really excited that all the people on *Hill Street Blues* are my friends now. I love being up on what's going on with the best TV show in the world. There is something to that. I have an in on the best TV show being made right now."

Then he became more calculating. "I'm primarily just friends with the guys on the show, but there are certain things I can get out of it. I'll get a Christmas show reel, you know, showing all the cast at a party. It's something the general public never sees, ever, but it can be used for business. Say, somebody comes in here from out of town and wants to know what you're doing. They come into your office, and they see you've got a hat and a jacket with *Hill Street* on them, and you've got posters. And maybe you can take them on the lot and see their favorite actor, and show them the Christmas party clip, and they think—'This is something heavy.' Now, it's not heavy, but it can be used. It can be used for me. I don't always like thinking that the only thing I am going to get out of something is what I can do for my own business. But this is how I'm starting to think."

Charlie's fun becomes general fun, which turns Charlie's fun into legitimate work. What could be more perfect?

While Charlie showed a commitment to his career that would impress most of his fellow rich kids, there was a certain kid's-stuff quality to it. Helen Strauss, the documentary filmmaker, had a work life with the requisite fun, but it possessed a greater solidity in the main. Of all the rich kids I talked to, she was by far the most dedicated. Indeed, her work had become practically an obsession. Orphaned at a young age and left in the care of her parsimonious grandmother, she tried to pull the disparate strands of her personal history together in her work and make herself whole once more.

She had been hard at it, practically seven days a week, for six years now. "Occasionally I take days off," she said, "but I usually write during them." She had rented a country house—"for only two hundred dollars a month," she stressed—on Long Island for the creative aspects of her work that require quiet. She worked there from Fridays through Tuesdays and returned to her home in New York City to attend to business aspects—chiefly grant-proposal writing, since even she couldn't afford to foot the bill for full-length films—the rest of the time. And that was just when she was planning her next movie; when she was actually filming she worked even harder.

She had written fiction before that, but she had always been interested in drama, at least since age five when she mobilized her brothers and sisters to put on plays that she wrote herself. Her siblings would act, her grandmother would sew the costumes—skills honed by mending those patchwork bedsheets—and assemble the sets, and Helen would direct. "That's how I operate now," she said. "I write and direct and produce—I do just about everything."

She had produced a film on the New England fishing industry and another on a documentary filmmaker, but others have been intensely personal: one on money as seen by representatives of various American classes, one on her grandmother, and one on her upbringing. "That's my luxury," she said. "I'm free, more than most people, to pursue things that interest me."

And for Helen, those things were mostly autobiographical. No less than the other rich kids, her work was self-referential. She was in it only to please herself. If anything, her work was more satisfying simply because it satisfied directly, addressing with almost surgical precision the traumas of her childhood. There had been two major influences on her life, she told me. One was the death of both her parents before she was three and a half, and the other was the unexpected fortune she inherited at twenty-one when she thought she was a pauper. She was using her inheritance to make films that somehow undid the deaths that delivered it.

She had been born on a cypress mill in Mississippi that had been in the family for generations. It was her ancestors who used to mint their town's money. The family itself managed to swing more than a few dollars its way, enough to free Helen's father from the burden of work. Although Helen's father died when she was so young, she still had keen memories of him. "They're mostly sensual impressions," she said. "He carried me around all the time. His office was right near the house, and I remember going there and sitting by his typewriter while he worked."

He fancied himself a writer, but he also found time to travel and record his observations in a quantity of home movies that Helen regarded as her most valuable inheritance. "My father was straight out of *Gatsby*," she said. "He'd lived in Argentina and India and Africa as a young boy. He went to Africa on safaries and went to India to play polo. He took footage wherever he went." And it was from those films that Helen caught the only glimpse she can remember of her mother, who died when Helen was two. "She was an amazingly beautiful woman," she said. "To this day, some thirty years after she died, people tell me she was the most beautiful woman they'd ever seen."

Helen returned to Mississippi regularly for business meetings concerning the family company; but of late she had also been back there to make a film. It's about an orphan who returns to her hometown to try to reconstruct her past. It's about Helen. In a way, then, her films were the home movies that her father never lived to make. And in the flickering images that Helen herself created, she could do more than just master her own fate. She could alter it, building out of her own imagination a more perfect life for herself, beyond death, beyond wealth, beyond work.

9

For the Love of Money

To celebrate his sixtieth birthday in 1936, Aga Khan III was placed on the scales by his grateful subjects and then presented with his weight in gold. His 220 pounds brought him $75,000. For his seventieth birthday's Diamond Jubilee, his loyal people weighed him in diamonds, which cashed out at $2 million. And for his eightieth, they balanced him against a pile of platinum, which netted $750,000 more.

Our domestic rich kids understand such equations. Like the Aga Khan, they are inclined to measure their heft in monetary terms. Often the rich kids feel this way to their sorrow. Like the sad, monkish Daniel Griswold, they don't see how they can ever measure up to their net worth. They look into their wallets and then into themselves, and feel anguish at the comparison. But others see the money in themselves more positively: it gives them special value. Either way, the money has worked its way into their souls.

After all, they have come from money, as the expression goes. Gold, precious minerals, and the other manifestations of wealth are the family's chief currency, fundamental language, and its main source of identity. The family was founded by money and is known for having it. Like the Aga Khan's devoted subjects, the rich kids' peers put a dollar sign on them, too. As the Mellon descendant, Heather, said: "The name Mellon only means one thing to people—big bucks."

With money so important to them, one might think that rich kids would try to make a bit of their own through their work, rather than just living off the family dole forever. And, indeed, some of them do try to make money. At the very least, nearly all of them would like to. As Candace Hooper told me, in the same breathless tone she used to describe those fabulous pistachios she'd eaten on Skorpios, "I want to make my own money, and I'm determined to do it. And I will! I'll make a *tremendous* amount." The thought was yummy. But then she added a qualifier, "It's not the money itself, it's *making* the money." And that's what discouraged so many rich kids from fortune making: they don't need the money, so when the crunch comes they think—why bother? I could be sailing.

Of the fifty-seven rich kids I interviewed, about a dozen worked in professions that could be classified as moneymaking, but only three or four of those had gone to work with the sole aim of pulling in cash. All the others, like the artists and movie producers, were distracted by the possibility of doing something "worthwhile" along the way. And of the three or four, only one, Richard Potter, the cowboy-booted Texan who liked to go dancing at the debutante balls, was pulling down the kind of a return that would impress a Family Founder. Not so coincidentally, he was one of the happiest rich kids I talked to.

At thirty-one, when I saw him, Richard had yet to come into the bulk of his inheritance from his father's real-estate interests and his mother's investments, which is due him at thirty-five. But he had already converted the first installment into such a fortune—rumored to be in the vicinity of $20 million—that any further inheritance would look a little silly beside it.

And it was so easy! His business partner Jimmy Wynne, also his cohort at debutante balls, compared their business to playing Monopoly. "You just want to keep getting the best properties and putting up hotels on 'em," he said. Of course, Jimmy and Richard started out with a little more cash than the other players around the board. Still, they had made the most of it. And as their winnings mounted up, they had discovered a deeper pleasure in the enterprise that made it seem like more than a game. Moneymaking made them feel fulfilled, and that made them happy.

It took me several tries to get in to see Richard, which clued me in to his success. But when I finally did, I only had to take one quick look around to see he had it made. Texas-sized, he wore a black leather vest and a four-week beard as he sat with his heels up—showing off his embroidered cowboy boots—on a big wooden desk in front of me. He looked like the man who owned all the best properties on the board. There was an eight-foot blue tuna, one of his lesser conquests, mounted on the wall behind him. A cover of the magazine *Aero* which pictured his twin-engine Piper Aerostar hung on one wall. Tacked up beside it were maps of Texas and Kentucky, the better to display Potter-Wynne's extensive land, oil-well, and mineral-rights holdings. He also had a few peripherals going, like a cedar-chip oil-distillery venture in Kerrville, Texas, a gold mine in Kentucky, and a pair of billboards in Dallas that are rigged up with a slide projector to show dozens of ads a night. And occasionally stray properties—the equivalent of Community Chest freebies, perhaps—came in pretty much by luck, he told me, such as the $200,000 stock certificate that had appeared in the mail the other day from a movie producer he'd helped out with an introduction.

Not bad for a kid who had only been at it full-time for a year. Like so many other rich kids, he hadn't spent his life working up to his current job. He'd never known what he wanted to do when he was growing up, or afterward. He had, consequently, ended up traveling much of the way around the 360 that Alex Trammel spoke of before stumbling onto this hodgepodge of oil and mining interests.

Instead of attending a regular college, for example, he had gotten his degree aboard a ship cruising the Pacific Ocean in a program called World Campus Afloat. "That gave me a chance to see a different side of life," he said, "and meet some new people. When I decided to do it, I just hopped on a plane to reach port in California and jumped on board. I didn't really know much about it. I just wanted to see what would happen." But Richard brought some of his rich-kid attitudes along with him. One of the friends he made was a Chinese man who worked on board. Although neither spoke the other's language, they managed to communicate well enough for Richard to discover that, as he put it, "the guy wasn't happy where he was." Richard helped him jump ship, then arranged for him to fly to Dallas to work as his parents' houseboy. "I gave him to my parents for Christmas," he said.

To keep his options open, Richard went to business school at SMU in Dallas after college. "I figured whatever I did, I'd do it better for going to B-school." After graduating, though, he took up sculpture. "I was never much of an artist on paper," he said. "But I found that I could perfect my designs in the metal. I like to work in three dimensions, in reality." And, working in reality, he found his first clue to what he really cared about, for he learned that he felt better the more money he made from his designs.

Rather than concentrate on personal expression, he took to designing hollow metal figurines to house topiaries in the shapes of rabbits or swans that had a mass-market appeal. One of them was signed up for the Neiman-Marcus catalog. But that, in turn, moved him up a notch from the individual artisan to the wholesale manufacturer. In making the transition, he started to evaluate his efforts by the profit margin. And that felt right to him, so right he didn't even comment on it as he told me the story, just said, "For the return, I wasn't getting the most out of my effort." So Richard moved on to another standard rich-kid fascination, trading classic cars—Rolls-Royce, Bentley, Mercedes, Ferarri—where the markups were better. He had married his first wife by then, and he had taken up residence in the penthouse suite of Dallas's Stoneleigh Hotel. He was living well, but everything came crashing down suddenly when some personal legal problems that he would rather not go into suddenly engulfed him. He attributed the crisis to his public personality, so he decided to pull out and return to the lines that had long been so provident for the Potter family, in oil and real estate.

And perhaps it was inevitable that he should have hit pay dirt. He had a dowser's feeling for where the money was. "I went through business school," he said, "but for what we're doing now, we didn't go about it by any particular guidelines. We got in just because we felt there was something there that we could work with to make some money." Richard had an instinct for buying low and selling high. He was, for example, raising ostriches at his villa in South Texas. The project had begun as a lark, but he soon discovered that there was good money in it. "The eggs go for five-hundred dollars apiece," he said, "and the ostriches lay about sixty eggs a year, of which forty will be fertile. That's twenty grand a year." He had the buyers lined up already.

Like the Aga Khan, Richard took the measure of himself in money. With each step up the financial ladder, he felt his own worth, his own legitimacy, rise. "I'd feel guilty if I were just taking what I was given and not doing anything more with it," he said. "I did that when I was younger. I didn't have to do much of anything, and I could maintain a good life-style. But I feel better now, because I know I'm doing it because I'm *doin'* it, and it's not handed to me. The way things are going now, when I come into my trust it's not going to mean peanuts, really. Whatever I buy, whether it's airplanes or anything else, it's money I've made. I've paid for them. I feel real comfortable with that."

His pleasure in "doin' it," however, went beyond the joy of creating a positive cash flow and went back to the larger measure by which rich kids gauge their value—against the efforts of the Family Founder. This mirrors the competitive tension felt between fathers and sons everywhere. In Richard's case, these tensions actually did come out against his own father. The sources of the family money were various, coming from both sides of the family, but the holdings were all managed by his father, so he saw the money as all Dad's.

His father, Richard J. Potter, Sr., had always carried on as if the family fortune was his own personal accomplishment, anyway. When Richard Jr. was growing up, his father set himself up as the big boss of the family and reduced Richard to the level of groveling employee. Richard's job around the house was to wash the family Rolls-Royce, Cadillac convertible, and limousine, and to act as caretaker of the houses his father had bought for his real-estate deals. "All the time my friends were out in the country club during the summer, I'd be mowing lawns and washing cars," said Richard. "I just accepted it. That was the deal my father laid out for me. 'We give you food, lodging, clothes, and education,' he told me, 'and in exchange we expect you to do this work.' I said, 'Yessir.' There was no negotiating with him."

In his own business affairs, Richard was determined not only to establish his own fortune but to conduct himself almost oppositely from his father. He took on the task of administering the family holdings when his father died in 1979. But in replacing his dad, he made his mark by doing everything differently. In business, he prided himself in developing his own deals, rather than just riding the family coattails as he felt his father had. While his father had set each member of his family against the others, Richard always tried to be as inclusive as possible. Part of his success can be attributed to his instinct to cut in others. He had rigged up a special telephone line for his investors to call for up-to-the-minute information about the latest drilling. "Drilling is excitin'," he said. "With this phone you can pass some of the excitement on to the investor." If profits should ever falter, that was also a good way to keep the investor coming back. And he had been even nicer to his employees. For Christmas, Richard gave his Iranian houseboy and his secretary each a piece of an oil well so they could share the pleasures of his wealth. And, interestingly, they got some of the perplexities, too. "My secretary told me," said Richard, " 'If I make all this money from the oil, what have I got to work for?' I told her, 'Because you want to.'"

Seeing Richard operate, I felt I'd met some benign new-style family founder, one who didn't pass the money down to unknown heirs to receive long after he was gone but distributed the profits to his employees and friends to enjoy in his presence. Imagine if the Aga Khan had weighed out his jewels and then handed them back. Richard's generosity multiplied his pleasure, and it also eased the isolation that rich kids tended to feel, alone with their bounty. "It can be lonely at the top," Richard said, "or you can be there with everybody. You can be at the top, but what have you got? What's that mean? If you can get a lot of people you like up there with you, then you can all enjoy it together. If I was by myself, I might say, 'God! Do you know how much money I made at that oil well?' They all would go, 'Golly! I wish I had that.' This way, everybody's excited right along with you, yelling, 'We hit! We hit!' They're all in on the fun."

But, pleasing as fortune building can be, there are dangers involved in creating a new private source of income, separate from the family money. Richard had avoided any nasty confrontations with his father, since his father was dead before he began his moneymaking in earnest. But such bold departures are bound to upset the balance of power. They tell the family in the strongest possible language: I don't need you. And the kids who do go off to make money often end up in the position of a renegade duke who has set up a competing duchy just outside the borders of the royal empire. They have violated the accepted order.

Of course, that can be part of the appeal of making a fortune instead of simply receiving one. They want to break out, make their own name for themselves. Ando Hixon, for example, said that part of his interest in his blimp, even above his quest to prove the worth of an abandoned technology, was to come up with something that was "bigger than AMP." And at 200 feet in diameter, Ando's blimp certainly dwarfed the tiny connector that made his family's fortune. But more importantly, he hoped that its profits would do the same, thereby making a place for Ando in the Hixon family pantheon. Better yet, it might establish a new one with Ando at the head.

At his little Hollywood production company, Selluloid, Charlie Chiara's financial ambitions were not so grandiose, since they were tempered by his determination to have some fun as well as profits. But he was still keen to show the builders of his fortune that he could make money, too. It was his way of establishing his manhood. He didn't want to go crawling to his trust fund for the rest of his life. "That shows a real weakness," he said. And that weakness emerged most poignantly in comparison to his mighty uncle Edgar Bronfman and his powerful grandfather John Loeb. He needed to prove his strength to them. "I know there's not going to be any problem for me financially down the line," he said. "But I'd much rather earn it myself. That would be much more of a kick. I'd love to go and rewrite the checks withdrawing money from my account in New York to put them back in, and have my grandfather see that. And I'd get a kick out of putting a new car in my uncle's driveway. My parents bought me a car. Well, I'd like to buy them a car."

The matter had become somewhat pressing ever since Charlie began his Selluloid venture, because Grandfather Loeb, the Family Founder himself, had been objecting to the way he had been spending the family money. "He wrote me a letter that was about as nasty as you can get," said Charlie. "He said that he wanted to have nothing to do with any of my projects and that he wished I would put it in writing that nothing I was doing at Selluloid was at all connected with any of his businesses. He didn't want anybody to think he was involved with me. Now, that was heavy." The elder Loeb must have been doubly irked—first that Charlie should try to make money out in Hollywood in a way that was entirely antithetical to Loeb's own approach on Wall Street, and second that he was using Loeb's own money to do it. "I immediately got on the phone and I laid it out to him that if he really felt that way, I wouldn't touch his money. He's an old man who doesn't want to die, and he's watching his money. And he sees his grandkids, who have done nothing in their lives, piss his money away. And he's right. He's right to feel that way. Since then, though, I've taken him aside and told him exactly what it was I was doing. I showed him the contracts and I laid it out to him. I said, 'You may not like the situation, but it exists.' And I've sent him copies of some of our shows. He likes to play golf, so I sent him our cassette of a golf lesson from Sam Snead. I think he likes that."

Only rich boys entered such head-to-head confrontations with their forebears, however. Of the heiresses I interviewed, none worked for the money alone. In this, they reflect female society at large, which has yet to produce an appreciable number of tycoons. The 1983 *Forbes* survey of the four hundred richest Americans included only four women who had made the list by their own efforts—cosmetics queen Estee Lauder and three publishers, all of whom weighed in on the nether end of the *Forbes* scale, with fortunes of around $200 million.

One of the reasons for young heiresses' lack of aspiration must be their lack of inspiration from their own mothers. Like Richard Potter, rich boys can be driven to make money to outdo their fathers, or that supreme father, the Family Founder; there is no equivalent drive on the female side of the family. For all their financial elevation, these rich families mirrored the standard fifties suburban arrangements for Mom and Dad and the kids. Even though the fathers rarely brought home much money, most of them did at least make a show of going off to the office with a briefcase every morning. The mothers in these well-to-do households stayed behind and rarely troubled their heads with business questions. While they might spend some time on their favorite charity, most mothers attended to social affairs and looked after the children—or after the nannies who looked after the children.

Sometimes this was by the husband's fiat, as with King Rancher Alice Tatum's father, who insisted that his wife drop her business interests as a fund-raiser to spend all her time with the kids. But mostly rich kids' mothers just followed the unspoken rules of society. It was an important display of a woman's privilege to spend her days in idleness. That's what the money was for. And the practice allowed some women to retreat to an earlier, more civilized age. "My mother is a real dinosaur," said Richard Potter, expressing a sentiment that many of his wealthy peers would certainly share about their own mothers. "She is a woman of the past who is the very picture of the Southern Belle. Servants did everything for her. They dressed her, did her hair, the whole thing. She's still that way today. She is a real smart woman, but she doesn't know a thing about business or finance or any of that. Her interests are social—the women's club, the garden club. She's something that doesn't exist anymore." But Mrs. Potter was still firm about some things. "She never allowed any harsh words in our house. One time I slipped and said 'damn' or something, and my mother went whap! and my face stung for a week. She was left-handed, and she really caught me."

To rich girls, the money itself must have had a masculine feel to it, as it suggested heavy briefcases, fat cigars, and cold leather chairs in boardrooms. After all, the money was made by men, converted into trusts by men, and divvied out quarterly by men. Rich kids of both sexes may feel infantilized by their on-the-dole existence. Yet men can ultimately divine the method by which they can grow up—they can master this system and make it work for them. Women feel they can't even open the boardroom doors. As one said, "Ever notice how heavy they are?" Sometimes rich girls are kept out more deliberately. In the Ridder family, the female descendants are expressly forbidden from taking a job in the family newspaper business. "There were so many Ridders," says one of the excluded, Cary, "that I suppose they had to cut it off somewhere. But I still think it's terrible."

For this reason, few rich girls ever got very far in business. Some had been swept along by the women's movement to take a job in the professions; others needed an occupation to absorb their energy; and still others went for paying jobs only because volunteer work has lost its cachet. But none of them exhibited much drive to get to the top. They just wanted to get in. Rich boys may have the idea of toppling their fathers to encourage them. Women who sought to improve on their mothers' lots could set their sights considerably lower. All they wanted was a basic knowledge of finance, for many rich girls believe their sheltered mothers have paid a high price for lacking one. Left in the dark financially, their mothers were forever dependent on men to show them the way. And the women were terribly vulnerable if their men packed up their alligator-skin suitcases and left. In this age of divorce, that happened all too frequently.

The Houstonian Emily Montgomery had taken a job as a financial analyst largely to gain greater security through knowledge. Although she would have preferred to be home writing or drawing, strong interests of hers ever since attending St. Paul's, she spent her days considering p/e ratios of such stocks as Bloomingdale's and McDonald's for a group of mutual funds. A refined and pretty young woman, she looked as if she'd be more comfortable behind an easel than an executive's desk. "I guess what I've done is a reaction to this whole dilettantish thing," she said. "I didn't want to be perceived as having taken the easy way out. I felt I'd be criticized if I'd gone into painting and just become a secondary artist. I have excellence as a goal in all aspects of life. But, perhaps more importantly, I knew I'd have a certain amount of financial responsibility in the future, and I always felt that I should know how to manage my own things. I don't want to be dependent on a man who might disappear, and then I'd be left feeling helpless. Women in my parents' generation weren't necessarily trained to handle their money. They weren't told things, so no matter how they tried later, they weren't conversant in it. They didn't have the tools."

Emily's mother had done charity work but had never developed any business expertise to fall back on when her marriage failed. Emily was barely a teenager at the time. "After my father left," she said, "I saw how difficult life could be for a woman. This world is not very nice to single women with children. They're really cut off. I feel that if what happened to her then happened to me now, my life would be much better. I have the currency now to enter the business world, or at least to communicate with someone managing my affairs. I know the buzzwords. I know the hocus-pocus. I still have my share of vulnerability, though. I see my mother as very sad and alone and broken by a man. That made me never want to be dependent on a man in that way."

Another factor had contributed to Emily's decision to enter

finance, one that women from less lofty circumstances would recognize—the feminist impulse to gain respect through a corporate job. Possibly because the money encourages restraint, wealthy families often take a while to accept the social changes that catch on so feverishly in other quarters. As Emily put it, "When you have more to conserve, you become more conservative." But, with their educations from prominent boarding schools and liberal arts colleges, rich kids eventually catch on to progressive ideas. Emily had clearly been affected by the suggestion that the woman's place is not in the home but in the office. She was now a solid proponent of the cause and had been appalled when she encountered a less liberated Houstonian woman recently who told her quite bluntly, "If I were as rich as you, I wouldn't bother to work." Emily said nothing at the time but wished now that she had the moment back. "I felt like telling her, 'Honey, there's more to working than just putting food in your icebox. There's something called fulfillment and wanting to contribute to society and furthering your learning and defining your sense of self.' "

But the lessons of feminist independence had come hard. Emily had fallen sick several times since she took the job. She thought her illnesses had come from exhaustion, stemming from her reluctance to cede so much time to her career. "Being a financial analyst doesn't interest me all that much," she admitted. "At the office, every minute of the day is work. It's not something that I *love* to do. But it is a skill I want to have for the future." She rather enjoyed the carefree rich life, though, and didn't want to sacrifice it for a profession. Consequently, she ended up wearing herself out partying or concert going or writing letters or reading late into the night all because, as she said, "I refuse to give up *everything* for my job." It had taken enough as it was.

Occasionally she fantasized about junking her career to get into a line of work she'd find more satisfying, such as starting a small press where she could run everything. "I've always loved the arts of printing and writing," she said. "You have the technical challenge of getting everything right—putting in all the little letters and so on. But you also have the artistic questions about where are you going to place those words on a page. It requires great talent. Everything's your decision." She had also contemplated writing a book, starting a restaurant, and making a movie but had yet to commit herself to any of them. "With all of these," she said, "you've got to take a risk, and that's scary. It's more secure to work for someone else. That way they set the rules." Sometimes, she was tempted to retire from the working world altogether. "I do occasionally lie back on the pillows and say to myself, 'Why am I trying to do it all? Why am I trying to be the superwoman?' "

But for now at least, Emily was committed to her job. The security she extracted was payment enough. Even though her ambivalence stemmed from her unique circumstances, it ended up bringing her in line with almost everybody else in the working world. It brought her in touch with reality. As she said, "I don't wake up in the morning dying to do it, but once I get started it's not so bad."

Leonard Russell, as I'll call him, had taken the very plunge that Emily Montgomery dreamed of and put up his own money to start a small publishing company in New York City. While Emily's gaze back up the family tree had made her cautious, Leonard was inspired by the examples that he saw above him to undertake an act of great boldness. In his case, it was his grandfather, the Family Founder, who urged him on. The most senior Russell had founded a major business magazine, then helped start a no-less-major publishing company before moving on to the even bigger businesses that made the family money.

As I sat with Leonard in his antique-filled parlor in Greenwich Village, I could see how heavily the history weighed upon him. He looked like an elongated version of Theodore Roosevelt, with a robust yet aristocratic bearing, horn-rim glasses, and a handlebar mustache. But he was born too late. In the nineteenth century, aristocrats could take charge of the world as though it belonged to them; rich kids in the twentieth felt something held them back.

Publishing had been his grandfather's first and strongest love, and it was the one young Leonard came to share. He did not find it immediately. After college he followed his father, who had used his inheritance to start a small group of investment companies. Leonard went into banking with the idea of someday taking over his father's business. But, like Emily, Leonard was bored with high finance. He also performed badly at it and was fired after six months, an embarrassing fact that he had admitted to only five people since. Russells were not accustomed to failure.

"I did nothing for a year after that," said Leonard, "and then one morning I just woke up and said, 'I've got to *do* something!' I counted on my fingers the things I enjoyed, and one of them was books." With the help of a friend, he got a job at a publishing house, liked it, and was soon looking for a publishing company to buy.

In a way, Leonard combined the interests of his father and his grandfather, since he looked on the publishing company not as a plaything but as an investment. "Deep down," he said, "I know that it's terribly hard to make a lot of money in books, if not impossible. But there are exceptions to that rule, and that's what keeps me going." Instead of the usual literary fare that most small presses turn out, Leonard's company had concentrated on the books that are most likely to sell, chiefly celebrity bios and self-help books. But he had still lost $30,000 in the previous year.

In order to spur himself on to maximize profits, Leonard had to screen out some critical facts about his own finances. In truth, Leonard was bound to receive far more money than he ever could make in publishing just by biding his time until the remainder of his inheritance came to him. He coped with this fact by ignoring it. "I operate under a very interesting assumption," he said, "and that is, I will never inherit another dime. It's not true—or at least I have been told it's not true—but that's how I live, that's how I think."

And what, I asked, if he could register the fact that this is all an illusion and that he will inherit money?

Leonard paused for a moment to blow out some air. "This is going to sound pretty dumb," he said. "But I don't think I'd be as successful at this job. If I knew that I was going to inherit several million dollars, I don't think I'd be doing anything."

To judge by his life-style, he didn't need any more money. Leonard lived with his wife in a fancy brownstone in Greenwich Village not far from his publishing company's offices, and the couple took nearly a month's vacation every year.

What more could he want? He didn't have any children yet, but he said he'd need more money down the line to pay for their college education, assuming, again, that he wasn't a multimillionaire by then anyway just for living so long. And he had a dream of building a library of beautiful books and then grandly bestowing it on the public, possibly with his own name attached. He wasn't fazed by the contradiction that he should sell books now so that he could give them away later. That was just a small part of the Leonard Russell paradox.

He felt the pinch of contradictions around the office. Situated in a former warehouse in SoHo that dates back nearly to the Industrial Revolution, his publishing house was a small capitalist universe as Adam Smith himself might have envisioned it. Bought with his capital, the house was his and he ruled it. "I'm the big boss, I guess you'd say," he declared. "It's my money." Although Leonard tried to run the place democratically, his four employees—a marketing manager, a publicity director, and two editors—were paid to do his bidding. "There's no question that I end up making all the decisions," he said. "That seems to follow in a good capitalist society." Although one of the two editors owned a small share of the company, they were both avowed socialists, while Leonard was, like his father and grandfather, a staunch Republican. And Leonard was irked that the two of them weren't always sufficiently conscious of the bottom line in their editorial decisions. "I insist that this company does not publish books to save the world," he said. "They forget that this company is trying to make a success of itself and create enough money so that we can all make a decent living."

Although Richard Potter had placed himself in a similar position as the father figure for his employees, he was able to create a happy family feeling by spreading the wealth around. Leonard was not so lucky, since there were, as yet, no profits to distribute. Just the opposite—any profits could only come by keeping salaries down to the paltry levels of the small-press industry, with $13,000 a year about tops. That didn't sit too well with the employees; no family feeling prevailed.

For the time being, the only one making a decent living was Leonard, who was pulling down a substantial income from his trust, and that made him very nervous. He tried to hide his financial superiority from his employees out of what he regarded as simple politeness, but considering the lengths to which he went, the explanation probably ran deeper. He had all of his personal bank and investment statements sent to his house, avoided talking to his broker when the employees were within earshot, and deliberately dressed down for the office. He felt quite awkward about this summer's four-week vacation to Texas and Bermuda. He emphasized to me that much of their trip west was for business and that he and his wife "don't stay in well-known, expensive places. We're not like that. We like to find really good little hotels that are inexpensive. It's become quite a challenge for us." The awkward part had come afterward, back in the office, when the UPS man kept delivering parcel after parcel of gifts they'd bought for Christmas presents. "This year's and next year's," said Leonard. The packages had to be shipped to the office because no one was home to receive them. "It got a little obnoxious," he admitted.

He also worried that his Renault station wagon might give the wrong impression, since his staff couldn't afford cars. Although his house was just minutes away, he had only invited one employee home, and that was a young man I'll call Brent, who was closest to his own financial circumstances, the son of a wealthy professional. Because of that kinship, he extended to Brent some of the prohibitions that he routinely applied to himself. "He has some beautiful three-piece suits that he got for a job uptown, and he wears them to the office quite frequently and it drives me *up the fucking wall!*" Leonard exclaimed with unusual force. "It's not the atmosphere of the office. It sets him apart in ways that it shouldn't set him apart. I have plenty of three-piece suits. I don't feel outdone. I don't feel it makes him the boss. I feel it makes the other people in the office uncomfortable. In fact, I know it does." Leonard reserved his flashy clothes for his nights out at the theater with his wife. Even so, he lived in fear that someone from the office would spot him after hours. "I've worried about that a lot," he said.

Since he paid the salaries, he felt personal responsibility for his employees' tight financial straits. He felt a terrible twinge when the favored Brent came into the office raving about a fabulous apartment he'd found that was fifty dollars a month over his budget. "That was tough," he said, "because I knew how much he wanted that apartment. But I couldn't say to him, 'I'll give you a thousand-dollar raise,' which is what it would take annually after taxes. So I didn't say anything. I just felt crummy." On the other side of the coin, when he gave another employee a raise, he watched her go out and get a better apartment. "You feel the effect on other people's lives," he said. "I hate controlling people. I hate the people who control. I *hate* it. When you're running a business, to some extent you are running people's lives. You're setting limits on them. I for one don't like to feel that anyone could put limits on me. That's why I'm doing what I'm doing. That's why I'm my own boss."

But even when you're the boss, Leonard was coming to realize, you can't rule everything. There are some facts he could not change. He could pretend that he needed the money, but he couldn't pretend that his employees didn't. In shifting from a life of leisure to a go-go business career, he had hoped to leave the inequities of society behind. But, of course, on the job the inequities are, if anything, accentuated, since workers know precisely where they stand, right down to the penny. In his job Leonard had gained a personal refuge: the company excited him as few things ever had. But the excitement he felt in the office was his alone. His employees would never share it, since their interests ran in such a different direction. He had gone into the publishing venture to break his isolation, but, despite the best intentions, he had only increased it.

As we ended our conversation, I asked him how many people he had told as much about himself as he had just finished telling me. "No one," he said. "Well, maybe my wife."

Then he thought for a moment. "I did tell one friend some of what I've just told you a little while ago. He took it OK. I'm changing. I'm getting to be less private about things. I've started to think—maybe I should start trusting people more. I mean, OK, so I have money. So what? What's the big deal?" But it would take time before he could bring himself to make such a full disclosure to his colleagues on the job, if he ever would. Meanwhile he passed his days at the office with a guilty secret, never knowing what would give him away.

As the profit-minded heirs seek to increase their fortunes, and to boost their self-esteem along the way, they sometimes find that they can indeed reach a better place. But it is never an entirely new one, and, like Leonard, they often discover there a new version of the same stigma that they had originally sought to escape. Leonard hadn't succeeded yet, but if he did, he might suffer another barrage of worries: that he only made it because of who he is descended from, not because of what he did. Rich kids might have thought success would free them from the burden of their past. But like a man charged with but never convicted of some terrible crime, they often find they can never fully clear themselves.

Shannon Wynne certainly appeared to have reached that better place. With his chain of restaurants and nightclubs around Dallas, he was at the height of Texas society. His places were so "in," they were almost in danger of going out, because of the frustration endured by all the diners waiting in line to get a table. The friends I was visiting in Dallas, in fact, wanted me to pass on their displeasure about the lines to Shannon when they heard I would be seeing him. When I told Shannon about it, he wrote out a pass for them on a napkin and signed it like a king creating the coin of the realm.

For all the glory of his star restaurant Nostromo, I had trouble finding it even though I knew the address. In the tradition of the reclusive rich, the hot spot bore no sign, and I mistook it for the fern-filled restaurant next door. When I was redirected, I found a white warehouselike building with a lot of square tables scattered across the inside—a lot of nowhere, I thought. But after my first impression faded, I realized this truly was unutterably chic. With its scuffed floors and tall ceilings and high-tech metallic furnishings, it looked like the backstage of some vast and unseen theater. And that's the whole idea: this was the in place, the behind-the-scenes place, the where-it's-happening place.

When I walked in, I happened to catch Shannon himself chewing out one of his waiters for delivering a rather poor example of lima beans. "Lima beans should be *shiny*," he was saying. "These are dull. Now take them back."

A tall, skinny but almost electrically charged stick figure of a man—a "hectic anorexic," he called himself—Shannon wore a pair of metal glasses that popped out unnaturally from his face like goggles on a racing-car driver. To judge by the energy with which he attacked the lima bean question, he had slimmed down for action. Shannon never planned to get into the restaurant business, but now that he was here he was making the most of it. Like so many rich kids, he had come to his job by a circuitous route. After college, he had toyed with the idea of being a veterinarian, gotten a degree in filmmaking, tried (and failed) to cash in on the nation's 200th birthday with a Bicentennial T-shirt, and then finally hit upon his life's work when his favorite restaurant in Dallas went up in flames leaving him no place where he felt like dining. So he thought, why don't I just build one myself? And he did.

Considering that Shannon knew nothing about the restaurant business at the time, one might think this was a quick way to kill off an inheritance. Indeed, when he built his first restaurant he neglected to put in a bus station for the busboys, because he didn't realize such things were necessary. He just concentrated on the aspects that he considered important: the decor, the lighting, and the music, all the things that contribute to the all-important tone of a place. His mother supplied the name, the 8.0, inadvertently when she said, "I done *ate* there and, *oh*, it was good." But the dining spot was better known simply as Shannon Wynne's place. Texans were curious to see what the rich boy would come up with. "People always played on that," said Shannon in amazement; "that I didn't need to be doing it, but I was doing it anyway. I think that's a silly reason to see somebody's club, but there you are."

And the gawkers came out in quantity. "The 8.0 took 'em

by storm," said Shannon. "It became a preppy hangout. *Women's Wear Daily* wrote about it, and all the preps attacked. At the time, I was *furious*! Business was already booming. But I've learned to be grateful for publicity."

So successful was 8.0 that Shannon soon opened a second high-tech, high-society hangout—Nostromo. Even without a sign, customers found their way to the place in quantity. Then he put up Rocco and finally Tango, the latter of which seemed destined for greatness as well, having made the national papers because of a controversy involving six ten-foot-tall acrylic frogs—four playing music, two doing the tango—that he placed on the roof. The Dallas Sign Control Board of Adjustments argued that the frogs violated the city ordinance against rooftop signs; Shannon believed they were exempt from such a statute because they were art. In 1984, the matter was still pending.

While Shannon was gratified by the success, he wasn't ecstatic about it. The prosperity of his restaurants had just validated his personal taste—in food, in atmosphere, in design. "I hate slickness," he said as he scanned Nostromo. "The glass blocks over there created a lot of slickness. So did the Italian tile, which is white and polished and clean, and so did the tablecloths. To balance that, I had to go to a really dry-looking chair. It's a Swedish Kreiger chair. It's no frills. They stack and they're functional. And the floor is unfinished. There's a really good sound system and fresh flowers every day. But you know what really makes this place? You can see everybody from one seat. Laugh if you want, but a good part of going out is being seen."

While he never felt much love lost on him as a rich kid, he hadn't felt the situation improve all that much now that he has emerged as an *accomplished* rich kid. His success had accentuated the standard love-hate relationship all Americans, even Texans, have with the rich. "A lot of people resent the hell out of me," he said. "They think I have financed my restaurants myself. I don't. I never spend a penny of my own money on any of it. I raise the money from other people. I see my money solely as my influence with the bankers. I use it as leverage against them, so they'll shell out. I use it as a threat—I'll jerk their chains if they don't act."

Even if Shannon had not used his personal capital for the venture, that did not mean he hadn't traded on his background in other ways. With this venture, he was investing some of the private cultivation that has been bred into the Wynne family here for generations and was going public with it. He was not the first in his family to turn cultivation into commerce. His mother, Joanne Ebling Wynne, is the Camay Soap Girl. Her wedding picture still adorns the Camay wrapper. And his father, Angus Wynne, Jr., strayed from the expected Wynne profession of the law to found the historical equivalent of Disneyland, the Six Flags amusement parks. But in Shannon's case the commerciality was higher-toned. He required male patrons to wear jackets. In *his* amusement parks, he would let the masses feel rich, with all the exquisitely understated style and flare and attention to details, like shiny lima beans, that wealth allows. And he was making a killing on it.

But even if Shannon's patrons came into his restaurants to enjoy the aura of wealth, they still disliked him for his own personal glow. It seemed a little much that he should now be both rich *and* famous. "A lot of people want to see me fail because I get so much press," he said. "They just did another thing on me in the paper this morning. I'm just a scapegoat, I think. They think I'm pompous because I'm from a well-known, old, social family. In one article, they ran this big picture of me at twenty-four and then superimposed on it a bottle of scotch and stuck me behind a bar at a debutante ball. They like to make fun of me.

"People either fear or hate me, without knowing me. It's very peculiar. Strangers either buddy up to me or are intimidated by me. I'm a little star here. In this little town of Dallas, I'm as much—don't take this wrong—as Warhol could be in New York. Out on the street I'm constantly plagued by people going, 'Oh! Oh! You're . . .' It's starting to get like this isn't that much fun. I don't know if it's the wealth or the profile. I think it's more the profile."

To Shannon, the most palpable aspect of his success, the money, didn't make much difference one way or the other. He was just thrilled that it had all worked out and, finally, he had found a good place to eat. If his nightclubs were all crashing failures I expect he'd be unchanged, with the same self-assurance, the same conviction about the same small details. In this, he probably took after his father who, besides starting the Six Flags chain, took a flyer on the New York World's Fair. He assembled the Texan entry to the fair, a little number with the theme "To Broadway With Love" that celebrated many of the tunes that Shannon played on his superb sound system at Nostromo. Unfortunately, the Texas pavilion was, like the fair as a whole, a total disaster. "It was a great big history of Broadway, a great big stage show, and everybody just lost their ass," said Shannon. And how did father Angus take it? "He threw an enormous bankruptcy party. All the guests brought bags of groceries. All the waiters ran soup lines. And everybody sang, 'Yes, we have no bananas.' "

10

The Volunteer Spirit

Michael Pratt, the ruddy-bearded Amherst graduate who as a child had gaily bicycled down the halls of his grandmother's Long Island mansion, first sensed the wide divergence between his life as a rich kid and his work as a community organizer when he went to work in a ghetto.

He was orchestrating a picketing campaign against a price-gouging grocery store in neighboring Queens. Every morning, he remembered, he closed the door to his plush apartment on Manhattan's Upper West Side (that even more handsome cooperative apartment by the Hudson came later), climbed into a taxi to cross the Fifty-ninth Street Bridge and got off at the biggest housing project in New York, a vast complex of grubby six-story buildings next to a power plant. There he worked the streets all day, banging on doors to meet the residents, holding neighborhood rallies, and finally directing everyone's efforts against the store. Every night, he hailed another cab and returned to his princely quarters across the East River.

"If the residents in the projects had known where I lived," he said, "none of them would have understood. Few of the people had any idea that I have money, or am related to money. And I wouldn't want them to. They already know how little the organizers are making, and they are amazed by it. At that time, we were paid by Vista and making at most six thousand dollars a year. That blows working-class black people away. 'You're white,' they say. 'You're smart. You went to college. What the hell are you doing?' After a while, they understood and they got excited about it. But there's always that confusion about why you're doing this stuff, and you have to explain it."

What the hell *was* Michael doing? Although Michael's money came from Standard Oil, he had picked up on his father's radicalism—forceful enough to win him an appearance before HUAC—in his teens. At Amherst he devoted himself to leftist causes, such as trying to remove companies doing business with South Africa from the college's investment portfolio, that would probably not have won him much love from the Pratt ancestors who donated so much money to the school.

He identified so thoroughly with the oppressed, in fact, that although he was a blue-blooded WASP he always thought of himself as Jewish. At Amherst, and afterward, he only went out with Jewish women. The first was a Jewish Marxist he'd met in a political science class who advocated violent revolution. Michael had to get straight with her just whom she was planning to shoot before proceeding with the relationship. "I was afraid it would be me," he said.

At Amherst Michael's own political philosophy rapidly grew so extreme—"I started spouting Marxist-Leninist dogma without knowing what the hell I was talking about"—that he decided he had better take some time off to think things over. So he dropped out for a while to work for a public-interest law firm. And it was that experience that led to his career as a community organizer.

"I've never worked just for the money," he said. "That's weird. That's definitely a separation from the average. It makes it hard for me to understand other people's attitudes toward work." Since the money had always been free for him, he had never known how precious it was for those who had to work for it, and such ignorance had affected his fund raising. "I don't really understand economic scales," he admitted. "I've asked people to give twenty-five dollars to causes. To me, that's nothing. I've had to find out how much it was for them." But he had also noticed that his work as a community organizer struck back at the consciences of high-salaried professionals he bumped into from time to time, returning the guilt trips so many people put on him for being rich to them for *getting* rich. "I try not to preach," he said, "and I don't think I do, but I have sensed that, as a community organizer, I can make banker and corporate-lawyer types nervous. It doesn't upset anyone who really loves what he's doing, but it seems to affect them. My work is a pain in the ass for them. I'm doing something about social issues, and they're just making a load of money."

Michael said he got paid about $9,000 a year for his work. Compared to his total holdings, he acknowledged, "That's spare change." Nevertheless he insisted on receiving it. "The groups I work for always struggle for money," he said. "But I still take my salary. If I didn't, we'd have nine thousand dollars more for leaflets, for trips to Albany to lobby. But I don't want to isolate myself by saying, 'Hey, I'll do it for free.' "

In a way, though, the true payment for his work could not be measured in dollars but rather in the very distance that it drew him from his upper-class origins. He saw such journeys as the one over the river to Queens less as trips to a different borough of New York than as trips down into some more central core of reality. His wealth lifted him up. He wanted his work to bring him down to earth again. "Instead of feeling isolated," he said, "my work makes me feel connected with the world around me. Other rich people I know feel odd, other-worldly, a little dizzy. My work gets me right down there, very excited about the world I live in. At that housing project, sixty percent of the people were on welfare, eighty-five percent were black, fourteen percent were Hispanic. Then there was me. That's a pretty intense situation for any white kid to find himself in regardless of income. Having been through that and come through to the other side— it's helped me. It's like I've paid my dues."

The work of rich kids always takes them on a journey of some sort. Free to choose their occupation, they can go wherever they like, hop from one thing to another as they please. As was true for a pleasure-seeker like Matt Trenton, who went off sailing in the Caribbean, some trips are quests for the ultimate pleasure, a deeper knowledge of themselves; for the few profit-minded rich kids, like the Monopoly-playing Richard Potter and Jimmy Wynne, the trip is a climb to the top, in search of the satisfaction of making their own fortunes, and thereby losing the stigma of having been given one. Then there are the rich kids like Michael who take low wages, or none at all, to perform social service. They are on a trip down, to reconnect themselves with the common men and women their families left behind so many generations ago.

These are the Good Samaritans in the ranks of the rich kids. As they labor at their storefront women's centers, prison therapy sessions, tenants'-rights organizations, and free walk-in clinics, they care little about their own comfort. They believe in their cause. They are daring. And, for the most part, they draw from their work a higher return than fleeting pleasure or cash. They attain a certain state of grace.

And yet, living lives so removed from the go-getter capitalist mainstream, they are also a little . . . peculiar. And most people react to them as if they'd heard that some young man of great promise had just entered a monastery. They think, what's *with* that guy? Why does he want to suffer so? Like monks, they abandon status, glory, fun, freedom, power. When so many other rich kids, indeed so many other people, think only of themselves, they are motivated almost entirely by a social conscience. Instead of working for rewards that society can measure with the exactness of, say, a six-figure salary, they *give* their time away, often to plead with others for grants and contributions. While their peers commute to work in shiny office buildings, the volunteers head the other way across the tracks to cramped work spaces in run-down neighborhoods.

But, crazy as such work appears, it is about the only kind that makes much sense for a rich kid. Can he help it if the very capitalist system that gave him the freedom to be so charitable should then mock him for taking advantage of it? After all, he has all the money he needs. Why shouldn't he work to help those who don't have enough?

The fellow I've called Max Perlman had been working for several years for a nonprofit agency he founded in Washington to encourage entrepreneurship by easing restrictions on business loans to the poor. He was a lean thirty-two-year-old with a forty-niner-style beard and a straightforward manner that may have come from recognizing that he was born with everything he'd ever want. We talked hurriedly at the conference table in his office, since he was eager to get home to his wife and kids. While Max himself had foregone a salary to devote himself to the cause, thereby taking a plunge in economic standing, his goal was to raise up the level of the common people. "The guilt that comes from money," he said, "is not because it isn't 'nice' to have money. It's because other people don't have it. That hurts their lives." He was trying to ease that pain by giving the poor access to the capital to make the system work as well for them as it had for the Perlman family. The family clothing business, one of the nation's biggest, not so coincidentally, owed its success to a stock of money the company had salted away when a highly marketable idea came their way in the previous century. They'd been riding that success ever since.

But capital, said Max, was class-conscious. For a risky new idea that the banks wouldn't touch, one had to go to one's friends and family for a loan. "That system obviously works for the wealthy," he said. "It works far less well in middle-income communities, and it works not at all in poor communities." As a result, he said, the budding entrepreneurs in poor communities have no chance to see their ideas come into being, and the potential workers in those communities are deprived of the employment that such ventures would bring.

His agency was dedicated to giving the lower class equal access to the cash. Through a textbook and a quarterly journal, it attempted to spread the word on how to redress this imbalance, and it made technical research and expertise avail-

able to its partisans in government as well as undertaking
some lobbying efforts on its own.

With the family business behind him and in possession of
an inheritance through his mother—a descendant of the company founder—that made him far richer than his own father,
Max himself never saw any need to develop an entrepreneurial project of his own. He had a great deal of difficulty
deciding what to do instead. He took three years off after
college to investigate various possibilities, working as an envi-
ronmentalist for the Arizona state government, and getting
a degree in public policy at Georgetown. "I took a long time
to decide," he said. "Sometimes I feel that if I hadn't had
money it would have been simpler. We always joked about
the burden of money in the family. Still, there were times
when I felt guilty. But I decided that what I would want
for others is that they have the same options I have. It made
no sense for me to feel guilty if by doing so I prevented myself
from exercising those options." Finally he decided to go to
law school at Yale. But before he graduated, he reconsidered.
"I said to myself, 'OK, time's up. What are you going to do
with your life?' " He resolved to do "what's worth doing,"
and that was his work for enterprise development. "I want
others to build their own family companies," he said. He
wanted the nation to be his heirs.

Even if these social workers do the work for free, or for
a pittance, their wealth still weighs no less heavily on them
than on the fun-workers or the profit-seekers. The volunteers
don't work for money; they work to release themselves from
money. They seek to defuse its explosive power, to tame it,
so they can settle down with it more comfortably. The fun-
workers do so by directing it, often extravagantly, to serve
their fancy. The profit-seekers diminish its hold over them
by earning a pile of their own, preferably one so high that
it puts their original inheritance into shadow.

The volunteers direct their efforts at the aspect of their
money that they find most irksome, namely the inequity of
its distribution. Like Michael Pratt and Max Perlman, they
try to even things out by climbing down from the pinnacle

of wealth and, at the same time, working to raise others up from the base. In this, they go beyond their peers who merely stay home and, in response to that wrenching money mail, write checks to ease their consciences. Their activism transforms their millions—turning what they had come to see as a liability back into an asset by doing good with it. And they do it pretty much the way Max had—by redirecting their money to the neediest, who naturally prize it wholeheartedly. As they say in the Murchison family, "Money is like manure. Pile it up and it stinks like hell, but spread it around, and it does a lot of good."

But besides performing obvious services for the poor, the rich kids also help themselves, by coming to see in the clearest possible terms, as they feed the hungry, shelter the homeless, cure the sick, what a singular blessing money can be.

"If the truth were told about money," said a glitzy, psycho-babbling West Coast heiress I'll call Phoebe, "it would be like water, and there would be a lot of it on this earth, and it would be flowing and luscious and feel good, and it would support people in being who they really are." All *right!* Phoebe smiled a thirty-two-tooth smile for me as she completed this sentence. And it did sound giddy to the point of lunacy—money like water? Lots of it? Feel good? Come again? But once I figured out what she was saying, Phoebe had a point.

An attractive, black-haired woman clothed in a loose-weave linen dress that looked like golden mail, Phoebe seemed to have been born to go to cocktail parties. But here she was at work in her nook office where she served as a volunteer fund-raiser for a Los Angeles organization dedicated to feeding the hungry around the world. She was given to extended metaphors about money as a vital force. To her, lucre was "love energy," "food," and "a wild animal," but mostly it was water—clear, flowing, natural, and essential to life.

Certainly it had been essential to *her* life, but that was something she had only recently come to accept. Born to money as an heiress to a vast and well-known fortune in kitchen products, Phoebe now recognized that her wealth was a critical aspect of her own identity. She had come to the conclusion that there was a fundamental psychic equation in which Phoebe equaled money, and therefore to give of it was to give of herself. And she could freely tell me that it was no coincidence, given her vision of money as water, that she was a Pisces, a water sign; that she had a "big swimming pool" at her house for her four children; and that of all the places she had been in the world, she was happiest at the beach, gazing out at all that water. If she redid her house, she said, she was going to bring the water inside, with waterfalls and pools running right through. She wanted to get in touch with the flow, to plunge into the never-ending stream of gushing money.

And that was what she did on a global scale at the organization's well-appointed L.A. headquarters. It was her job to get the water flowing, she explained, by rechanneling it—out of the ample reserves of the industrious or, like herself, the well-born and into the communal pool of the organization which in turn piped it about the world in an attempt to feed the starving masses. In so doing, Phoebe saw herself performing a vast therapy: physical therapy on the hungry children fed by the project; psychological therapy on the wealthy donors by helping them feel good about their moneyed selves; and a little of both on herself—by finding a satisfying outlet, both physically and psychologically, for her own "love energy." To her metaphorical mind, she was feeding the "hungry" of all sorts—both in the Third World and in the first. "I think in this country we are hungry," she said, dropping into the talk of the human-potential movement in which she is a believer. "Our hunger is unexpressed potential. We're all hungry, and our hunger runs deep."

Phoebe had felt the pangs herself. They came out early as a discomfort with her surname, which she felt had little connection with her true self. "People would always be asking me, are you related to the kitchen-products people?" she said. "They all had a connotation, an expectation, sometimes for better, sometimes for worse. They had a definite picture." But, of course, her squirming over her name was only a token of a more fundamental angst over the millions the name represented. "I was almost trying to get rid of it," she remembered, "to keep the money down. It's like a wild animal when you don't know what to do with it. You corral it. But when you let it out, and it runs on the beach, and you see the beauty and magnificence, it's thrilling! It's exciting!"

It took her some time, though, until she got up the nerve to let the beast run free for her to observe in all its glory. It was a gradual transformation. "I didn't go into therapy," she said. "It was nothing heavy like that." It occurred instead through the simple act of charity, and that began with a contribution to the food organization. By giving money away, she sensed herself coming to grips with her fundamental nature. "As I began to contribute," she said, "I came to life more and more. The more money I gave, the more I was also giving of myself. Before that, I was fairly unconscious about my money. I didn't pay attention. I avoided it. I didn't want to be separate from people, you know? But when I let go, I saw how much I could feel together, together with myself, and together with others."

Eventually she concluded that she had no reason to feel bad about being rich. She recognized that so long as she overlooked amounts, money was common to everyone, a universal bloodline. It can unify as much as it can divide. As she said, "I came to see that what I thought made for separateness in the world actually does the opposite. Money is a vehicle for understanding. When you talk to people intimately about their money you have more of a real experience of who they really are. When people let loose with their money, they let loose with themselves. It doesn't matter how much they have. It's just a matter of how they express themselves with it. It's an ongoing process, coming to terms with money. I don't hold my money as mine so much. I hold it as something to share, and it comes through me because I'm a good channel for it."

As a fund-raiser, Phoebe could establish bonds with her donors that provided a vital connection with her fellowman. "I just go right into their hearts," she said. "It's very intimate work, *very* intimate. It's like getting to know someone, like having a relationship where you know someone better and better. They start to loosen up, and it keeps on going. It never stops." She admitted, though, that it did help if the prospective donors were "open personalities" to begin with.

And through the work, Phoebe felt much happier with what she found when she looked into her own heart. "I think I have my money for a reason," she said. "God wants His children fed, and money is put here to feed them. And that's what I'm doing. I'm giving my money, and I'm getting other people to give theirs. There are all kinds of illusions and mind games going around that lock the money up. It's great to shake people loose and let their money flow. People *can* make a difference with their money. Once they see that, they no longer worry about guilt. They have a purpose in their lives. I know I do."

The idea of volunteer work for socialites is hardly new. At the turn of the century, according to Cleveland Amory's *Who Killed Society?*, Miss Mary Harriman, daughter of railroad tycoon E. H. and sister of ambassador W. Averell, looked out on all the flowers gathered for her debut and burst into tears when she realized there were far too many for any one person to enjoy. In 1900, she formed the Junior League, through which debutantes like herself could redirect some of their blessings to the less fortunate. Yet long before that, starting in the 1820s, upper-class women had taken it upon themselves to help the needy, first with female-sponsored orphan asylums and homes for indigent women and then with more general care for the urban poor. This movement culminated in the progressive era in the 1890s, when wealthy women by the thousands followed Hull House founder Jane Addams, herself solidly upper-class, to establish and staff inner-city settlement houses around the country.

Phoebe had spoken of "going right into the hearts" of potential donors in order to feed hungry children. Such efforts have a female quality—extending the traditionally female values of compassion and nurturing to the poor. While men have certainly done charity work—John D. Rockefeller, Jr., being perhaps best known for it—they are less likely to dedicate their lives to the cause. Their role has always been to make the money; women have been free to do other things.

The men who have gone into social service see it as one aspect of a well-rounded life and perform the work at a certain remove from the people they serve. The robber barons are the classic examples of this. They all gave substantial sums of money away eventually, but they were proud to have accumulated it first. And in giving it away, they employed the grand style that used to come naturally to billionaires, as they directed their names to be inscribed in block letters on the massive institutions they created for the public good.

Largely because business has traditionally never been considered a fit place for a lady, women have felt that charity was the only work for them. Despite the women's movement's encouragement of work-for-pay, this attitude still held for many of the rich girls I interviewed. While rich boys like Michael Pratt, Max Perlman, and others did their bit of volunteering, their gender was definitely in the minority. Men showed far more interest in making money or spending it than in working to give it away. Rich girls threw themselves into social work in greater numbers with greater gusto just as their socialite mothers had before them. And they may have done so out of fear. Several expressed a reluctance to mix it up in what they saw as the capitalist hurly-burly.

That may be wise. Even more than rich boys, rich girls are softer than their peers in the lower classes. Never having had to hold jobs, many had never formed the hard outer coating required for survival in the marketplace. The only brittleness about them, in fact, often stemmed from the sensitive subject of the money itself. About that they could be quite defensive.

Rebecca Berendt, as I'll call her, was decidedly uptight about her money. A slinky, girlish twenty-eight-year-old, she twisted her rubber-band body into unexpected shapes when I raised the subject of her wealth as we sat together sipping water in her sparse kitchen at her apartment in Boston's Fenway. The dollars got her all wound up. She had only revealed the actual amount of her inheritance, which came down from a wealthy uncle, to her parents and her grandmother. And she quickly grew hostile when I tried to inquire about it. "Why should I tell you?" she asked. "I'm not going to tell you. I've decided for no rational reason that I don't want to say the figure. Clear statement?" The very idea of high finance, in fact, made her head spin, and Rebecca had to ask for a definition of a million dollars. "How many thousand is that?" she wanted to know. "I operate on a twenty-dollar and hundred-dollar basis." Indeed, the money itself caused her discomfort, for when I handed her a five-dollar bill in a little psychological test, she held it daintily by the edge, as if it were somehow contaminated.

Rebecca was a volunteer at a women's outpatient clinic, where she provided counseling to rape victims. She also gave lectures on rape prevention to women's groups around the country. At the clinic she was one of two dozen workers on the nonmedical staff, of whom two were paid; all the others fitted their volunteer efforts in around their professional lives. Rebecca alone had no other job, but she sought no payment for her work at the clinic and tried to refuse it when offered. That sometimes happened after she had accompanied rape victims to court and they expressed their appreciation by pressing some money into her palm. She reacted to it the way she greeted my five-dollar bill. "When people force a few dollars into my hand I'll take them, but it's really against my will," she said. "I try to say no, but they say, 'Please take this. Please.' So I do. I don't think it's right to accept money too readily."

Rebecca had held a number of arts-related jobs in the Northeast, ranging from art gallery clerk to movie producer's assistant, but she rarely received a salary for them. "I didn't need the money," she said, "so I didn't go for regular nine-to-five jobs. I figured they'd be too draining." Even this one at the clinic preserved her energy and independence, since she could work out of her apartment and set her own hours. That way she could make time for her artistic pursuits as a composer and short-story writer. In her threadbare apartment, the only luxuries in evidence were a good stereo system and an electric piano. "I've taken the fall into possessions," she said grandly.

While Rebecca said she was perfectly comfortable working as a volunteer and ascribed any uncertainty to her mother's nagging her to establish a career for herself like other college-educated women, she admitted that it did feel awkward at times to be the odd one out. "It's hard being different from most of my friends," she said. "In our society, it's practically like I'm unemployed. It would be a lot easier for me to say, 'I have a job and I do this and I get this much for it.' Then it would be like I had my little place of importance. In a way I have that with my work with rape victims, but not entirely. And I'm not publishing the things I write, so that's not too glamorous. With my music, I'm not giving performances. I keep very busy, but I don't have the official 'I make so much money and therefore I'm worth this' type of thing that's socially acceptable. The words 'volunteer worker' don't get much respect. Somehow it seems more serious if you're getting paid for something."

Her volunteer work did, however, have its benefits, even if they weren't pecuniary. Most importantly, she felt she was doing a lot of good for the rape victims she assisted at the clinic, who tried to express their thanks in what they took to be the universal language of money, and for the women in the audience for her speeches, who felt more secure for hearing her speak. Despite the coaxings of her mother, Rebecca found some reward simply in being clear of the grubbier aspects of the capitalist world. Sensing that relations with colleagues at a corporation were rife with competitive tension, she appreciated the relatively calm and supportive atmosphere at the clinic. "It's more comfortable going to our meetings," she said, "than to others where there's a lot more stuff going on, where people are trying to climb the ladder to more money, or more power. There aren't any ladders around for us to climb."

By the same token, at the clinic she also escaped the greater combat over how the spoils of capitalism have been divided, since she clearly wasn't turning her share to personal advantage. Still, as an heiress, she had been one of the big winners, and that fact got Rebecca all twisted up.

While she was pleased to have the money, glad about the way it allowed her to pursue her interests, she was conscious of the way her blessings might look to others and felt she was the target of nearly universal envy. She was very sensitive to the veiled hostility in comments people made about the rich. When she had once overheard a friend remark jokingly about a wealthy acquaintance, "She's so rich, she can laugh at cripples," she smarted for weeks. And she had grown anxious when a popular song came out, called "Eat the Rich," that had detailed the pleasures of consuming Mellons and Oysters Rockefeller. "I see friends of mine tapping their feet to that and I think, 'Hey! Wait a second!' " she said. "And I've been in classes at school where people start talking about revolution, and it sounds like they're going to take out all the preppies and shoot them. When I hear that I start getting alarmed.

"Sometimes I talk to people about it. I say I'm really uncomfortable. I'm an OK person. I'm rich. I'm not going to give away all my money now because it wouldn't do any good. I would be willing to give up all the materialistic benefits I have if we had a good society, but we don't. I would do without my car, even without my record player."

Possibly her own sense of being unfairly singled out helped explain her work. The fear of rape affected all women. It knew no class distinctions, imperiling rich and poor alike. By addressing that issue, Rebecca could escape the isolation of her wealth. Further, she could identify with these victims and thereby expiate her fear that actually she was the attacker.

She said she had never given rape much thought until she took a women's self-defense course at college along with her literary studies. Curiously, the words she used to describe her new awareness could apply just as well to her condition as an heiress. "That course made me really aware of the burden I was going around with," she said. "It was a big thing in my life that was never spoken about. And all sorts of myths surrounded it. You know, like the idea that if you don't wear a bra, you'll get raped. All those experiences that I'd had growing up but never talked about. The self-defense class was a very positive thing, talking about all that for the first time. It was a wonderful experience for me. It changed the way I looked at things, and changed the way I walked down the street. Now, instead of being afraid, I was prepared to fight."

But rape was a subject she could address publicly. It is doubtful that she could ever bring herself to open up about her wealth, or, if she did, that she would get much sympathy.

Rebecca's motivation, like Phoebe's, might be clouded by some personal peculiarities, but her essential rationale was as compellingly straightforward as Jane Addams's or any of the other female social workers of the past: she saw injustice in the world and sought to end it. Since she needed no money, she asked no greater remuneration than seeing her work do good. The Mellon descendant, Heather, was possibly a purer example of this nobility.

Believing it the best way to help mankind, she was training to be a nurse. "My long-term dream is to do pediatric nursing," she said, "in both maternal and child health care. I don't care about making money. I want to go to a developing part of the world, or maybe the rural U.S., just someplace where it is really needed." Like Rebecca, she had received some comments from her family for not showing more ambition, in her case for not pressing to become a full-fledged doctor. Still, Heather was pleased, even excited, by her decision.

Besides, she was continuing a family tradition in another way. For she said she had been inspired by her great-uncle Dr. William Larimar Mellon, Jr., called Larry. Once a cattle rancher in Arizona, he had been moved by a *Life* magazine article about Albert Schweitzer's mission to the poor and sick in Africa. Although nearly forty, he quit ranching and went to medical school. When he got out he looked for the area in the world that most needed medical help. It was Haiti. There, in 1956, he celebrated his forty-sixth birthday by opening L'Hôpital Albert Schweitzer, which he had built for $2 million, most of it his own money, and endowed at $200,000 a year after that, pretty much cleaning out the rest of his assets. Now in his seventies, he has been working there ever since.

Her grandmother introduced Heather to her great-uncle's good work. Heather had regularly made trips to her parents' vacation retreat in the Bahamas. Her grandmother made sure that Heather and her siblings occasionally went a little further to see the other side of the Caribbean paradise. "She takes two of the grandchildren down there every summer to show them the hospital and to see him," said Heather. "I remember the first time I went to the island, I couldn't believe what I was seeing. That was the first time I had ever been taken aback by poverty. The river is where everyone bathes, washes their clothes, and drinks, and it's where all the animals drink. There's constant begging and people washing in puddles in the streets, and crippled people in corners asking for money. What they have on their bodies is all they own. And there are animals with their pelvic bones sticking out. I've been in poorer sections of the U.S. but never seen poverty so intense. It's sad, and the worst of it is in Port-au-Prince, where the dictator lives in a huge white palace with all this squalor around. It's disgusting!"

Heather was proud that her great-uncle was trying to help. "It's neat to see what he is doing," she said. "There's certainly a different spirit at his hospital than at Port-au-Prince. Besides treating people at the hospital, my uncle goes out into the community and teaches them things like building wells. He has worked on cotton spinning, and he tried to get into education. My aunt has set up shops in the hospital for woodworking, weaving, pottery, and painting and has a little store where she can ship things out and make some money for the hospital. My sister and I were there for four days a while ago. We were just visiting, but we worked in the malnourished ward, just playing with the kids. They'd been fed and would be going home soon. That was wonderful. It was just neat to see what you can do."

As soon as Heather was through her nursing program at Georgetown, she was going to make a voyage out like Uncle Larry's and do her part to help. "When you have your dreams," she said, "that's one thing. When you go out and do them, that's another. I would like to go somewhere long enough so it would make a difference. You can go to the Peace Corps for a couple of years, and you get personal growth, but it's hard to say if you've made any impact. Long-term means a lot. If I got there and liked it, I'd stay. I like the idea of getting down to basics. I like simple things, the fundamentals; food, health, love. Maybe the thing that symbolizes best the way I am is that I like to go barefoot. I like the feeling of the earth under my feet."

Yet the money doesn't always free up the heirs for volunteerism. Sometimes it weighs them down so heavily that they just fall into it. While that may sound like a bleak description of a saint's calling, it only reflects the way many participants speak of it themselves. In this view of the world, a paying job stands on a mountaintop and a nonpaying job down in the valley. It's where you end up if you can't muster the energy to start climbing.

"What am I doing?" asked Daniel Griswold, the self-sacrificing San Francisco therapist to wife-beaters. "That's my least favorite question in the world. I would *love* to have a good answer to it. There have been years when I have almost had to make something up to say what I'm doing. Even now, when I'm . . . when I don't have as much free time as I'd like, I still don't feel as though I'm doing anything at all." Actually, Daniel was able to list five things, all of them volunteer. Besides the counseling, he served on various committees for the Vanguard Foundation, the San Francisco equivalent of George Pillsbury's Haymarket, and he met weekly with like-minded heirs to discuss the common problems of wealth. "We don't discuss the positive aspects," he said. "It's hard for me to think of any positive aspects."

Daniel dropped into the counseling when he couldn't think what else to do. He said that he had only done one "adventuresome" thing in his life, and that was to teach English in night school in Taiwan after his sophomore year in college for a program called Volunteers in Asia. He had been to Europe so many times with his parents that he wanted to travel somewhere different. He had been studying Chinese in college, largely on a whim, and so his thoughts went eastward. The teaching did not go well. "I made it through all right," he said. "But inside myself I knew I was a failure. I hated the teaching. I didn't feel like I had enough personality or enough ego to be up in front of a classroom. I didn't feel I was qualified to be the focus of all these people's attention and directing things and making decisions."

Partly to figure out what had gone wrong, he enrolled in

a graduate program in counseling. "That was a psychological ploy on my part," he said. "I saw it as a way to improve myself. To become a counselor, I had to learn all sorts of things that I thought would be good for me to learn, like becoming less shy, more outgoing, more extroverted, less self-absorbed, better at making contact with people, better able to communicate. Maybe that's just not in my nature, though."

Once he had the degree, he felt obliged to put it to use, and that led him to the counseling job. But it hadn't satisfied him. "I can work hard," he said, "but I don't feel stimulated to do it. I feel I lack the stamina. It's funny, too, because I used to spend hours absorbed in learning Chinese. These days, I find myself quickly turning away and doing other things. Like in the counseling sessions, I'm supposed to do write-ups right afterward, but I always put them off."

Partly, the problem was that he had so little empathy for the men he was counseling. With his girl friend Carole, he never got so worked up that he could imagine hitting her. If anything, he had the opposite problem: he didn't care enough either way. "I don't love Carole," he said, with a frankness that was softened by his gentle manner. "That's what it comes down to. I have fantasies about falling in love, but that's about it. About the only way I'm violent toward her is the way I withdraw affection. I'll hold out from her for a period, and then I'll feel contrite afterward the way these men do."

But that disposition reflected a deeper and more widespread attitude toward the world that was doubtless aggravated, if not entirely caused, by his wealth. It allowed him to withdraw not just from Carole, and from the men he counseled, but from the world at large. Like the Buddhist monk he had failed to become, he could live life at one remove. Because of his money, he saw himself as different. With his money, he could stay that way.

While other volunteers felt the same way, they went one step further and used the money to join back up with their fellowman. In their non- or low-paying social work they could, as Heather put it, feel the ground under their feet once again.

But Daniel was too caught up in the striving capitalist mentality to take any comfort in that. He felt that the value of a job was only determined by how much it paid, and, what's worse, that he was only worth what he could earn. That made him feel pretty low when he wasn't making anything. "It would be wonderful to have confirmation that somebody else feels I'm worth paying, that what I am doing is valuable both to that person and to society," he said, "But as it is . . ." His voice dwindled away. He had bought the capitalist vision totally: you are what you earn. In his *pro bono* job, he was doing work that only he seemed to value. And that wasn't enough.

Should you go after money you don't really need? Like so many other issues raised by inherited wealth, the question went to the heart of the prevailing social order. Do you establish your own value system separate from that of nearly everyone else? Or do you get along by going along? Cary Ridder, of the newspaper chain, had faced this question for the ten years of her working life. A cheery, vivacious young woman, Cary talked to me while she fixed some veal and scallions for dinner at the colorfully decorated house she had bought for herself and her husband in a middle-class section of Washington, D.C.

Cary was executive director of a group lobbying to retain the discount mail rates for nonprofit institutions. Personally, Cary operated for profit, and she was thrilled to report that she was making one. "They pay me," she said, her face lighting up. "Yeah! That's important. Nonnegotiable! I have taken the long road from volunteerism to pay-me-when-you-can to this job where I'm paid just like everyone else. And it's the best thing I've ever done."

For Cary, it had been a long struggle, in which she not only had, like Daniel Griswold, to overcome doubts about her own self-worth but also to overcome what she saw as a prejudiced and exploitative attitude toward the rich. In her last job, for example, as a consultant for another lobbying group opposed to strip mining, she had been doing a project for the National Wildlife Federation when the funding ran short. Cary's directors had an idea about where to economize. "They cut me off," she said. "I had a fit about it! My boss took me aside and said, 'Nobody is going to cry elephant tears for you if you don't get paid. We know you'll eat whether you get paid or not. I said, 'I quit.'

"I decided that if I wasn't going to get paid, I wasn't going to work. I was really freaked out about it. Totally! I thought I'd finally reached a point where my boss understood that I expected to be paid for my work. That's the way the world operates, and I'm no different. Just because I had money doesn't mean the organization should benefit from it. That's *my* benefit. My money is for *me*—not for them! If I want to give it away, that's great. If I don't, that's great. I really think that. There was a time when I thought, 'I've got money. I'm rich. I'm privileged. I should do this or that.' That was my guilt phase. Well, people just took advantage of me. Not just one too many times. Ten too many times. I said, 'Screw it!'

"Now I work with a group of professionals, and the subject of my money hasn't come up once. They're professional. They're in it to make money, and they don't sit around and wonder why I work. They figure I need the money or I wouldn't be there. And I do need the money. I want to live very well."

Like other rich kids, Cary had to work hard to reach a conclusion that others might have come to automatically. But she had further to travel. The money had swept her away. To get back, she had to fight her way through the expectations of her family, then of her class, and finally of the world at large. Only then could she assume her position as a regular hard-working person "like everybody else."

She thought that her troubles started in her childhood in a family of overachievers. She felt she wasn't worthy of the wealth she was born into, and that she had to strain to become its equal. "My family had very high expectations for us," she said. "I played a lot of mind games and went through a lot of uncertainty about who I was. Being a Ridder, I was expected to be just brilliant. I felt a lot of things pushing in on me. I had to be socially outgoing, successful, and lead a brilliant career. When it turned out that we children were just mortal—well! We always felt that we had to be something more."

In Cary's case, the results were nearly tragic. After graduating from high school, she considered herself a failure at eighteen because she only got into Stanford, not the prestigious Radcliffe. Perhaps as a consequence, her politics drifted leftward, she fell in love with an activist, and in 1968 she found herself in a radical collective house outside Stanford University. Her housemates included a gang of Marxist-Leninists who ultimately turned into the Symbionese Liberation Army, the ones who nabbed Patty Hearst. For the time being they had another heiress in their grasp.

"They had guns all over the house," Cary remembered. "Shotguns, pistols, illegal M-1s and M-19s. They had them stashed everywhere—under the bed, in the umbrella stand. And some were not only loaded, but cocked! I thought to myself, 'I'm living in a nuthouse. These people are nuts!'

"I'm lucky to be alive. My boyfriend went to jail for throwing rocks and leading violent riots. When he got out, he brought home this guy who'd been in jail with him. That guy screwed us! He stole money from us. And he hid drugs in the house. He was going to snitch on us—squealing to the police so he could get better terms for his parole. That was the lowest of the low. I decided I wanted out."

So discouraged was she about the way she had been treated by the men in her life—her boyfriend and his friend primarily, but also her father and, possibly, even the four brothers of her grandfather's generation who founded the newspaper chain and the family fortune—she went to live in a lesbian household that wouldn't even let men in the door unless they were specifically invited. "It was very intense," said Cary. She quickly became disillusioned with the gay life and headed into therapy—group therapy, California style. "It was a mix, a couple of therapists in encounter groups—touchy feely, with a little bit of *est* and 'body stuff' thrown in. There were lots of weekend marathons where we'd sit together in a room with thirty to fifty other people for two days. We'd play these little games, and one person would stand up and say, 'I hate my body,' and others would pick it up—'What can you do not to hate your body?' and, 'What specific part of it don't you like?' I was involved with that for two years. I was pretty screwed up."

RICH KIDS

As I listened to her tale, I thought of Annie Owen's sister Carole, the one who committed suicide because she could never get a hold on her good fortune, and the other rich kids who felt they stuck out in the antiwar generation. Cary suffered from the same disjunction between her privilege and the world's pain. Since then, she had come to recognize that her involvement with radical politics and hostility toward the "owners of the means of production"—a phrase that often rolled off her lips in her Marxist-Leninist days—reflected a deeper antagonism within herself. For Cary, it all boiled down to one monstrous feeling of, as she said, "self-hate."

After finally graduating from college with a degree in medieval history, she moved to San Francisco and pondered what to do next. Possibly the most natural choice was to go to work for one of the family newspapers, but that was blocked by the family policy of excluding Ridder women. Nevertheless, as it often does for rich kids, her indecision derived from too many choices, not too few, and she reacted to this wealth the same way she reacted to her other one. "I could do a million and one things," she explained. "If I'd had to make a living, I'm sure I would have buckled down and selected one. But as it was, I felt overwhelmed by all the things I figured I could do in theory but couldn't do in fact. I felt like a failure, and anything that I decided to do would be doomed to failure. I was depressed—catatonic."

In her depression, she retreated alone to her bedroom and didn't come out. "It was a dark little room in a working-class section of San Francisco," she said, "and I just couldn't get out of bed. I wasn't totally alone. Friends came by occasionally. I played records and smoked a lot of dope. All I wanted to do was throw the covers over my head. I gained tons and tons of weight. I just wanted to hide. I was so scared! I thought I was worthless and stupid and ugly. I just couldn't, *couldn't*, get up in the morning."

Throughout this trauma, in which she was so completely out of touch with the world, she thought it was pretty ironic that the money continued to roll in from her trust fund month by month, dependable as the phases of the moon. In the last few months before she went into hiding she had started concealing it more methodically than in the past. "But it wasn't so much that I wanted to hide my money," she said. "I just wanted it *away* from me." As she sank into her depression and her lethargy, however, one of her few pleasures was seeing how little the trust-fund checks affected her. Compared to everything else that was happening, the money no longer mattered. It had lost its sting.

"I stayed in bed for weeks at a time. I started seeing a therapist and she knew what was happening to me, but she couldn't stop it. She just said: 'OK, go to bed. When you get bored and feel like doing something you'll do something.' She felt I'd pull myself together. Her therapy sessions at least gave my life some structure. All the rest of the time I was in bed."

The therapist was right, for Cary got up for good when a friend asked her to manage the office for David Harris, then the husband of Joan Baez and a leader in the antiwar movement, in his congressional campaign, and Cary didn't want to say no. That job was unpaid, a tentative early foray into the world of work. She liked it. It made her feel purposeful, even though the campaign was ultimately unsuccessful. When the campaign was over, she gave herself the "luxury of not working" and took a brief trip to India with her grandmother. When she returned, she got into her lobbying work in Washington and began her professional life in earnest.

"I always knew that I was a candidate for going over the edge," she explained. "And when it finally happened that summer in San Francisco I felt a whole lot better. I wasn't waiting anymore for doom to descend. It descended. That was really the bottom of the barrel for me. I went past what I thought was socially acceptable to a state that was clearly socially unacceptable. I went past the point of stability, past the point where the facade of sanity can be maintained. I acknowledged that I was not in balance, that things were not working for me. But I survived. I thought: I went through all that and I'm still here. And I could go on. And it was through all that, that I came to terms with the money. It kept coming in. And in the end I learned not to think about it anymore. I was so far gone, it wasn't an issue."

RICH KIDS

And now, Cary had reached the ultimate goal—doing work she valued and the world valued by paying her for it. And in doing so, she had done what so many other rich kids had tried to do, many failing: she had taken her fortune and made it hers, and then she had moved on.

PART V

Places

11

There's No Place
Like Home

In lieu of cash, a young woman I'll call Wendy inherited
what she termed "an unusual piece of property": a million-
dollar Frank Lloyd Wright house. It's a flat-topped, Persian-
looking structure made of wood, glass, and precast cement
built over a reflecting pool on a hillside in southern California.

A friend in Boston told me about Wendy and her property;
it turned out that I would be staying with friends right nearby.
So as soon as I got out there, I called her. After some initial
confusion over who I was and what I wanted, Wendy sounded
jovial. She told me to come right by and take a look at the
house. But what she didn't say was that she wouldn't be there
to let me inside. At least she didn't answer my buzz. So I
found myself conscious once again of the many barriers to
entry into rich kids' lives.

RICH KIDS

But Wendy and I had at least enjoyed a good chat over the phone. She'd grown up in the house, and since inheriting the place in 1975, she told me, she had devoted her life to maintaining it. "It's easy and nice not doing a nine-to-five," she said. "I was never caught up in the women's-liberation business of achieve, achieve." The house itself was built of stout redwood sealed to a nearly hermetic tightness between a pair of chunky wooden pillars. The only homey touch was a freestanding mailbox by the driveway, the kind with the metal flag, that bore no name. While such stout defenses naturally arouse curiosity, Frank Lloyd Wright seemed to have expressly designed his structure to keep such curiosity from being satisfied. The fortifications were virtually impregnable. The walls were so sheer and the joints so tight, they'd keep a spider from sneaking in.

As I looked the place over, first standing on tiptoe, then jumping, to try to peek over the wooden fence into the ravine that was Wendy's backyard and squinting the wrong way into the fish-eye lens of the door to get a look at the house's interior, I remembered something that Wendy had told me over the phone. "This house is my inherited wealth," she had said.

And so it was. She meant those words literally: she had received no other inheritance. But the words had a deeper figurative truth. For all rich kids, their wealth is a kind of private house. They live in it. It shelters them and walls them off. The nonwealthy have their own structures to their lives, but the houses of rich kids are bigger, grander, more astonishing. Theirs are like Wendy's: of unique designs, with a long and meaningful history behind them. They are built by an ancestor, lived in by their parents, and now the rich kids' own to tend and decorate in a continuing effort to make them truly theirs. While they may entertain other careers, their mission is simply to keep their house in order. And that task is long and arduous, for it so often seems that the whole business is in danger of pitching down the hill. Although the house may appear to others to be a museum, to them it's their home, their one true home. They don't treat gawkers kindly. Only the rich kids themselves will ever truly know what it is to live there.

But while the rich kids' money may provide the metaphorical structure to their lives, they also have a real house, a visible one, that approximates this figurative version. At least I suppose it does; I guess I'll never know for sure. It's nearly as hard to get in to see this residence, though, as the other invisible kind. Just like Wendy with her Frank Lloyd Wright creation, other rich kids weren't too keen to let me into their private abodes. It was one thing for them to tell me all about their lives. It was quite another to show me their houses. So, for my interviews, we usually met in restaurants, or coffee shops, or their office. But a few more trusting rich kids told me to come on over to their houses, and I certainly heard about the others, for interior decorating is one of the rich kids' greatest passions.

Like Wendy's, again, the homes of the rich kids today don't welcome attention. The Vanderbilts might have spent their lives vying with each other to see who could build the most opulent château on Fifth Avenue. They wanted everybody to see how rich they were. For the rich kids of today, a different standard applies. All that is left of the castles are a few nondescript stout walls and, as in Annie Owen's case, an occasional moat. Just as the kids rarely dress for show, they don't as a rule buy houses for effect either: no turrets, no porticoes, no banners flying. To judge by the exterior, you would never guess a rich kid lived inside. True to their essential character as foreigners in their own country, they live behind blank walls that look blank precisely because of their careful conformity to the rest of the neighborhood. Some of this is by economic necessity: the family fortunes have been divided and subdivided with each passing generation since Vanderbilt days, while real-estate prices have doubled and doubled again. So, as the great-grandparents' house overshadowed the grandparents', and the grandparents' the parents', the parents' now generally dwarfs the kid's. Even rich kids face some limits.

But they are still a lot better off than other kids their age, better off, even, than most of those kids' parents. And so they face a big decision as they contemplate where and in what style to settle down. It's a decision, like so many others in their lives, with numerous options, but no obvious choice.

RICH KIDS

Wherever they settle—and they can settle anywhere—rich kids are always interlopers. While other Americans sort themselves out into different neighborhoods according to their social status or ethnicity, rich kids have no place where they naturally feel they belong. They don't necessarily identify with their "own kind," but even if they did, they would be hard pressed to produce sufficient numbers to populate much of a neighborhood.

So they slip into social strata other than their own and buy up houses or apartments that look, on the outside at least, perfectly average for the locale. But because of their own hidden differences, they are always significantly at odds with their neighbors. Roberta Bernstein had gone into a closet at age three because of her wealth, but she was no less closeted from the world in her adulthood. To stay within the means of her husband, she lived in a middle-class neighborhood in the Midwest. And she kept her neighbors in the dark about her background—until the week Roberta and her husband went off on vacation. They asked the people next door to take in their mail while they were away. On their return, Roberta encountered such amazed looks as the neighbors delivered a cardboard box full of fat envelopes bearing stock information, bank notices, and investment advice, not to mention all the money mail, that Roberta was sure her secret was out for good.

Rich kids are misfits wherever they end up. If they select a well-to-do neighborhood in, say, Washington's Georgetown or Dallas's River Oaks, they are probably a good deal younger and less accomplished than the rest of the community, most of whose members have been working much of their adult lives to afford such a place. If they opt for a middle-class section of Arlington, Virginia, their neighbors might not exceed them in age or work experience, but they would fall quite short in taste, education, or worldliness. If the kids take the plunge and move to a factory town like Lansing, Michigan, they are sure to find themselves in a community of one. If, finally, they decide to get away from it all to live in rural isolation like Laurance Rockefeller's daughter Marion—off in caboose number 694 somewhere in the mesa of northern California—

they may indeed escape curious neighbors, but who knows what they'll find?

Wherever the rich kids settle, their home truly is their castle (even if it lacks the turrets), their place of refuge from a pestering world. While the house may present a blank exterior to the world, the rich kids decorate the interior as they please. At home they can drop the appearances they affect out on the street and finally be themselves. And I was surprised sometimes at what I found there.

I had a wondrous moment in Alex Trammel's apartment on Wilshire Boulevard. Having quit his job as an I-banker to spend six years "thinking," he was obviously a strange bird, and I never knew what to expect during my brief visit one afternoon in the winter of 1983. We sat in his library, he stiffly in a straightback, I struggling to stay afloat on some huge and fluffy pillows on the couch across from him. Although it was nearly four when I arrived, he was wearing a bathrobe and slippers, his neck warmed by a silk ascot. Alex looked at me coldly, never ruffling his smooth features with a smile. As he filled me in on his career as a street person, I asked him if he had ever had any trouble with muggers. "No," he said. "People don't approach me. I'm an expert in physical intimidation." And with that he turned down the temperature on his Frigidaire looks a couple more degrees.

With all this in mind, I was a little alarmed later when I needed to visit his bathroom. Instead of giving directions, he escorted me down the hall, opened a door to a small dark room, practically pushed me inside, and then shut the door tight behind me. That might have been all right, except I couldn't find any light switch. And the door wouldn't budge when I tried to open it. Thinking that Alex was still out in the hall, I yelled out to him but received no answer. I felt around with my hands. No switch. Then, as I walked about fanning the air, a cord brushed against my face. I gave it a yank. A light came on, and I found myself inside a tent, an elaborate Arabian one with flaps and tassels, looking out at a broad and shimmering expanse of sea, sand, and sky. There was a gusty wind, for whitecaps had appeared on the waves, and the tent's tassels bobbed. I could nearly feel the breeze on my cheek.

As my eyes adjusted to the light, I could see that this was all a painted illusion, created by murals covering the four walls and the ceiling. Actually, I was in Alex's bathroom, complete with all the amenities right down to monogrammed towels. At least I thought I was. The toilet flushed, in any case, and water poured from the tap.

By putting my shoulder to the door afterward, I was able to get out, and I found Alex seated once more in the library. When I asked him about the bathroom's sea view, he seemed surprised that I should remark on it. "That scene is a fantasy for me," he said. "It's not reality."

Interesting that he should make the distinction. In his apartment, the line between fantasy and reality had grown as hazy and indefinite as the distant horizon in his bathroom murals. He could create whatever reality he chose and make his fantasies tangible. I could tell just by looking around his library that money was certainly no object. Besides being packed with hardbound books and glossy magazines, the room was stuffed with electronic equipment, from the color TV and VCR in the cabinet to the tape deck, stereo system, portable "boom box," and several other machines I couldn't identify on a shelf beside it. "There is not an electric appliance *made* that is not in this apartment someplace," he told me.

Possibly because so much was to him so cheap, the whole place seemed dreamy and insubstantial, like the soft pillows into which I'd sunk in the library. And as I wandered later among its many rooms, I felt I was floating in a cloud. If one of those shore breezes in the bathroom had ever really whipped up, it could have blown the whole place away. The walls of all the rooms were painted in such soft pastel shades, they seemed hardly like walls at all, more like lighting effects I could have put my hand through if I'd reached out; and the rugs on the floor were so deeply piled I sank into them nearly up to my knees, fearing momentarily there was no true floor beneath.

To decorate the place, Alex had assembled an impressive if idiosyncratic collection of objets d'art. Dominating the living room was a nearly billboard-sized pop-art neon-enhanced image of George Washington, an oversized version of the portrait on a one-dollar bill. In the library were a set of demure English hunting scenes. On a counter in the kitchen were a series of glass-covered boxes on such humorous themes as Barnyard Animals Disguising Themselves As Chickens. Along the hallway were original Toulouse-Lautrec posters. In the dining room, one lampshade was in the shape of a hat.

And those were just the highlights. In places, his collection was so densely packed that some select pieces were actually hidden away inside others, the ultimate, I suppose, in classic understatement. On a shelf in the library stood a miniature wooden bureau. Alex pulled out one of the drawers and held up a tiny card, a prize from a turn-of-the-century pack of cigarettes, showing four camels with liveried drivers walking in step across the desert. "See that?" he said. "That's a *great* image."

Despite the apparent eclecticism, however, one theme predominated, and it was an unlikely one at that—Alex's affection for pigs. They were lurking nearly everywhere I looked: porcelain pigs, neon pigs, pig paintings, stuffed-animal pigs, piggybank pigs.

"Why pigs?" I asked.

Alex allowed himself a moment of levity. "They're real cute, and they're real round," he said. "They're soft, cute, fun images." And as he spoke, the corners of his mouth curled up into the most childlike smile.

Here on the inside of this Fabergé egg of an apartment he has fashioned for himself, I had the creepy sensation that I was wandering through Alex's subconscious. He had brought his house into perfect conformity with his innermost desires, and now I could see them all—the cuddly ones left over from his childhood, the more sophisticated ones he had developed in his years of "thinking," and the deep need for peace and tranquillity that he'd had throughout.

Everyone reveals his secret self to some extent by the way he lives, I suppose, but Alex was curbed by none of the normal restraints of time and money. So he could make manifest every little quirk of his inner life. Rather than conform to the natural limitations of the world, as most people do, Alex had created another world entirely to his liking. If he had sought to reverse the direction of gravity, he could probably have arranged it in his apartment.

He'd already gone to work on some natural laws he considered petty, like the distinction between night and day. He ignored it. He started his day at nine or ten in the evening and went about his business—dancing at his favorite nightclubs. Then he retired at two in the morning for a nap until six, and stayed up until five in the afternoon, when he hit the hay until his "dawn" once more at nine.

I asked when he ate.

"Whenever I'm hungry," he responded with a look that added, *"obviously."*

"No schedule?" I persisted.

"I don't particularly like to eat," he said. "I think for most people eating is a sexual substitute, and I don't need any substitutions."

He looked quite well fed regardless. He added that when he did get around to eating, he usually went out to restaurants. But he watched what he ate and preferred natural foods. "To me," he said, "everything is a drug. I drink an occasional beer, but that's about it for alcohol. I stay away from coffee. If I want to be stimulated in the evening, I'll drink iced tea. I get *wired* from iced tea."

Alex had made iconoclasm into a fine art, expanding on his consciousness to the point where it filled the cosmos. He had jettisoned normalcy by quitting his job to "think"; he had jettisoned reality by building his own version for himself at home. For Alex, being independently wealthy meant being independent—of everything.

There was a quiet knock on the door during our conversation, and an abject face appeared calling Alex to the phone. With a scowl, Alex replied that he was not to be interrupted and that he would call the person back later. The face meekly disappeared. I assumed that this was Alex's servant or houseboy, but it was in fact his lover, "Ted," whom he'd met half a dozen years back during the filming of a *Colombo* episode. Since then, Alex said, except for one vacation, they had almost literally never been apart. Although Alex had spoken highly of Ted, he treated him like an inferior. And Ted appeared to have resigned himself to a lower caste. He had bent to Alex's will, too.

Even though he spent lavishly for electronic appliances, Alex didn't like to hire personal servants. It was a matter of maintaining his privacy, but also of keeping his temple to self uncluttered. "I try to preserve my independence," he said. "As soon as you become dependent on anybody for any-thing, nuisances arise. I'm not interested in having a household staff because I'm not interested in having anybody underfoot. Instead I use people. I invest in them. The only things I do in life are the things that I can't find other people to do as well or better than I can. When I get my car washed, I just have them do the outside. The inside of the car I do myself. There is nobody who can clean the inside of the car like I can. *Nobody.* It doesn't take a long time, just twenty minutes. I don't have a system. I don't always start in the same place. Sometimes certain places in the car are dirtier than others. I have never found anybody who can clean the inside of my car in any satisfactory way. I've tried continually. There are people who can shine my shoes, but very few."

Silly as this diatribe sounded, Alex delivered it with great conviction, as though he had discovered the cure for cancer.

My patience wearing thin, I asked Alex if he could sum himself up in a sentence. "I could," he said. "But it would be a *very* long sentence." He began it fairly promisingly: "Cir-cles are important in life, the yin and the yang . . ." But he began to digress and never did complete his thought, and I took my leave, summing him up for myself as I left, with one last look around his pastel-shaded apartment.

Alex Trammel was the sort of person who could bend life to his will the way psychics disfigure spoons. Within the con-fines of his palace, he could make his world whatever he chose. If that meant turning day to night, or a bathroom to a pasha's tent, small matter. Inside so many layers of financial insulation, what could touch him? For him, life did not proceed from the outside in—from objective reality to his inner soul—but from the inside out. His ego swelled to the limits of the universe. That's what money can do: it doesn't change these rich kids' inner lives so much as reveal them. It provides the colors with which they can paint their characters on the sky.

But not all rich kids are so secure with this power as the imperious Alex Trammel. Such a rarefied, isolated life is unnatural, almost hubristic. Other rich kids may try to cut themselves off from the aspects of ordinary life that don't suit their fancy, but eventually, one way or another, reality comes barging in.

In Fitzgerald's allegorical story, "The Diamond As Big As the Ritz," the wealthy Washingtons live in splendor by chipping off particles of a secret diamond mountain. To keep their treasure to themselves, they tightly control the knowledge of it. For fear that word might leak out, they kill off visitors at the end of their stays and imprison chance explorers who stumble upon their magic mountain. Finally, however, their splendid isolation is broken. One prisoner escapes and sends back bomber planes that end up—despite a last-minute attempt by the elder Washington to dodge his fate by buying off God Himself—blowing their precious mountain to worthless bits.

Wealth can breed that kind of insulated self-absorption. Possessing the one thing that everyone wants, the rich kids retreat with it into their own private world, safe from both the daily cares that don't affect them, and from the rest of the world, which naturally begrudges them their privilege. Yet the temples they oftentimes build for themselves are also temples to their money. For theirs is an existence thick with cash.

Living in a big-city pad scarcely less princely than the jewel-studded palace of the Washingtons, the young man I'll call Albert Kapstein had built a universe for himself in perfect conformity with his desires. But now that it was complete, he told me when I popped in for a visit not long after my encounter with Alex, he was undergoing a change of heart. When he looked out on his creation, he was not pleased. Everything was exactly right, but nothing was right at all.

"Apartments aren't like people," he told me in an inadvertently revealing phrase. "You can't just discard them." But he admitted that he was awfully tempted, and if he didn't have a half-million-dollar investment to recoup he might just let this one go. It was a five-room corner apartment on an upper floor of a proper brick apartment building overlooking a small park in New York City. It was the sort of place that might have found particular favor with Albert's parents' generation, largely because they're the sort of people who could afford it. Indeed, the building was populated mostly by retirees. But Albert did have some neighbors his age just across the hall. To make the mortgage they had had to cram five people into an apartment only one room larger than his. In Albert's five-room palace, there were only Albert and his dog.

The moment I stepped into the building, I could detect the unmistakable aroma of wealth. It was like the scent of a freshly dry-cleaned suit—nearly imperceptible, but there. The lobby floor was freshly waxed, the tiled walls recently polished. Rather than spoil the decor with a bank of clanking mailboxes in the foyer, the management delivered mail individually to the residents, leaving it on small tables outside their apartment doors. The uniformed doormen wore white gloves that were pearly white right down to the fingertips, like the gloves on debutantes. "The service isn't that great," Albert sniffed. "But the guys downstairs usually open the door for you."

Inside Albert's apartment, the same tidy formality reigned. Albert asked me to remove my shoes at the door lest they muss his oriental rugs. I placed them by the wall, next to his Irish setter, Zip, who had curled himself up decorously to snooze in the front hall. Then Albert took me on a tour of his rooms. With its hunting prints and mahogany tables, the place bore the timeless look of an exclusive men's club. Albert's house, though, was a club with only one member. The rooms had some of the club's anonymity, too. The only personal touch in the place was a framed photograph of Albert's college fraternity, and he only displayed that, he said, "because a framed photograph looks good in that spot."

His bedroom was practically barren except for a set of crinkly, silvery curtains on the window and a swelling quilt on the bed. Only his closet had much life in it. It was bursting

289

with clothes; the tie rack on the door could compete with a haberdashery's. His office was cozy, with a desktop that wrapped around him from three walls, and all his books and papers in easy reach. Despite the quantity of possessions, there were some oversights. When we sat down with some coffee in his parlor, he realized he lacked a hot pad for his coffeepot. He had to set it down on an ashtray.

Although not done in pastel shades, the color scheme seemed designed like Alex Trammel's to be easy on the eyes— the perfect place, I imagined, to recover from too much champagne. And, like Alex's, the apartment revealed a side of Albert's character that might otherwise remain hidden: in his case, a longing for security.

Only twenty-six years old, Albert had a middle-aged bearing that might have come from being saddled with so many possibilities at a young age. Dressed in Brooks Brothers clothes, he sank uncomfortably into the soft pillows of his white couch like a man in over his depth. Black Mr. Peabody-style glasses rested no more gracefully on his wide nose. "I'm basically a schnook with a lot of money and good taste," he said.

Albert was the son of a well-known and spectacularly successful entrepreneur in electronics who had created the family fortune. His grandfather, however, had been a tailor. And Albert betrayed some confusion over which line of the family he was continuing. Despite his money and cultivated tastes, he thought of himself as thoroughly middle-class. "I come from peasant stock," he said. "Basically, my family was in the rag business. My father climbed two steps up by virtue of his education. He worked hard, got lucky, and did very well."

His class identification was an issue because, with his inheritance, Albert could select his level of affluence the way ordinary people might decide on a brand of detergent at a grocery store. After some soul-searching, Albert opted for the highest quality and started climbing the golden arches of consumerism to their peak. With this apartment he felt he had finally arrived. But now that he was here, he found himself looking longingly down the far side.

The ascent began shortly after Albert received the first spoils of his father's success at twenty-one. "It was a strange feeling to be a multimillionaire in college," he said. "My father put a lot of trust in me to see if I'd be corrupted." Corruption to both Kapsteins meant spending the fortune "lavishly." Albert tried to fight the urge but ultimately couldn't resist. "I went through a stage of extravagance," he admitted. "I set myself up as a little king in my senior suite. I felt I'd reached the pinnacle of life. After college I flew to France every year and dined at three-star restaurant after three-star restaurant. I bought my girl friend tons of clothing. We'd zip around the country to have my suits made, three or four every season."

The big extravagance, however, was his fabulous apartment, which he bought in 1980. Although initially he had shared his father's scornful attitudes toward "corruption," he now felt that spending money wasn't in itself so awful, provided it was done in good taste. Besides, it allowed him an avenue of competition with his father in which he could win. He knew that he could never equal his father in production, so he tried instead to keep up with him in consumption. "I bought this place to keep up with my parents," he declared. "I felt it was important to match their basic possessions. They have a large place across town, and I saw the opportunity of living this way slipping away from me. I thought that it was necessary to live this way to be happy."

He secured one of the city's finest (or at least highest-priced) interior decorators and went to work. "I'm an artist creating my environment," he said. He outlined for me his decorative philosophy, which stemmed from a canny appraisal of his fundamental nature. Like Alex Trammel, he was constructing himself in three dimensions. "There are three ways to live. There's the modern apartment; the traditional apartment, either English or French; and there's fine antiques. I figured I couldn't afford the antiques. The modern sleek style wasn't for me, because I'm much more formal than that. I don't walk around in leather pants, or sit in a leather sofa with a big arc lamp higher than my head. I don't like high tech. It's cold. That modern stuff just isn't me. It doesn't last. And French traditional was too froufrou. But this sort of thing"—he gestured around at all the mahogany—" is timeless and it's nice. I like to make a long-range investment. I don't like to think of having to change everything every five years. I have been in some of those modern places. Just the other day I was in one that was renovated in 1976, and you know what? It looked like it was done in 1976. It was dated."

Little by little, Albert put his house in order, but it did take time. And, of course, it took money—over a hundred thousand a year for three years. He went for months with an empty dining room because he couldn't find just the right table for the space. And the coffee table in his living room was an even bigger decision. "I agonized about it for a long time," he said, "because I wanted it to be right. Every piece in this apartment has meaning and place. I thought about all of it with my designer to make sure it looks right. I like everything to be in its place. I don't like to walk into somebody's house and feel that it's just been put together. It makes me think that they don't care about how it feels." For the coffee table he finally settled on an English boat table, the rounded kind with hinged flaps that fold up. As it happened, Albert was going to put the finishing touches on his creation and fill the blank space on the wall behind the living room couch with two more English prints the very afternoon we spoke. "Now I feel at peace with myself because everything is settled, everything is in place," he said with all the contentment of the octogenarian who, having apportioned his estate, was looking forward to his heavenly rest.

But all was not completely harmonious, it turned out, no matter how well the furnishings matched. The more Albert delved into his true feelings about his abode, the deeper into unhappiness he sank. The turning point, he confided, had come only recently. Eight months back, Albert had gone through a massive life change in which he broke off his engagement when he concluded that his fiancée was less interested in him than in his money. A few days after that he'd quit a $55,000-a-year job as an executive for Xerox to return to his apartment and heal his wounds. He signed on with a psychotherapist, but a more important way to remake himself, he felt, was to pull his apartment together at last.

Now the place was the highest and most perfect expression

of himself. That was fine. The trouble came with other people. Alex Trammel hadn't had to worry about this because he rarely let other people in and didn't bother too much about them when he did. Albert got lonely if people didn't come around from time to time, and he cared about them. But the problem was, the place was so exquisite, his friends were reluctant to drop in for fear of mussing the decor. "They seem to feel they need a formal invitation," he said gloomily. "They don't come unless I invite them. Even close friends don't invite themselves over. It's not that casual a place. *I* don't even feel all that comfortable here."

Like Frankenstein's monster, Albert's creation was starting to impose its own will on its creator, requiring a high standard that even Albert felt a bit put out to attain. He gave parties that were more formal than he might like, just because they would "go" with the setting. For the upcoming New Year's he was planning a black-tie party, the latest in a series of social events that he staged every two months. "It'll be a big production," he said grimly. "It's a real pain in the ass. But I have to do it that way because of this place." Just the other day, he had tried spreading the Sunday paper out on the living room couch to read it in utter relaxation with his feet up. He couldn't do it; he had to tidy the pages back up and read them properly in a straightback chair. "It was a violation," he said. The windows that he had once loved for their golden light and splendid sunset views now left him feeling too exposed. "I don't feel that secure here, actually," he said. "I prefer a place where I can't see the world all the time. Here I see out into the world too much. I want to be more insular. I feel I'm on the inside looking out all the time. I don't feel protected. I'm too aware of the elements—*all* of them, noise, people, weather." Even the very peace of the apartment had started to mock him, because it left him feeling so isolated. "I feel lonely in a place this big," he said, and then added enigmatically, "I cannot encompass this space in a single thought."

He had decided to move on; he couldn't take any more. After his years at the top, he'd decided to check out the view from a lower altitude. "Being where I am isolates me in society," he said. "It's lonely at the top. My friends are resentful—they don't live like this. This is an awesome place. I want to be like my friends. I don't want to set myself up on a pedestal. If I bring a girl home, she's blown away by this. It would be different, I suppose, if I were going out with the Princess Sophia of the Duchy of Izvestia or somebody, but I'm not. I just go out with middle-class women. So I'm consciously moving to someplace less opulent. I'm going to have to live more modestly. It doesn't look good."

Now Albert had decided that all he needed were the "simple" things in life, such as "fresh water, fresh fish, fresh bread." And into that category he now would put a smaller apartment, "a bachelor pad, with just room enough for me and Zip." But he wouldn't push simplicity to the point of austerity. "I'm not going to slum it," he said. He'd like to have a terrace and a garden to look out on from his bedroom. "I want to get in touch with the natural world.

"Rich people are totally misunderstood," he concluded. "The richer they are, the more unhappy. People who live in the finest places, jet about the globe, take limousines, and are untouched by all the crap, they're miserable. I know them through their designers, and they're so fucked up! And you can see how little wealth does for me. When I was in the depths of my depression, when I was breaking up with my girl friend, and this place wasn't finished and it was noisy, I realized how little wealth does for me. All the stuff I could buy didn't do a thing for me. And I realized how vulnerable I was. And now, emotionally, I'm more in tune with the simpler things—fresh bread, coffee. I have fewer things of greater quality. I don't have any crap, any clutter. It's pretentious to be too perfect. I don't add any more, I get rid of things." And now he was going to get rid of his apartment.

Albert's place was a one-bedroom, a pad for him alone, and that was a big part of his problem. He'd love to share it, but since it was designed to his rarefied taste, it was not the kind that attracts company.

Richard Potter, the multimillionaire who was "doin' it," turning his inheritance into yet more money, had adopted a different and more inclusive strategy at his thirty-acre country place in Kerrville, Texas, which he called "the Villa." It was a former girls' school, built in 1890 on a hillside in a Spanish style with arches and painted tile floors. His father had bought the property but never done anything with it. When Richard came into it, he saw the school's gymnasium, stables, guest-houses, ponds, and greenhouses and immediately recognized its festive potential.

"The Villa is really becoming kind of a game place," he told me at his office, his cowboy boots up on his big desk, in the glowing, happy way he discussed much of his life. "It's pretty much your ultimate 'Let's go have fun someplace' place." If life for him really was a big game of Monopoly, as his friend and partner Jimmy Wynne had said, then this was Park Place. So far, he'd put about $300,000 into it. And, in accordance with his investment philosophy, he wasn't spending the money just to profit by himself. His idea was to pull others in. This was no private retreat. It was more like a hotel with Richard's friends as nonpaying guests.

He'd installed a big swimming pool and set up a jukebox beside it for "little sock hops." He'd got those moneymaking ostriches going behind fences by the house, and, if he could resist the $500-per-egg selling price, he was thinking of trading a few of them for some other animals to start a small zoo, starting with zebras and llamas. "The animals can just wander there along beside you," he said, "so you can walk in and pet 'em or play with 'em or whatever. They can't mess up the yard." He'd already stocked the ponds with goldfish which had procreated so fast that the water had a golden hue. He'd refurbished the basketball court in the gym for some intra-mural action. He'd put in a regulation horseshoe pitch. And he'd gotten thoroughly hooked on croquet.

That all started when an antique croquet set turned up at the location for a promotional photo he'd hired an agency to take for his exotic-car business. He had the Dallas Cowboys Ed "Too Tall" Jones and Tony Hill in the picture, too, along with some antique Rolls-Royces. But what caught Richard's eye were the croquet mallets and colored balls and spindly wickets. He'd bought the set on the spot, taken it back to the Villa, set it up on the lawn, which he had always kept trimmed to "golf-green-like" height, and let her rip. "Me and Jimmy and some of the guys started messing around with it and playing some and it was really fun, so I ended up making some heavy-duty hoops and refinishing the whole set, repainting the balls and all. We just got into this real, like, regular thing playing croquet. We'll play anytime. I've got lights up for the evening, and if it gets too hot, you can always jump right into the pool. It's great. We had a big party on July fourth and we had a whole play-off. Jimmy and I were the last two. Jimmy won, but that's fine with me. My yard is so perfect for it, and everybody has such a good time doing it, we went on to get a certificate that I've got framed here on my office wall saying that we're members of the United States Croquet Association. There are only three clubs in Texas. We are the Kerrville chapter, at the Villa Seralita Country Club. That's my house. We're invited to play in Central Park for the championship in September. I may just do it."

In the meantime, Richard was thinking of other fun to have. With his Iranian houseboy, Meir, and a couple of migrant Mexicans, he spent last summer reclaiming acres of the surrounding hilly shrubland for his yard. "We really got into sprinklers," he said. He's not sure exactly what he's going to do with the newly conquered terrain, beyond its being "for some kind of game." He's thinking of acquiring some ultra-lights, flying bicycles, so he can take to the air to view his estate from a new angle, or, possibly, buying a two-man helicopter to complement his small planes. But for certain, any future activities will be games that more than one can play. Just as he found it fun—and profitable—to bring other people in to share the excitement of his drilling, so he found that the fun of others redounded to enhance his own. It was like an investment that way: the more he put in, the more he got out. As he said, "One thing that I have noticed is that, with all the things we've got going at the Villa, the greatest enjoyment I get comes from seeing other people happy. I don't really do the stuff there for me, so that I can sit back and think, 'Isn't money nice.' I do it so other people can enjoy it. *That's* what's fun for me." I pictured everybody frolicking by the pool, knocking croquet balls about the lawn, flying through the air in the ultralights. I was a little sorry not to receive an invitation to witness these pleasures firsthand, but I figured I'd intruded far enough on Richard's life. As with other details of these rich kids' lives, I'd have to leave the Villa Seralita Country Club in Kerrville, Texas, to my imagination.

Living in their little pockets of affluence, all the rich kids saw their isolation as the primary burden they had to bear. Richard Potter eased his by turning his country house into an adult camp. That was fine for a vacation, but, eventually, all vacations have to end. What about their homes in town? How can a rich kid keep his home from reproducing the "lovely prisons" of his childhood as Albert Kapstein had, wiling away his days in a gilded cage? How can life be structured, without being confining? How can life be free, without losing all its bearings?

I had met the filmmaker Helen Strauss at a SoHo coffee shop for our first talk. She said her place was too messy for visitors, but I suspected that she simply wasn't sure she wanted me inside. Even more than the other rich kids, Helen was careful about what she showed of herself, and to whom. I had enjoyed meeting her for coffee and had come away impressed with the way she was managing her film career with such dedication. I felt an increasing curiosity to see her home. She had spoken of it so warmly, saying she was so glad to find a place that was truly hers, that I thought it might solve the mystery of who she was as tidily as her work answered the question of what she should do.

After I returned to Boston, I let a decent interval pass and then called her back up. I told her I wanted to ask her a few more questions. Would she mind if I came back down to see her at her house? There was a long pause on the end of the line, and then we set a date.

The directions to a rich kid's house can get complicated, I'd already found. In Helen's case, the problem was that her door bore no street number. And, as usual for rich kids, there was nothing about the place's outer appearance that would make anyone think that it was anything special. Her building was a former warehouse in what she termed a "low rent" section of New York, and it was indistinguishable from the other warehouses around it, except that most of the others were still in their original use. The street was filled with delivery trucks and grimy warehousemen. Because her front door lacked a street number, I had to scrutinize all the other entrances on the block before I found hers. I was relieved when, after I buzzed, the front door clicked open. I climbed up a dark staircase one flight to her floor. As I approached I could hear the sound of several bolts and locks being released, and then her door swung open. And there Helen was. As she ushered me inside, I felt immediately that I was entering a new dimension of light and color—and time.

Sunlight streaming in the windows turned silver and golden as it passed through a collection of old glass jugs perched on the sill and poured into the living room. It made the colorful, angular-patterned rug shimmer electrically, and the towering Rhapas tree glowed as though its roots and leaves were filled with neon. The crystal glasses and shiny new countertops of the adjoining kitchen sparkled as if they were in a TV ad for the wonders of Spic 'n' Span. Everything was sun-spangled.

"What you are seeing," she admitted sheepishly, "is total ostentation."

But it was not all brand-new. While the functional items, from the white couch to the Advent TV (for showing her movies and those of her friends), were of recent vintage, the adornments Helen displayed were all antique, as if to say: I live in the modern world, but I am proud of my past. The furnishings were all early American of the highest and most expensive quality: a bench from the 1640s; an eighteenth-century chair with whimsical duck feet; a patchwork quilt; an ancient bronze rooster; and, on one wall, a whole series of primitive American chairs, last sat on, I imagined, by the pilgrims. I sensed them now being occupied by the spirits of her ancestors. Lit by track lighting, the furnishings were displayed like museum pieces.

Like Wendy's Frank Lloyd Wright house, though, Helen's

place was not a museum but a home. However impressive her collection, Helen's furniture represented to her the most significant aspects of her past; along with her father's movies of her mother, it was her most valuable inheritance, for it was all she had left to remind her of the grandmother who brought her up. And she felt as comfortable with all the antiques as she did sleeping in the darling lace-covered canopy bed in her bedroom next door, or, for that matter, as her childhood stuffed animals looked tucked into the doll's cradle beside it.

"I decided to make a home for myself that was comfortable," she said. "I simply faced the fact that I had an anthropology," she said. "I had a history. I had a personal history, and in my history I was used to certain things that I enjoyed and had expected as a child. I grew up with wealth, even if I didn't recognize it as that at the time, so when I went to make a home, I needed the elements of wealth to make a place feel like home to me. These antique pieces were in my grandmother's house. And I wanted a place where I could have them. I knew I was in for a beating in my profession. I was living alone. I needed comfort. And it has given me infinite pleasure. I love this place. It's a great comfort to me. I have friends in, and I'm alone here and I write alone here, and it buoys me up. I've never had a moment of regret about it. The experience has been so positive, because it just gave pleasure and it didn't take any away."

Because the apartment was so much more visibly rich than she ever was in person, she had to think awhile about whether to invite people—like myself—in. To see the place was to tell them she was wealthy; it was to take them into her confidence. "There is tension when I bring people home to the house," she confided. "Because I have faith in myself as a human being, I say my friends will come here and accept it. And if they can't handle it they will express that, but they won't be my friends and that's the reality."

So far she had had only one bad experience, and that involved one of the few people she knew who could compete with her fortune. "That woman," said Helen, "became visibly angry that I was living in such a nice place. She thought it was ostentatious and self-indulgent. And I realized then and there that she would not be an intimate friend of mine. She couldn't handle the reality of who I was." She hadn't been invited back.

But for the most part Helen was overjoyed to live here, to have a place where she could be herself, and to be at one with her past. And so it was most satisfying to have her grandmother's priceless collection of antiques. It was a way of still having her grandmother. The collection represented both the old lady herself and the fortune that came to Helen through her. The furniture was her grandmother's only indulgence and the symbol of Helen's confusion over who she was as a child, since the priceless antiques had always looked worthless to her. "It was very hard to separate my grandmother's miserliness from her art," said Helen. A specialist in this furniture, Helen's grandmother was courted by many museums, but she suspected she was wanted only to secure her collection. So she spurned them all and left her collection to Helen.

There was a photograph of her grandmother in Helen's bedroom showing her peering at some paintings by her friend Jamie Wyeth at one of his early shows in New York. She was wearing her customary beret, sensible oxford shoes, and Scottish woven stockings—"the kind you can't see through," said Helen—and an Irish tweed skirt suit, one of several that she would journey to Dublin to have made and then "wear for thirty years." While all the people around her were gabbing in the customary fashion at art openings, the grandmother was totally absorbed in the paintings, even though she was nearly blind. "She was a person who knew what the important things were," said Helen.

The important things were here in evidence in Helen's house—art, tradition, family, warmth—although her life was solitary. Helen thought about her grandmother a lot in this place. The place returned her to childhood and made it into the childhood it should have been. What had made her feel poor now made her feel rich, rich not just in money, but in memory, in commitment, in the deepest kind of happiness. Helen had repaired many of the pieces, and in a way they were here in her apartment just for safekeeping. She would turn her attention to her grandmother's extensive collection of paintings, now residing in a warehouse, soon. But for now, she just took comfort in tending these antiques and having them close by. "These are all the things that she owned," she said, "but never sent to the doctor. So in a way I feel that I have been taking care of her after she is dead by taking care of her things. I am very aware that she would have loved it here. She would have felt it was very cozy, and she would have liked it."

12

Ah, Wilderness!

When Albert Kapstein, the millionaire saddled with the old English apartment that was *de trop* even for him, was in his most miserable phase of isolation and romantic frustration, he did a very interesting thing. From the city public-works department he acquired a license as a tree pruner after taking a brief course in the subject. And now, he told me, "I can go out with a hacksaw to do whatever I want to any tree on any street in the city."

But Albert was no arboreal Jack the Ripper letting loose on the innocent elms and maples of the city sidewalks. Nor did he plan to bring the kind of decorum to the trees that he had given to his apartment, turning New York into a garden at Versailles. Rather, he was giving his most loving attention to the trees because he *felt* for them. Watching from his apartment window, or strolling by on shopping trips, he had been appalled by their suffering. Some strained pathetically against guy wires stretched tight as banjo strings; others were rot-infested; still others had been mutilated by lovers inscribing their devotions in the bark with a penknife.

Albert had taken it upon himself to help these trees as if they were his foster children. He tended them regularly on weekends, going out into the park by his apartment with a pair of clippers, garden shears, and a hacksaw to loosen the guy wires and lop off the dead limbs. "I've helped about three hundred trees," he said proudly. "I was completely neurotic about it. I felt I was helping them to grow."

So absorbed had Albert been in his mission of mercy that he hadn't sensed any connection between the trees' struggle for life and his own: it might be he himself who needed tending, clearing away of the dead wood, and loosening of the restraints that had tied him down so tightly. His mania about the trees, I noticed, had sprung up around the time he had started feeling so confined by his apartment and by his money.

When I gently suggested to him that he might identify with these saplings, Albert's eyes brightened with the idea of his kinship with trees.

"I never thought of that," he said, "but it's true." Then he warmed to the notion. "I want to get in touch with the natural world," he announced, "with sun and light and air and water." Covertly, he had long felt this way. Some nights, he told me, he had slept under the trees in the park—right there with the bums and the muggers and the drug pushers. He just wanted to feel the air on his skin all night long. "I love to be outside," he said. "Not in the winter, obviously, but in the summer. I love to see the sunset. I love to watch the sky and the moon and to feel the hot breeze flow in from the city. I love that tormented, angry blast of heat that comes across the city. I like the heat, and I like to feel it when I walk down the street. I like to *sweat*."

It was a remarkable confession from the citified Albert, but he was not alone. Most of the rich kids I spoke to expressed similar hankerings for the simple pleasures of nature. It may seem a strange fantasy for those whose money can buy them the best of the material world. But it's one that unites them, as common to all as the rarefied air they breathe. Remember Annie Dale Owen and her log cabin in downtown Houston? Or Matt Trenton, who sought his fate at sea, first sailing the Caribbean, then rounding the Horn? When Phoebe spoke of money as water, she wasn't describing her love for money so much as her love for water, its clarity, its freshness, its depth. Even the urbane Alex Trammel admitted to the pull of nature, with his bathroom murals of the thrashing sea. Sonia Belahovski, raised on a gentleman's farm, still thought of a log cabin in Vermont as her dream house. Continuing a family tradition of environmental activism, the Rockefeller heir, Terry, worked on a country newspaper in Vermont and in the environmental office of the mayor of New York. Not so coincidentally, he compared his future inheritance to a darkening storm cloud that might bring forth a thunderstorm or a "warm spring rain." Elizabeth Meyer was happiest aboard *Matinicus* with the wind up and the waves pounding on the hull. Ando Hixon believed that a major reason he felt so strongly about his blimp was its ecological purity, the way it floats so gently up there in the sky, as beautiful and natural as the clouds themselves. "My blimp leaves the campsite neater than I found it," he declared. "Just like Dad always said." And the Mellon, Heather, called herself a "barefoot kind of person," keen to feel the earth under her feet.

All the rich kids feel for the natural world, and they spend their money to protect it. While rich kids were inclined to give away their money to a wide range of charities, one interest that overlapped was conservation, as exemplified by such organizations as Greenpeace and the Sierra Club. Although the department-store heiress Roberta Bernstein had solved her money-mail dilemma with the purchase of a large wastebasket, she made an exception for environmental groups. She had invested in land trusts to save selected parcels from the ravages of development. She did so not just to preserve the surface beauty of the landscape, its rolling hills speckled with wildflowers, but, with an antivivisectionist's powers of empathy, to save it from the pain of being gouged by bulldozers and pierced by oil wells. "The earth is a living organism," she said. "It's not inert. It's vital. There is something called the Gaia hypothesis, which says that the earth is a living being and the forests are its lungs. I believe that. Taking care of the earth is not just a matter of cosmetics. It is a sacred duty."

Economists cite a "hierarchy of values" that ascends from the most basic needs of food and shelter up to the luxuries of fashion and philosophy. The richer one gets, according to the theory, the higher one rises into the ranks of increasingly less pressing concerns. Or, viewed in another way, the hierarchy proceeds from the near to the far: individuals attend to their own hunger before they concern themselves with the general question of world hunger. Either way, near the top of the list of such inessentials would come a rhapsodic feeling for mother earth. As Lester Thurow notes in *The Zero-Sum Society*, "One is struck by the extent to which environmentalism is an interest of the upper middle classes." It's a privilege of rich kids, whose immediate needs have all been met. Such remote terrain is their natural territory.

Less philosophically, it makes sense for rich kids to go for the wide open spaces. The rich of all ages, and all eras, have sought periodic respites from the grime, danger, extreme temperatures, and ugly poverty of the city to enjoy the balm of country living, whether in a glass house on the slopes of Mount Tamalpais in Marin County, one of the palaces of Newport, an eighteenth-century farmhouse in Vermont, or a twenty-thousand-acre ranch in Texas.

These rich kids, however, who were so shaped by the sixties and early seventies in other ways, may also be carrying on the back-to-nature movement of their formative years, celebrated most famously on Earth Day, April 22, 1970. Since they alone are not subject to the economic restraints that forced their less wealthy peers to abandon the dream of chemical-free homegrown, they can maintain their original trajectory a little longer than everybody else.

Yet a more complete explanation for these rich kids' nearly universal affinity for the natural world must go further. The enjoyment that rich kids derive from it transcends its value as a consumer good, philosophical ideal, or vacation spot. It is their ultimate home, where they can finally strip away the confines of their money and be free. Their wealth may form the structure of their lives, but they can escape it in the wild. The country offers a wider, freer version of the pockets of peace, tranquillity, and harmony that they create so painstakingly in their house or apartment. The land is where they truly belong, the final destination.

The hardscrabble farmer toiling over his ten-acre plot, the weekend backpacker hitting the trail in a national park, and the backwoodsman cutting mountain timber he's grown from seedlings obviously have their own affection for the earth. But the devotion of the rich kids is of a different order. In the wild they find relief from the tensions that pull at them from every side in civilized society. There is no poverty in nature; there is instead a kind of universal richness—in the shine of a silver birch, the luster of goldenrod. In wildness the rich kids can flee the confines of civilization, where everything has its price and everyone has his rank. In nature, rich kids can be, finally, at one with the world, just another of God's creatures, neither above nor below.

Alice Tatum found this feeling of oneness on horseback at the King Ranch. Friends called her an "Indian," she rode so naturally, her body in perfect rhythm with her steed pounding over the grassy range. Even though she did most of her riding to help with the branding and the castrating of "the poor little bulls"—two practices that asserted the King Ranch's dominion over the natural world—she loved riding because it brought her down to the level of the animals, her hide right down against theirs. "A lot of people are taught to ride rigid," she said, "not working with the animal, not feeling the animal. But I'd rather feel a part of the animal, and feel what he's doing. I don't want to feel like a dominant figure on the horse."

It was the same story out at sea. She had almost become a marine biologist, she was so entranced by the ocean's vast breadth and all its mysterious sea creatures. She had sailed with some college friends in twenty-five-foot Fireball yachts off the Connecticut shore, but that was too removed. She needed to get down into the water. So it was scuba diving in the Gulf that won her heart. "I love the scuba," she said, "with all that incredible expanse of water, and the variety of colors from the shore out to the great depths. And when you get down into the sea, you're surrounded. You're not the dominant figure anymore. And the closer you get to the floor, the more you see all the different grasses and all the coral, and the fish and the colors, the more you're just overwhelmed."

For most rich kids, such a feeling of being overwhelmed, of being completely *blown away*, is what they're after. In a world where they themselves, inflated by their money, are so oversized, it is oddly pleasing to be humbled by something even bigger. And it is just as gratifying to pass beyond the tiresome influence of their whopping bank accounts. In nature, they've reached a higher level and found a greenness, of ocean, leaves, and grass, even richer than their cash.

"For me," said one rich girl, "there's nothing so beautiful as something terribly wild. You cannot possess it. You really lose yourself in it. You're human and this is nature, something so much bigger than yourself. That's what I like. I can't make a tree. I can't buy a tree. And that brings you back into the right perspective, at least for me. That's why I feel so exalted in the wild. There, things assume their natural sizes again. You are man in nature, as opposed to man in the environment you create, with all the status symbols and all the associations of money and power. Out in the wild, you don't have any of that. Everything is in its proper relation. We're all part of a big universe."

Rich kids often describe their glorious retreats in the Mediterranean or the Alps as "paradise" or even "the garden of Eden," and, although they are speaking loosely, that's what these places are. Theirs is an ancient dream, the mythic return of mankind to the garden. But, as they attempt to undo the first fall, absolve the first guilt, and put the apple back on the tree, their quest takes on a highly personal nature. In the wild, surrounded by the herbs and flowers, the lakes and rivers, they can, for a time, cleanse themselves of their original sin of coming into money. Like Alice Tatum scuba-diving in the deep blue sea, they are just one of many creatures, all of them strange and beautiful in their way.

Of course, as the world grows smaller, it gets more difficult for rich kids to obtain a stretch of wildness to fit their needs. So most have to compromise. Instead of acquiring utter solitude, they find themselves in the company of their fellowman pretty much wherever they go. That's tolerable so long as he is sufficiently primitive, or at least different, to maintain the impression that "civilization"—meaning the oppressive, status-conscious society they know all too well—lies elsewhere. Cary Ridder likes traveling in India for just that reason. "I always feel really relaxed when I get back from there," she says. "In India, the push just to survive is so strong, it wipes out the push here in America to excel and be successful and make thousands of millions of dollars. Also, I feel India can face its own problems, so I don't have to solve them. I don't have to take responsibility for them the way I do in the U.S."

The black millionairess Shiela Waters has bucked this trend and, instead of going to the primitive outback, confines her impromptu getaway flights to such civilized places as Scotland and France. But in doing so, she provides the exception that proves the rule. She tried to vacation in the less-developed islands in the Caribbean, but she always returned from these visits vaguely dissatisfied, never fully cleansed by the sparkling sand and the azure sea. Gradually it dawned on her why. The black islanders who seemed so charmingly uncivilized to white visitors were to her cruel reminders of her special privilege. Except for a stroke of fate, she could have been one of the young women peddling scarves and seashells to tourists on the beach. "How could I possibly enjoy myself sitting cheek by jowl with them?" she asks. She longed for a "castaway island" where she and her boyfriend could be alone with all the natural beauty. But she never found one. The best she could do was to rent a villa on a deserted strip of the coast of Spain. "There we created something on our own," she says.

* * *

The more popular resorts for rich kids, like Martha's Vineyard off Massachusetts, St. Barthélemy in the Caribbean, or Club Med around the world, cater to this secret hankering of the well-to-do to leave the burdensome trappings of society behind. Even when it is a tightly controlled illusion—one can easily imagine the puppet strings in such places, although they are of a gossamer thinness—the effect is deeply appreciated.

The world traveler Candace Hooper flew into raptures when she remembered her vacations to Capri, tempered though her enthusiasm must have been by the fact that the husband who joined her on them has since left her for a younger woman. She let her ice cream melt there in Schrafft's, she carried on so about it. To tell the truth, the place did sound inviting.

"It was pure bliss," she said. "Capri is supposed to be the oldest resort in the world, something like two thousand years old, and it can get very touristy. You've got to go there in May or June. That's the best time. It's so incredibly beautiful! All the streets are paved with old stones, the houses are lovely, and everything is covered with bougainvillea.

"I've spent the best days of my life there. Do you want to know a typical day?"

I nodded, and her eyes lit up at the memory.

"Well, I'd get up in the morning to have breakfast on a terrace overlooking the sea," she began. "There are two enormous rocks out there, the Ferrioni, that poke out of the water. I'd have the most delicious breakfast, and then I'd walk down to the sea for a swim. There is a path down that takes about a half-hour. It's long and winding, and all the way down you pass through these deep green pine trees. It's one of the most beautiful walks I've ever taken in my life. It's the path the Romans took.

"I'd usually spend the morning swimming and snorkeling or just lying in the sun. There are places I would swim to and lie on these very flat rocks. Nobody can see you there, because it's in a little cove, so I'd take off my bathing suit and lie in the sun with no clothes on. There's nobody around to bother you.

"Afterward, I might swim back to one of a couple of places

for lunch. The food is so fantastic! It's all fresh fruits and vegetables and fresh fish that's caught by the local fishermen. I'd usually have the fish grilled, with salad and tomatoes and mozzarella cheese.

"After lunch, I might go water-skiing or swim some more. Or I might take a walk. It's wonderful in Capri that you can get so much exercise, because there are no cars, so you walk everywhere. I might have a game of tennis with friends, or maybe go home to read a book or have a nap.

"In the evening, I'd go out to a restaurant for dinner. Again, you have to walk to get there, and that might take up to an hour and a half. But that's fine. The food is always delicious.

"One feels very well after a day like that. No pollution, and all that exercise. It's the closest thing I've found to the garden of Eden. There are no cars. And the island itself is so beautiful. It's all mountains, with the valleys all filled with little farms and little vineyards. All the people who live there are all so sweet. There's no crime. It's the most heavenly place I've ever been in the world.

"I used to go there every summer with my husband, and then I went there every summer by myself. It's better with someone, but it's wonderful alone, too. There's something magical about the island. It's supposed to have radioactive rock that can give you a tremendous amount of energy, and I've found that was true. When I went dancing at night, I found I could just dance and dance and dance."

So powerful is the radioactive energy of nature that it can revitalize rich kids far more fundamentally than the usual vacation respite. It can remind them of their basic humanity, so easily forgotten in their preoccupation with the uniqueness of their position, and, by liberating them from the cares of wealth for a time, help them see what bounties they truly possess.

The tasteful Houston heiress Emily Montgomery often felt drained by the demands of her job as a stock analyst, and she was really down in the dumps one Friday evening in the Denver airport when she missed a connecting flight to Aspen for a three-day weekend visit to some new friends, which she'd been looking forward to for months. She couldn't get another plane until the next morning. Because her purse had been snatched at the country-club locker room a few days before while she was playing golf, she had no credit cards to pay for a hotel room, and foolishly she hadn't brought enough cash. It suddenly struck her that instead of having just about everything in the world, she had nothing at all.

But gradually the tide started to lift. She remembered the name of a friend in Denver. When she called, he offered her a bed for the night and even took her to a party. In the morning, she flew on to Aspen and was overjoyed to discover her friends lived in a stunning house way up in the hills, in the thick of the wildness. There was an "amazing" group of people—a pair of powerful Washington lobbyists, an accomplished jewelry designer, and a Sotheby's art consultant among them. But best of all, they were in the country, and they all took to it with children's zest. In the space of forty-eight hours, the group managed to cram in rafting trips down the white water, horseback rides in through the valleys, and hikes up into the mountains for scenic picnics. "It was like adult summer camp," she said. She conjured up images of the pastel mountains, the whipped-cream clouds, the trees shimmering in the heat, the furtive wildlife darting through the forest, and the wine flowing freely the better to appreciate all these wonders.

Emily came back completely recharged, and although this all happened almost a year before we met, she said that weekend changed her life. "Sometimes I concentrate on the things I don't have," she explained. "At the time, my job was boring. I wasn't going out with anyone. And I kind of dwelled on this misery. I was so unhappy. But then I went on that weekend, and that was the start of the really wonderful rest of my life. It was so great! I thought to myself—'Emily, you're crazy! You have everything in the world!' Since then, I've tried to maintain a more positive attitude, because I basically have so much, and I can get tripped up concentrating on the small negatives of life. It's paid off, too, because a few months later, during hunting season, a friend invited me down to her ranch for their annual dove hunt. And that was glorious, too. And that's where I met the boy I'm going out with now."

Virtue rewarded.

RICH KIDS

*   *   *

Nature can be a placid refuge from the struggles that rich
kids face, a place where they can discover the joys of merely
living. But, as many rich kids found out at the abrupt conclusions of those lovely joyrides in their sleek and expensive new
automobiles, nature can also provide an important reality
check to lives that too often float free of all conventional
restraints. Rich kids may be able to flout some of the legal
niceties with high-priced legal help (John Hinckley being a
prominent example), but the natural laws are not so easily
contravened. And this truth can be reassuring to some giddy
inheritors. It reminds them that there is something stronger
than themselves—or their lawyers. Wilderness-survival
courses like Outward Bound, which features a weekend solo
in the wilderness with only bush berries for food, are popular
with rich kids for this reason. But some of the kids have to
find out on their own the force of nature.

One might think that the shipping magnate's son Edward
would have learned his lesson about the immutability of nature
when he nearly met his death in his brand-new Saab with
his pot-smoking friends on the German autobahn. But no.
He continued to test the limits. In renovating his house, he
said his favorite tool was his buzz saw. He wanted to cut
through life the way it took care of two-by-fours. He still
dreamed of becoming a racing-car driver. "I need fast action,"
he said. Bored by conventional sailing (even though he had
been terrified the time he had to deliver a yacht to the Caribbean), he preferred to windsurf. That way he could get right
down into the elements and fight the wind with his entire
body. And, to make the sport even more challenging, he substi-
tuted a narrow surfboard for the usual fairly broad hull. So
hooked was he on the recreation that he kept going right
through the winter. He'd go out on a lake in a snowstorm
so long as the wind was up. He wore a wet suit—complete
with boots and hood—and scanned the waters for icebergs.
"The surfboards are great for lousy weather," he said. "You
need thirty knots just to get out of the water. But once they're
out, it's screaming wildness. Man, they really shoot."

But he had known nature to get the better of him, and

he remained humbled by the experience. That happened one winter at a Swiss resort where he was working as a ski instructor. He and a friend took one afternoon off to indulge themselves in some recreational skiing and resolved to go where no other skier had ever been. The two almost didn't live to tell about it.

There had been such heavy snowfall that one of the runs had been closed off because of the avalanche danger. But to Edward that just meant virgin powder. So off they went, *wedel*ing down in the soft white stuff, nearly intoxicated by that fabulous weightless feeling, when suddenly Edward heard a terrifying roar. Then the whiteness that had been only below him was everywhere, and the whole mountain was shaking. Avalanche!

"I managed to stay above it," he said, "but my friend didn't. He started above me but ended up about a thousand yards further down. He was buried. He got some air down through one armhole, fortunately, or he would have suffocated. I was only in up to my waist, but the snow was like a body cast and hard as cement. I couldn't get out. They sent out helicopters to find us, and dogs. I was pretty much out in the open, but it took the dogs to find my friend. He said the scariest part of it was afterward, when he looked up his air hole and saw a German shepherd staring down at him with his tongue out. That freaked him out. But we're both lucky to be alive. After they found us, they balled us out and took our passports for a while. But I was just glad as hell we got found. You can be damn sure I've learned my lesson. I don't ski off the *piste* anymore. The whole thing was pretty heavy."

Most rich kids' need for nature is more peaceable. Instead of pounding them into submission, the elements show them from where, and what, they come. These forays into the wild are not so much journeys out as journeys back, back to the point where the wealth was made. While some of these fortunes were made by invention, some by shrewd manipulation of stock, some by mere connivance, fundamentally all the money came from the earth, from its oil and minerals, its crops and timber. In returning to the land, the rich kids come

313

full circle, reuniting themselves with the ancestors who first pulled the money out of the soil and then passed it down to succeeding generations.

There is something very American about this. The European landscape, of course, has been divvied up for millennia. Only Americans can go back to the time when their world was new, a seemingly untouched universe before the first explorers, pilgrims, and pioneers took it over in their inexorable march west. And in the process of rediscovery the rich kids can make themselves whole again—by coming to terms with their origins, by reaching down to touch the fundamental element. As Cary Ridder said, scorning the heirs who affected working-class accents in their attempt to escape their past, "I like people who are centered." And they can become centered by coming back to the earth.

The rich kid I'll call George Blanchard made such a journey, although he would be the last to describe it in such grand terms. He was a prematurely grizzled, straight-talking young man of twenty-seven, his bearded face sunburned because he didn't believe in hats. Jeans, a western shirt, and dusty cowboy boots completed the picture of the dedicated rancher. Since I hadn't known what sort of a ranch to expect, I'd worn a suit and dress shoes when I came out to see him. George thought that was pretty funny. "Quite an outfit," he harrumphed when he first saw me. If I hadn't known that George grew up in the plush suburb of Grosse Pointe, Michigan, I might have thought that he'd sprung up from the ruddy south Texas soil along with the barley and sorgum. He had come down here to run a 48,000-acre ranch outside of Houston built by his great-great-grandfather, a legendary cattleman I'll call "Hawkeye" Sanders. Although George had other illustrious ancestors, including a meat-products distributor and a confederate general, in his past, his money came from this ranch, chiefly from the oil it happened to be sitting on.

Except for the tenure of one nephew, the ranch had been run since Hawkeye's death in 1885 by a series of hired managers, the last of whom had to quit when it was discovered he was having an affair with the nurse for George's ailing grandmother. "It was a scandal," said George, "but it really wasn't. He was just a guy who fell in love with a woman."

After that, a local veterinarian had taken charge of the place, but he proved a disaster, and after nine months the family determined that they'd better do something fast if they hoped to have much of a ranch left. That's when George decided to come on down and see what he could do.

At that point he'd had a somewhat checkered academic career ever since he was booted out of prep school—a place attended by "every Blanchard in the world"—for what struck the academic authorities as a bad attitude, but to George was only being natural. "I've always been a flower child," he said, suddenly modulating his hard-bitten manner. "I've been a hippie basically since hippies were around. My attitudes go that way. I rebelled against authority at school. I was trying to be a cool guy. I thought it was cool to rebel. They thought I was doing drugs, which I was, but they didn't catch me."

Afterward, he was packed off to college in Switzerland, a school primarily for the rich, where he ran into—and from— such kindred heirs as Pulitzers and Lawfords. The chief advantage of the college, he said, was its "central location." It allowed him to scoot about Europe and beyond, down to North Africa and up to the Arctic Circle. "I wanted to see the midnight sun, so I did," he explained. "I wanted to see the desert, so I did." He came out of the experience with a knowledge of French, German, Italian, and some Spanish—and an ambition to work in foreign relations, possibly in the agricultural branch of the United Nations. He'd gotten as far as business school at the University of Illinois when he got the bad news about what was happening to the ranch. He decided to apply the agricultural ideas he was developing on a global scale to the 48,000 acres of wheat, barley, rice, sorghum, and cattle on the Gulf.

"We always complain about how managers quickly get out of hand and start to act like they own the place," he said. "It's a natural feeling. I backed myself up with that theory and said, 'Let me do it.' I didn't really like business school and didn't like corporations. But I do like the idea of agriculture and people taking care of their own things. I figured, here we have this ranch that is a big part of this area and this community, and nobody knows anything about it. Nobody knows anything about *us*, the family. As a secondary thrust, I wanted to bring the ranch and the family into the public eye a little more. But just around here. I wanted us to be more visible. I wanted to show people that we didn't walk six feet off the ground. We were pretty normal people. This wasn't a mystery island of land. It was part of something. People had this misimpression that we were these mystery people, these auras off from Detroit. And it's true, we have been absentee owners. We came down here every year. I'd do some work here in the summers, and we'd come on Thanksgiving or Christmas. But we came as visitors, without taking an active role. That always bugged me. It didn't seem right. Here we owned all this stuff, and we weren't taking active responsibility for it. I just thought that if you owned something you should take responsibility for it."

He was doing that now. He lived in a small barrackslike cottage by the main house. "I've never had extravagant tastes," he said. "My mom says that I could be happy living in a cave." A beautiful plantation-style mansion that Hawkeye built to show that his establishment values had prevailed over his essential renegade nature, the main house looked like only a slightly smaller version of Tara. Inside, it had been done over in a style that might be called Grosse Point modern, with cheery yellows and greens. There was a swimming pool and sculpture garden in the back. George stayed out of the place and used it only to house his parents in their accustomed style when they came down from Detroit for a visit.

His job was to take care of what are termed the "surface rights" of the land—its agricultural uses, in other words. The mineral rights down below have been licensed, for a hefty fee, to Exxon. There were a number of spindly oil derricks cranking away around the property, hauling up the Texas crude that accounted for much of the land's value and that had made so many generations of Hawkeye's descendants so rich. "I have a different sensitivity to the land and what's below it," said George. "What's below I never really see. It's in figures and in logs and in pipes. It's abstract. You can't get too close to an oil well. But you can love the land. You really can.

"I do this for love," he went on. "That's why I'm here. I want to maximize profits as much as I can, but I want to do it in a human kind of way. I don't want to do it in a technical corporate way." This meant that he was planning to keep the land essentially the way it was, with its marshes, rivers, and stands of pine. He had introduced a triangular rotation system of rice, cattle grazing, and row crops to get the most out of the soil but scorned a more vicious agribusiness philosophy, which would dictate that he strip it clear of trees to farm it more efficiently. He preferred its wildness, with its tangled forests and herds of deer that graze on the property and geese that splash down on his ponds. "This is pretty much a nature preserve," he said, "and I like it that way. I could level it and farm it from fencepost to fencepost. But I've seen that happen and it's not good. It's not the way it *should* be."

He had tried to be just as good to the thirty-four employees on the ranch and the neighbors from the town. When one of the townspeople died recently, George quietly bought a horse at the county fair to give to the man's five-year-old daughter. And on the ranch, he said, "we take care of our own. When somebody has some trouble, we take a collection for him and bail him out. The wife of one of the guys here died recently, and we all pitched in to help him out. I like to think of this place as family. Maybe that's something I have about inherited wealth. I don't have to maximize profits here. So I'm allowed to do that sort of thing."

Hawkeye Sanders would probably have snorted at such a lily-livered attitude. George's ancestor was known for a discerning gaze when evaluating property and its owners—chiefly to see what it would require to separate them. George said that Hawkeye liked to hang people who got in his way. He told me one story to illustrate: Hawkeye once was stringing up a gang of three brothers for cattle rustling on his property—even though the three might well have had a more legitimate claim against him. After the first two were dispatched, Hawkeye suffered an uncharacteristic bout of penitence and told his men to let the third and youngest rustler go. As he was being released, the boy cried out, "Damn you, Hawkeye. I'm going to hunt you to the end of my days." So Hawkeye quickly reconsidered. "On second thought," he said, "string him up, too."

"Hawkeye was a rogue, no doubt about it," said George. "Plain and simple. He was shrewd, probably cutthroat, because he had to be. He was farsighted, energetic, all the things it took to be successful." He was also six foot five and two hundred sixty pounds. Part of his unlikely progress from his tiny hometown in a corner of Connecticut to one of the largest ranches in Texas was probably just to find a place big enough for him. Once he found it, he wanted all of it. He ended up with a half-million acres along the Gulf of Mexico. He named the town after himself, Sandersville, along with its church, Sanders Church, and two railroad stations—one Sanders, one Hawkeye. Finally, to make sure that his gravestone was to his liking, he commissioned a sculptor to erect one well in advance according to his ideas: a full-sized statue of himself in the manner of the kings and emperors he'd seen in Europe, mounted on a stately pedestal "higher," he specified, "than any statute [*sic*] of any Confederate General." The whole monument soars nearly thirty feet into the air. It's still the highest thing around.

George sought no monument himself. The role of the rich kid starts as a passive one—just to take what he has been given. Moneymakers try to stand out; heirs do their best to fit in. Hawkeye was six-five, his statue even higher; George was a mere five-ten. There is a lesson in that. If Hawkeye stretched the law a bit here and there to get his way, that was his way of doing things. Nothing George needs to feel guilty about today. That is just something for him to accept, along with the money.

"I respect Hawkeye," said George. "He was doing the best he could. The fact that he was dishonest—well, businesses are dishonest today. My values are different from his, but that's in the nature of inherited wealth. When you're just managing it instead of building it, you have a different attitude."

Around town, some of the folks kidded George by calling

him "Chickenhawk." George took the ribbing good-naturedly. After an initial icebreaking, they'd come to accept him and to appreciate what he was trying to do for the ranch and the town. "People make snap judgments around here," he said. "People come into meetings with me here expecting me to be a real jerk, a real snot. It's up to me to deal with it. I just try to be myself. I don't think I'm snobby. I think I'm just the opposite. I think I'm more accepting of everybody than a lot of people who aren't wealthy. Maybe it's guilt from having so much money—feeling I should relate to everybody. I don't think it was the way I was brought up. My dad was brought up to hang out with other monied people. It's much more segregated. He's very big in favor of servants, for example. That created another kind of gulf.

"But a lot of people here, before they get to know me, they think that I'm standoffish or shy. I'm going out with a girl now who hated me. She's from money, too. She's from around here. She couldn't stand me! And I didn't like her very much. That was because I didn't put out any effort to get to know her. We were just two shy people. We get along better now."

But George still tried to maintain an inner reserve of privacy, a strength that was his alone. He seemed to draw it out of the earth. We had a quiet lunch on the terrace overlooking the pool. Since his father was down for a quarterly meeting, George had opened up the house. We looked out at the small, tiled pool and the sculpted cupids that stood around it. Weeds were growing up in the grass and cracks were appearing in the pool. The wooden clapboard house, too, was fragile. Built on pilings, it sagged with age, causing doors to stick and windows to bind. At the tinkling of a glass bell, a young white-coated Mexican came around to serve us chicken and assorted vegetables formally, from the left. I felt that our small patio was one small enclave of civilization, surrounded by a wildness that crept in from all sides. And beyond that there was something wilder still.

That's what George had come here for. "I really get off on a place that is really wild, really nature," he told me. "Everything here is happening as it does in the wild." He had bought a barnstorming Citaborea airplane, a rusting, stubby craft he parked out back of the main house, to get up into the wildness, to feel the pressure on his body with each loop of the loop. "I'm somebody who likes thrills," he explained. "I like living on the edge."

But he wanted to soothe the wildness inside him, so he meditated and did yoga every evening after work to relax. Although he attended the local Sanders Church, an Episcopalian denomination, he said he was actually a Buddhist. "But there aren't too many Buddhists around here, so I end up practicing what I do by myself." He usually meditated at one of his favorite spots on the ranch, near an old "picnic house" by a lake. "I'm pretty fond of the place," he said. He wanted to show it to me, so we climbed into his Caprice "Classic"— "an executive's car," he noted—equipped with air conditioning and a mobile phone, and took off down a dirt road that ran past the house down into the woods.

We passed a creaky metal windmill and some cow barns and reached the lake after a quarter-mile's drive through the bare trees. It was a pleasant but somewhat mournful spot— a place beautiful for its decay. The lake was small and man-made, with weeping willows arching down all around it. Some swans glided about on the water. They'd been imported from Michigan. "The first batch we got died out," he said, "but these ones are doing real well."

We sat down on the bank by the picnic house, a small shingled building that had seen sunnier times, and looked out at the water for a while without speaking. It seemed to me everything was falling—the willows, the house, even the swans with their long drooping necks. Although he didn't speak of it, I expect George saw only a stirring and primitive beauty. It is in the nature of things to fall. It was up to him to lift them back up—to raise the crops, to hoist up the roof beam where it sagged, to uphold the family name.

Then we drove on. As we passed a herd of cattle, George told me that he liked to peer into cows' eyes; he imagined he could see clear through into their murky minds. Some deer leaped through the fields beside us as we drove along, and then some sandhill cranes rose up overhead, their heads capped a radiant pink.

Finally, way out in the field, we reached a crossroad. George stopped the car and got out. He'd brought me here because it was the one spot on the ranch where, whichever way the wind blows, you never heard any noise from the distant highways. All we could hear was the howling wind and the sound the tall grass made as it whipped back and forth. Now, in midwinter, the fields all around were a dull brown, just crumpled straw. The crops had fallen, too. But in this final decay, George saw the hope of renewal. "Too bad you couldn't see this in the summertime," he shouted into the wind. "When the crops are up, it's one of the most amazing things. It really gives me a rush. It's the colors, the sounds, the smells, all the sensual things." He looked at me with a smile. "You know," he said, "it's amazing how it all comes together when you stand outside on a hot day."

EPILOGUE: *Pennies from Heaven*

From George Blanchard's ranch, I would travel on to see other rich kids, but as I crossed the cattle guards that marked the limits of his property, I felt I had gotten as deeply inside the life of the rich as I ever would. There, in the remote crossroad deep in his property, I had reached the center. I had been impressed, as I looked around, with the great sweep of the landscape and its history. I could imagine old Hawkeye driving the cattle by here, his skin leathery as cowhide. I'd love to come back some summer and see the crops up and blazing with life.

But the field only looked wild. Actually, it was, like most things the rich kids owned, built by man, for man to use. George's family had laid out these crossing roads; and he'd planted the crops himself. Standing out there with George, I couldn't hear the cars on the highway, but I could see them in the distance. And, closer in, I could see the oil derricks cranking away, hauling up the crude. The money was there, too, right beneath us.

His ranch wasn't the wilderness at all; it was a garden, one that he had grown and tended. And that took a lot of hard work. Much had been given to him, but he had provided much more himself—initiative, grit, vision, wisdom, hope. Only with those qualities could he maintain such a spread, keep the house up, keep the weeds down. It was his ancestor's money, but it was his life.

In this respect, George was unusual. Unlike so many other rich kids, he never allowed his money to get the better of him. I thought about this often as I traveled about the country. I was fascinated by all the rich kids I met; their lives were so unusual, their backgrounds so exotic. And I liked them, or at least most of them, far more than I would have expected, considering rich kids' reputations. But I admired only a few. I did admire George. He saw what he wanted to accomplish in the world, and he was getting it done. I admired the ones who, in Richard Potter's words, were "doin' it." As one rich kid's father had told him, quoting Saint Luke, "From those to whom more is given, more is required." And he was right. That means doing something, making something, contributing something. Their money had lifted rich kids to a great height at birth. They can reach even higher in their lives. But, unable to grasp their good fortune, few rich kids ever manage it.

The rich kid I've called Harold, who discovered what it meant to be rich looking out the train windows at the shacks of migrant workers on a childhood trip to Florida, had spent much of his life worrying about the inequity of his position. Why should he be so rich when so many others were poor? Like several other heirs, he'd taken an interest in American history as a young man in an effort to track his dilemma back to its source. He had been particularly troubled by the phrase at the very beginning of the Declaration of Independence, about all men being created equal. "How could all men be created equal if I wasn't?" he wondered.

He was still pondering the issue at twenty-four when he joined the Peace Corps in the 1960s. Stationed in southern Brazil, he worked to improve agricultural practices in the poverty-stricken countryside. One night he had dinner with an educated Brazilian couple, he an agronomist and she a home economist, who were also trying to help the poor farmers in the Brazilian hills. They told Harold a story he's never forgotten. One of the girls in town had been horribly burned when an oil lantern toppled over on her while she was making dinner. Because the family had only a donkey cart for transportation, and the nearest medical help was over a hundred miles away, there was nothing the parents could do for the child. Without crying out once the whole night, she died the next morning from her burns. "It was the educated couple's reaction that was so extraordinary," Harold said. "I was horrified that nothing could be done for the girl, but they praised her for suffering in silence. In these supposedly primitive countries, the people are resigned to fate and to man's inability to control events. But in America, we assume we can manipulate life and death. We try to control, dominate, and direct events to make a human utopia of equality of condition and circumstances.

"But by her actions, I was relieved of guilt for that child. In her dignity, I felt there was an acceptance of her fate, no matter how harsh it was. And it seemed to me that if she could accept the fate that had been so cruel to her, then I should accept the fate that had been so good to me."

His thoughts returned to that line about equality in the Declaration of Independence. "What I now understand it to mean is something different," he said. "What it means to me now is that we are all equal to ourselves, to becoming who we are. We all have inherited wealth. We have the inheritance of our traditions, our attitudes, our beliefs, and our talents. That perception was a great release for me."

Like any cultural or genetic advantage, the money was there to be used. So many rich kids were imprisoned by their wealth, yet they didn't need to be. Theirs was a wide world, and their love for the shimmering earth may, ultimately, have been for the way it represented the true scope of their opportunity—so wide, so green, so fresh. In their rich young lives, the whole world lay before them.

A behavioral psychologist named Martin Seligman once conducted an experiment with caged rats. He taught one group of rats to push down a metal bar by rewarding their successful efforts with a few pellets of food. That group caught on quickly and took to pressing the bar for their food with zest. Then he tried out another group of rats in the cage, but, before putting them to work on the bar, he released a shower of pellets in a great gush from the top of the cage. The rats feasted delightedly on the lovely pellets at their feet. When they were finished, Seligman watched to see how well they performed the task. These rats did not learn to pull down the bar for their food nearly so quickly. Some of them instead just sat around in their cages looking up at the ceiling, waiting for more food to drop down. They didn't make their way toward the bar at all. And the more free food Seligman showered on them, the worse the rats performed. But they didn't enjoy their indolence. Given the choice between a cage where the food just rained down upon them and a cage where they had to pull the bar for it, they preferred the box where they had to work for their food.

Seligman discusses this experiment in his book, *Helplessness: On Depression, Development, and Death*. He calls it the "spoiled brat" study and concludes that the randomness of the rewards for the second group of rats upset any emerging sense of an ordered universe. The rats were frustrated that they couldn't control events through their own actions. Applying the idea to humans, Seligman writes, "What produces self-esteem and a sense of competence, and protects against depression, is not only the absolute quality of experience, but the perception that one's own actions controlled the experience. To the degree that uncontrollable events occur, either traumatic or positive, depression will be redisposed and ego strength undermined. To the degree that controllable events occur, a sense of mastery and resistance to depression will result."

So good fortune can be as disruptive as tragedy. Rich kids find this out to their sorrow, although few would pity them for it. Just as they are setting out into the world, these lucky heirs come unexpectedly into huge sums that make any further effort unnecessary. No less than Seligman's rats, the rich kids greet their windfall joyfully, but soon end up profoundly confused and dejected. There is no clear connection between what they have done and what they have received. Why should they be so lucky? More importantly, what should they do now?

Hard as it must be to make a fortune, it is easier than receiving one out of the blue. Earned money is clearly one's own, an affirmation of talent, energy, self. An inheritance is none of these things. Instead of being a source of pride, it is a subject of embarrassment; instead of rewarding accomplishment, it fosters sloth; instead of belonging to you, you belong to it.

Average Americans, struggling to get by, may not have all that much in their lives, but at least they have a reason to get up in the morning, and, most likely, a feeling of accomplishment when they go to bed at night. They have a sense of structure and a system of values that rich kids lack. With their tight finances, average people have clear limits on what they can do and what they can't. This can certainly be frustrating, but a much deeper frustration awaits those who have no limits.

When I began this book in the fall of 1982, I wanted to know many things about the lives of the rich, but one of them was quite personal: would my life would be better if I had inherited more money? Should I envy rich kids? As I listened to the rich kids' stories, examined their possessions, and toured their homes, in the back of my mind I always wondered—would I want this for myself? I was certainly interested in seeing their cars and houses; I enjoyed the exotic foreign beers they served me; I liked hearing their tales of wealth and power. But only once did I ever feel that I would like to swap places with the rich kid in front of me. And that was when Richard Potter was telling me about striking it rich with his oil wells. It sounded like such a thrill—the pipes going down into the ground, the oil gushing back up, and the money flooding in. My heart leaped at the thought. But then I realized that, of course, it wasn't his inheritance that excited me. It was his success.

Possibly this is just a foible of mine, but I don't think it's so much fun just to *have* it. The pleasure is in earning it. That's the American way. Yet personal achievement is precisely what inheritances so often prevent rich kids from ever attaining. As they measure themselves against their illustrious ancestors, their standards of success are almost impossibly high. So well supplied financially from birth, they lack the incentives to strike out on their own. And, used to immediate gratification, they don't put in for the kind of training that would lead them to a big payoff down the line. They received their fortune in an instant; they expect to make their fortune just as quickly.

So when I came back from my travels with the rich kids, I looked at my own life with new appreciation. I had everything I wanted. My own inheritance had given me an advantage in life, but not such a large one that I wouldn't work hard to give an even greater gift to myself, my own accomplishments.

Considering the confusion that so many rich kids suffer, one might think—maybe the makers of these large fortunes should do their descendants a favor and withhold from them the burden of so much cash.

But that is not so pleasant for a prospective heir, as I found out when I spoke to a documentary filmmaker named Richard Rogers in New York City. He had been cut off, and he found the experience highly traumatic.

Richard had grown up in luxury. His grandmother's family had been one of New York's august Four Hundred and owned a big house in the ritzy suburb of Tuxedo Park. As Richard saw it, his father had taken advantage of the family assets to pursue a career in social work. Richard always regarded himself as "the scion of a great family" and looked forward to the freedom his wealth would bring. So he was in for a shock when he bounded down the stairs on the morning of his eighteenth birthday. His father greeted him solemnly and ushered him into his study. Finally the big moment had arrived! His father opened up a strongbox and, with some ceremony, presented Richard with the following: three shares of IBM, a letter from George Washington to an ancestor, and Richard's grandfather's gold pocketwatch. As far as Richard knew that was the total of his inheritance. His parents had spent all the rest.

Richard was mortified, and he had never gotten over it. When we spoke, he still felt pained as he contemplated the difference between the person he was and the rich person he always expected to become. "I believe that rich people are magical, more intelligent than I, and that they can do anything," he said. He had gone into the documentary film business with some success and fallen in love with a series of wealthy women, but he had yet to marry.

Others would no doubt feel the same bitterness to find themselves suddenly penniless after a childhood of luxury. Being cut off so peremptorily, they are, in effect, disowned not only by their parents but by their class, and by practically everything they'd ever known. On the other hand, for parents to bestow a huge fortune upon their children at that age amounts to a kind of possessiveness, forcing the kids to live forever on the family dole. Eugene Meyer struck the right balance between the two extremes when he said that he wanted to leave enough money so that his heirs could do anything, but not so much that they could do nothing. He may have overshot the mark in the cases of Elizabeth Meyer and Steve Graham, but the principle is a sound one. Other Family Founders would do well to follow his advice.

Despite the strange difficulties rich kids faced, I still found myself enchanted with them and their lives. Yet I did so less for what the kids themselves delighted in than for what they took for granted. Rich kids were by no means insensitive to the uniqueness of their position. But there were certain things about them that had sunk into their consciousnesses without examination and were now a part of their identity along with their gold credit cards. It was this that made the rich kids so different in my eyes. In an often cynical world, they maintained a kind of dreamy innocence.

There was the offhand way that Cary Ridder told me about how she went up to Elliot Richardson, when he was secretary of defense under Nixon and she was barely twenty, at one of her parents' cocktail parties and tried to argue him out of the war in Vietnam. When he wouldn't go along, she snubbed him, refusing to speak to him ever again. Or the tone of wonder in which Steve Graham told me about a gambling trip he'd made to Reno. He'd gotten so flustered about some bad luck at the crap tables, he went back up to his room and started chucking all his furniture out the window and onto the roof of the casino below. When the manager heard this rain of chairs and tables on the casino roof, he raced up to ask him what the hell he was doing. "Oh, don't worry," Steve calmly told him. "I'll pay for it." To Steve's surprise, the manager let it go at that and merely wrote out a bill to settle the damages. "I guess at Reno they let you do anything so long as you pay for it," said Steve, as though it had never before occurred to him that money could have such power.

EPILOGUE: PENNIES FROM HEAVEN

Or the blasé manner in which Elizabeth Meyer told me about how, in building her house on Martha's Vineyard, she had done everything the "right way" with "real" French windows, oak floors, a genuine lathed banister, and tiled bathtubs. "It was so nice to do it right," she concluded with a smile. "We found you *can* build a house with quality. We had been thinking, 'God! You can't afford to build a quality house anymore.' Well, you can! It costs twice as much, but it's twice as nice."

It is twice as nice, and it's even nicer to hear these kids talk about it.

In preparing this book, I only started out calling these young heirs and heiresses "rich kids" because everyone else did. But as I talked to so many of them, I began to realize how appropriate the term was. They are rich, that goes without saying. But, more important, they are kids, practically regardless of age. This is, of course, one of their great frustrations. They can never get out from under the shadow of their elders; they will always, in some sense, live in their fathers' houses. But there are pleasures in it as well. Protected from the harshness of the world by their money, they maintain their soft innocence long into their lives, and they have a kind of breeziness and naiveté that I'll always find endearing. To them, everything will always be free, always be theirs, always be new. No matter how much they grow in experience, rich kids will always remain kids at heart.